TALES FROM THE
ROCK 'N' ROLL HIGHWAY

MARLEY BRANT

BILLBOARD BOOKS
An imprint of Watson-Guptill Publications
New York

Executive Editor: Bob Nirkind
Editor: Elizabeth Wright
Cover designed by Cooley Design Lab
Interior designed by Michelle Gengaro
Graphic production by Hector Campbell

Copyright © 2004 Marley Brant
All photographs are copyrighted © by the persons credited.
First published in 2004 by Billboard Books, an imprint of Watson-Guptill Publications,
a division of VNU Business Media, Inc.
770 Broadway, New York, NY 10003
www.watsonguptill.com

Library of Congress Cataloging-in-Publication Data
The CIP data for this title is on file with the Library of Congress.
Library of Congress Control Number:
ISBN: 0-8230-8437-X

This book is dedicated to those who have traveled the rock and roll highway in any capacity or mode of transportation.

For my family, whose moral support sustained me during my own years on the road and for whom I breathe each breath.

ACKNOWLEDGMENTS

This book would certainly not exist without the stories, and I offer my sincere appreciation to the following musicians who have personally shared their memories with me: Sam Andrew, Robin Bachman, Eric Barao, Bobby Berge, Rory Block, Eric Bostrom, Debbie Boyer, Robin Brock, Tom Brumshaw, Dallas Bryant, Mel Carter, Neal Casal, Johnny Chester, Mojo Collins, Dick Dale, Zak Daniels, John "Marmaduke" Dawson, Lee Dorman, Ray Dorset, Steve Ellis, Frankie Ford, Tony Franklin, Donna Frost, Gloria Gaynor, Nick Gilder, Andrew Gold, Supe Granda, Paul Gray, Randall Hall, Barry Hay, Larry Hoppen, Brian Hyland, Janis Ian, Jimmy Ibbotson, Jinno and Jigga, Marty Jourard, Carol Kaye, Ed King, Al Kooper, Wayne Kramer, Tommy Mandel, Jocko Marcellino, George McCorkle, Goldy McJohn, John McKuen, Barry Melton, Terry Morris, Peter Noone, John Novello, Alice Nutter, Nigel Olsson, Panama Red, Graham Parker, Dan Peek, Andy Powell, Prairie Prince, Rick Rose, Ralph Saenz, Justin Senker, Scott Simon, Ken Skaggs, Chris Spedding, Rob Squires, John Strohm, Lee Underwood, Violent Jay, Bruce Watson, Kayt E. Wolf-Strong, Gary Wright, and Rusty Young.

Thanks also to those close enough to the action to have a worthwhile tale of their own: Dave Anderson, James Bleseus, Ian Cooke, Arlo Hennings, John Hurd, Karl Kuenning, Matthew Greenwald, Kathie Montgomery, Mitch Lopate, Willie Olmstead, Ed Preman, and the roadies, record execs, promoters, et al, who helped supply the anecdotes.

Thanks to all who contributed photos—what a terrific lot!

My thanks to the dozens of fans who contributed stories for consideration—I wish we could have included them all.

Thanks to Dave, Tim, Glady, Red, Kathie, Willie, Carol, John, Jen, Will, Francie, Jean, Bob, Steve, Ralph, John, Rosie, Cha, and all the rest of this big ole family, for their love and support. I love you all so much. Mae and Pete, you're always with me. Thanks to those many friends who support what I do, whatever that may be.

Thanks to my terrific executive editor, Bob Nirkind, who is—even more than a consummate professional—a man with vision.

Most of all, thanks as always to Jesus for the music and the voice to shout about it.

May the music continue and may the road never end.

CONTENTS

THE CONTRIBUTORS:

Sam Andrew: Guitar player with Big Brother and the Holding Company and the Kozmic Blues Band; writer of film scores and classical suites; currently with the Sam Andrew Band

Robin Bachman: Drummer with BTO

Eric Barao: Lead singer and songwriter with The Cautions

Bobby Berge: Guitarist with Tommy Bolin, Black Irish, Buddy Miles, and others

Rory Block: WC Handy Award–winning blues guitarist/vocalist; recorded with Bonnie Raitt, The Band, Stevie Wonder, Mark Knopfler, Jorma Kaukonen, and others

Derrick Bostrom: Drummer with Meat Puppets, accomplished artist

Debbie Boyer: Vocals and keyboards with the Austin Pettit Band

Robin Broch: Singer, produced by Keith Olsen

Dallas Bryant: Lead singer of Street Survivor

Tom Brumshaw: Guitarist with Rick Nelson and Buck Owens

Mel Carter: Vocalist whose hit songs include "Hold Me, Thrill Me, Kiss Me"

Neal Casal: Singer/songwriter/guitarist whose *Basement Dreams* album was named Best Americana Album by *Mojo Magazine*; plays and tours with Smashing Pumpkins, Sheryl Crow, and others

Johnny Chester: Australian singer/songwriter; has shared stage with the Beatles, Roy Orbison, and others

Mojo Collins: Award-winning blues and rock singer/songwriter/guitarist

Dick Dale: Legendary, award-winning guitarist: "King of the Surf Guitar;" inventor of the Fender Reverb Guitar

Zak Daniels: Singer/songwriter/multi-instrumentalist with Zak Daniels and the One-Eyed Snakes

John "Marmaduke" Dawson: Guitarist/vocalist with New Riders of the Purple Sage

Lee Dorman: Bass player with Iron Butterfly, Captain Beyond, Spencer Davis, and others

Ray Dorset: Songwriter/vocalist of Mungo Jerry's hit "In the Summertime"

Steve Ellis: Singer of "Everlasting Love"; with Love Affair, Ellis, and Widowmaker

Frankie Ford: Singer of Number One hit "Sea Cruise"; solo artist

Donna Frost: Songwriter/vocalist/guitar player with solo career, appears regularly with Skeeter Davis, B. J. Thomas, and others; niece of Elvis Presley's record producer, Felton Jarvis

Tony Franklin: Bass player/songwriter/singer with The Firm, Blue Murder, Jimmy Paige, Carmine Appice, and others

Gloria Gaynor: Award-winning performer whose "I Will Survive" is *the* disco anthem

Nick Gilder: Singer/songwriter of such hit songs as "Roxy Roller" and "Hot Child In The City"

Andrew Gold: Songwriter/singer/musician of hits "Thank You For Being A Friend" and "Lonely Boy," among others; has worked extensively with Linda Ronstadt, Don Henley, Brian Wilson, Paul McCartney, Jackson Browne, and others.

Michael "Supe" Granda: Multi-instrumentalist with the Ozark Mountain Daredevils, The Dog People, The Garbanzos, and Supe and the Sheetrockers

Paul Gray: Bass player with Slipknot, The Damned, UFO, Eddie and the Hot Rods, and Captain Sensible

Randall Hall: Guitarist/songwriter with Rossington-Collins Band, Lynyrd Skynyrd, Randall Hall Band, and World Classic Rockers

Barry Hay: Singer/guitarist/sax player with Golden Earring

Arlo Hennings: Guitarist, manager of Shawn Phillips

Larry Hoppen: Singer of such Orleans hits as "Still The One" and "Dance With Me"; multi-instrumentalist who has appeared on albums by Screamin' Cheetah Wheelies, Blues Traveler, and others

Brian Hyland: Singer/songwriter with Number One hits "Sealed With A Kiss" and "Itsy Bitsy Teeny Weeny Yellow Polka Dot Bikini," among others

Janis Ian: Grammy Award–winning singer/songwriter of such hits as "Society's Child" and "At Seventeen"; has also written songs for several films and television shows

Jimmy Ibbotson: Founding and current guitarist/songwriter of Nitty Gritty Dirt Band

Jiga and Jinno: Members of psychedelic trance band Analog Pussy

Marty Jourard: Multi-instrumentalist with the Motels, author of *Start Your Own Band.*

Carol Kaye: Session and performance Fender bass player with Sam Cooke, Quincy Jones, Brian Wilson, Lou Rawls, and many others; respected music book author

Ed King: Guitarist/songwriter of "Sweet Home Alabama" and many other songs; with Strawberry Alarm Clock and Lynyrd Skynyrd

Al Kooper: Legendary musician/songwriter/producer/author; one of the founding members of Blood, Sweat and Tears; keyboardist on such mega-recordings as Dylan's "Like A Rolling Stone" and the Rolling Stones' "You Can't Always Get What You Want"

Wayne Kramer: Guitarist with MC5 and Gang War

Karl Kuenning: Roadie who has worked with over 200 artists; author of *Roadie: A True Story*

Mitch Lopate: Journalist/playwright

George McCorkle: Guitarist/songwriter with Marshall Tucker Band; solo recording artist

Goldy Mc John: Founding keyboard player with Steppenwolf, solo recording artist

John McKuen: Founding banjo player with The Nitty Gritty Dirt Band; Emmy Award–winning composer; has performed or recorded with artists such as the Doors, the Band, Hootie and the Blowfish, Phish, and many others.

Tommy Mandel: Keyboard player with David Johansen, Dire Straits, Bryan Adams Band, Hunter-Ronson Band, Little Steven, Ritchie Sambora, and others

Jocko Marcellino: Founding and touring member of Sha Na Na; television and film actor

Barry Melton: Cofounder/guitarist/vocalist with Country Joe and the Fish

Terry Morris: Artist/sculptor/comedienne/costume designer/actress/author

Peter Noone: Known as "Herman" of Herman's Hermits; television and stage actor

John Novello: Composer/arranger/producer/keyboardist who has played with A Taste of Honey, Andy Summers, Edgar Winter, Manhattan Transfer, Donna Summer, and others

Alice Nutter: Vocalist for activist band Chumbawamba

Willie Olmstead: Emmy Award–winning television producer and director; began behind the scenes career as security for Led Zeppelin and Alice Cooper

Nigel Olsson: Drummer/singer with Elton John, Spencer Davis, Uriah Heap, The Who, Rod Stewart, and many others

Panama Red: Songwriter/guitarist with Billy Shaver, and Kinky Friedman and the Jewboys; solo artist

Graham Parker: Singer/songwriter/guitarist with Graham Parker and the Rumours; solo artist

Dan Peek: Founding songwriter/guitarist with America; solo artist

Andy Powell: One of *Rolling Stone* magazine's "Top Twenty Guitarists of All Time"; co-founder of Wishbone Ash

Prairie Prince: Founding drummer of The Tubes; plays with Jefferson Starship; renowned artist and set and stage designer for music acts such as Michael Jackson, Bonnie Raitt, Shania Twain, and others

Rick Rose: Songwriter/singer with solo career in music (produced by Mick Ronson) and film; band involvement includes Lennex and Perfect Affair

Ralph Saenz: Singer with Atomic Punks and Metal Shop; actor

Justin Senker: Bass player with the Atlanta Rhythm Section

Scott Simon: Multi-instrumentalist/songwriter; Sha Na Na's Screamin' Scott; records also as Hong Kong Tailor

Chris Spedding: Guitarist; has played with Jack Bruce, Elton John, Brian Eno, John Cale, Tom Waits, and others

Ken Skaggs: Guitarist with Glen Campbell

John Strohm: Guitarist with Blake Babies, Anthrax, and Lemonheads; multi-instrumental session player; solo artist

Rob Squires: Vocalist/bass player with Big Head Todd and the Monsters

Lee Underwood: Guitar player with Tim Buckley; poet; author of *Blue Melody: Tim Buckley Remembered*

Violent Jay: Member of Insane Clown Posse

Bruce Watson: Guitarist with Big Country

Kayt E. Wolf-Strong: Keyboardist/vocalist; has performed with The Coasters, The Platters, Chris Montez, Peaches & Herb, and others

Gary Wright: Singer/songwriter; has performed with George Harrison and others; Number One hit with "Dream Weaver"

Rusty Young: Singer/songwriter/steel guitar player; founding member of Poco

INTRODUCTION

In "Midnight Rider," Gregg Allman sings that the road goes on forever. Most rockers would certainly agree with that sentiment. From the advent of the extraordinary and distinctive musical phenomenon known as rock and roll, musicians have been traveling from town to town, state to state, and country to country in pursuit of an audience. The venues and faces change as rapidly as the days on the calendar, and the rocker may not know exactly where he is at any given moment, but he knows what he must do: entertain. Only through live performances can a music act reveal its distinctive talent (or sometimes lack of same) in the pursuit of album deals, CD sales, fame, or whatever else it might be that it desires to attain through its association with rock and roll. Perhaps there *are* those who live only to make music, regardless of whether or not they have a large audience. At least that's what they might say. But the fact of the matter is that musicians can't live off the emotional highs they may enjoy performing in an off-road honky-tonk or local club. They are forced by financial concerns to expand their listening audience and connect with those who appreciate them enough to support their careers. Those who have successfully established themselves in the music industry have traveled many miles, visited countless venues, and lived a life unlike many others in the pursuit of their dreams. The lifestyle they have chosen has demanded that they embrace the "elements of the road."

The "elements of the road" are as varied as the musicians who experience this unique way of living. Yet in some ways, the fundamental components are

1

remarkably the same: extremely long hours of travel, broken-down half-assed vehicles, constipating fast food, flea-ridden motels and cheesy hotels, cheek-to-jowl living, fatigue, boredom, and loneliness. No matter how exciting the prospect of finding an audience who not only gets the music but also actually appreciates the effort, there are some things that those who decide to undertake a career in rock and roll can't circumvent. Consequently, those who travel the road are undeniably privy to some exclusive, attention-grabbing, head-scratching experiences.

Having been involved in the music business some twenty-seven years, I've been fortunate enough to hear some incredible road stories. Inevitably, when rockers get together, the tales flow fast and furiously. Sharing experiences with kindred spirits is somehow comforting to those living an atypical and isolated lifestyle. One of the most popular pastimes of rock and rollers—apart from the sharing of the music of course—is "Remember the time . . ." While the stories that unfold are always good for a laugh, a smirk, or a nod of the head, there's very little that musicians tell one another that is shocking or surprising to them. They've been there, done that. In spades. Yet those who haven't been privy to the intricacies and outrageousness of life on the road don't necessarily realize that what normal society might view as conventional is sometimes completely alien to touring rock musicans. They are, to put it succinctly, in a world of their own.

The more I thought about the possibility of inviting musicians to share their experiences in a public forum, the more I began to realize how idiosyncratic life on the road truly is. Through MTV and VH1 clips, rock biographies, concert tales, and the like, those not directly exposed to the road experience have had a glimpse of the kind of life a musician must lead. We've seen the excesses, the failures, and the triumphs. But those high and low points are hardly representitive of the lives musicians lead. By having artists from the '50s to the present share a story or two, a more complete representation of what they experience, how they handle events, and how they remember things in retrospect emerges to define the intricate "life on the road" experience. By sharing their stories, these artists have given us up-close-and-personal insights into who they are and how they live.

Tales from the Rock and Roll Highway is a collection of memories, stories, essays, quips, and reflections pertaining to the life lived on the road and all it encompasses. Entertainment is a challenging business, sometimes having more to do with the distinguishing dynamics of the various elements of touring than the actual show itself. *Tales* introduces the reader to the life musicians lead on a daily basis, warts and all. These stories reflect the complex artistic and day-to-day living experiences of rock musicians, an extraordinary group of people who must accept the commercialization of their art to familiarize an audience with their music. Stories of promoters, venues, roadies, groupies, hotels, buses, drugs, parties, shows, fans, and out-of-the-ordinary incidents are viewed from the perspective of individuals who have adopted an unusual lifestyle for the sake of their creative expression. What appears on the surface to be a pleasurable life of adulation, fame, and monetary reward is really quite different in reality. The stories range from the outrageous and funny to the poignant and reflective. We see what happens back stage, on the bus, at star parties, and behind the scenes. *Tales* takes the reader inside the beast—the rock and roll machine—to provide an extraordinary, introspective look at musicians who must endure all manner of experiences to establish themselves as artists and hopefully reach millions with their musical presentations.

It has been terrific to have so many rockers participate in this project and contribute their stories. The cross section of artists demonstrates that while each musician is unique, there truly is a rock and roll camaraderie that transcends time and subgenres. It may be a tire-worn musical highway, but thank God it's one that the people who entertain us continue to travel.

—Marley Brant

CHAPTER ONE

LIFE ON THE ROAD

L ife on the road. We hear whispers and tales about rock musicians frolicking around the world, being rewarded with vast amounts of "money for nothing" and enjoying a multitude of "chicks for free." They ride in limos or tricked-out tour buses, eat at all the "in" restaurants, go to the cool clubs, meet all the happening people, and party, party, party. Sounds like a sweet life. Sure, they've got to rehearse at least a little so they can play music that will make their fans want to come hear them, but that's not so bad. Wouldn't we all like to "work" by noodling on *our* guitars, keyboards, or drums? On the whole, they're just playing their music and enjoying their fame, aren't they? Well, yeah. But there's usually more to the story than what we see or think we know.

Until you've actually been "on the road," it's hard to identify with its long, tedious, lonely hours of travel in vans, buses, and airplanes and how difficult it is to get quality sleep. The food is monotonous and serviceable at best—certainly not your mother's—and there's a special stench that only a twice-worn stage shirt can generate (most artists are your average Joe, low- to middle-income musicians and not superstars who have people to take care of tiresome little chores like washing clothes). In other words, artists on the road have forgone the decency of daily life in their own comfortable homes with the people they love. Their music is their life. It has to mean everything in the world to them, otherwise the chaotic lifestyle they've chosen isn't worth a damn. Being on the road is routine, uncomfortable, and hard. Artists move from gig to gig, peddle their music, and live for that brief hour-and-a-half or so when they can share their love of song with people who actually appreciate what's being offered to them. The lifestyle is seductive, the opportunities limitless, and the dangling carrot of fame and fortune ever present. In the end, though, it's still life on the road.

DECENT FOOD: THE GREATEST SWAG OF ALL

SCREAMIN' SCOTT SIMON (SHA NA NA):

The interesting thing about being on the road is that no one, even the most seasoned of rockers, can predict what might happen on any particular day. It is true that some aspects of the experience can be painfully predictable. There's the travel (by bus, by plane, by train), the hotel (usually one of a half-dozen chains, if the act hasn't worn out its welcome), and the food (usually grabbed on the go or gobbled backstage). And always, THE SHOW—that magical time when the weary traveler comes truly alive for anywhere from forty-five minutes (if he or she is an opening act) to two hours or so (if he or she is the lucky headliner).

Yet it's also predictable that each day will contain at least one thing that can throw the touring performer and his professional entourage for a loop, such as box office screwups, cars that fail to show, temperamental artists sharing the bill, lack of adequate power or lighting or acoustics, promoters who fail to live up to the contract, and ad nauseum. Life on the road can, in some regards, be pure heaven. Or it can be—for an hour, a day, or months on end—its own kind of hell. Even with all the variables, however, the road never fails to provide an important life experience for the musician who travels it.

A working band that's on the road for weekends, weeks, or months at a time has a unique problem: how does it structure its day so that when it comes to "Showtime," the band is in the optimal physical, mental, and emotional state to best "rock the house." Everything leads up to "Showtime," and everything leads away from it.

The human body has only two ways to replenish energy expended: sleep and nutrition. Given the rigors of the road, made even more exhausting by the post-9/11 constraints on air travel, getting good sleep is rare. Different hotel rooms nightly, strange pillows, early wake-up calls after late nights, noisy maids in the hallways—all these varying conditions make good sleep an enviable commodity. If you happen to "sit down" in the same place for a few days, you may—after

Sha Na Na. Top (left to right): Jocko Marcellino, Buzz Campbell, Franklin Adell. Middle: Donny York, Jim Walkbilling. Bottom: Screamin' Scott Simon, Paulie Kimbarow, Reggie Battise
From the collection of Jocko Marcellino

getting adjusted to time zone differences, the taste of the local water, and the heating or air conditioning unit in your room—be able to saw some serious "z's." But you can't count on it.

Eating is then the option of choice when it comes to staying healthy and doing your job well. The truth of the musician's life is that his gig is pretty much a "swing shift" schedule, one that begins at the four PM load-in and ends at the midnight (or later) load-out. Many bands are able to negotiate one meal out of their employer of the night, and it is scarfed up between the end of the sound check or rehearsal and the beginning of the actual performance. This is the musician's favorite hour, the "Free Food Hour." Sure, there's a "rush" to being onstage making music, but nothing beats being fed a civilized meal.

If the band has some clout, it can dictate the menu of that meal right down to the salad dressing choices. This may be the only nutritious food that the musicians enjoy in a twenty-four-hour period, the only time the color green hits their plate in any form. "What is the problem?" you might ask.

Let's begin a midnight-to-midnight "day" in the life of a traveling musician.

Midnight is usually when the show is over, the equipment is all packed up, and it's time to find a bite to eat. The feeling is one of having earned some comfort food at the end of a long day and a hopefully successful show. So what's available? Back at the hotel, the bar is open but the restaurant's closed. Room service is long gone. The local pizza places might deliver if it's not too late or a weekend. We all know about the nutritive value of pepperoni. Or the guys pile into the van to seek more choices. They may come upon the "Awful House" (Waffle House, a twenty-four-hour staple in the Southeast), or they may find a drive-through of one of the regular fast food joints with their burger-an-fries menus. The band, having now been sated with high saturated-fat, carb-laden goodies of one kind or another, heads back to the hotel to wind down and eventually fall out. Who says you shouldn't sleep on a full stomach?

If travel plans don't necessitate it, musicians sleep until noon, when their breakfast, before moving on, consists of coffee and muffins, the caffeine and sugar-laced combo that gets most of America going each day. Fresh fruit? A luxury or an afterthought. Egg-white omelettes? Not currently available at chain restaurants off the interstate. Whatever it takes to get to the next gig determines the travel plans and eating opportunities. Airplanes no longer serve more than snacks and drinks, yet it may be many hours between the time you pass through security and the time you get to the next hotel. With notable exceptions (there's a joint near Gate 56 in Denver's airport that has a great fresh grilled tuna sandwich), the food in airports is no better or different than that on the highway. So food throughout the day is catch-as-catch-can.

By late afternoon, we're setting up for the next show, hopefully followed by the real dinner that actually has some vitamins and minerals, one that doesn't have to be eaten in a moving van.

And then on to the main event: the working musician's performance. After the show, the cycle begins all over again.

Some people think the greatest moment of the day is when you get paid. (Some claim it's when you get laid.) But that sit-down dinner between sound check and show is the one that keeps a band going. SWAG (stuff we ain't got) is free stuff that you can pick up along the way on the road—the T-shirts with the club's name on it that a friendly waitress might bring the band in the dressing room at the end of the night, the occasional hat with a logo on it that some promo person slaps on your head, the sampler CDs that local bands offer to trade with you. But the greatest SWAG of all is a free meal provided by the promoter.

GETTING THERE IS HALF THE FUN

In an airplane while on tour, Guns N' Roses' Izzy Stradlin didn't want to wait for an in-flight lavatory, so relieved himself in the galley.

Travel is an accepted necessity in the lives of musicians, but the hours they spend on the road making their way from venue to venue are certainly more than just an aggravating footnote to their professional lives. *Most of their time* is spent in transit. The standard form of transportation used by most rock bands is a tour bus. For most bands that haven't hit it big, the "tour bus" is, at first, actually a car or a tour van. Everyone in the band, regardless of its size, plus a roadie or two, jams into the van along with all the band's instruments and equipment. Also tossed into the mix are their clothes (clean or dirty, usually dirty) and the typical remnants of junk food packaging and other assorted trash. You get the picture.

By the time the band has developed a nest egg and has secured sufficient bookings to warrant the expense, it can upgrade to an actual bus. Now you've got the band, the roadies, and all their stuff in a slightly larger vehicle. At least there's a storage bin underneath to hold the amps and dirty clothes and maybe some of the instruments. That, in and of itself, is a much-appreciated bonus.

Now all there is to deal with are the endless miles of riding in the bus. See the U.S.A. Eat McDonalds or Burger King. Use the gas station toilets. Read a magazine or book. Listen to some music through headphones. What could be more fun? Well, they're doing this for weeks, maybe months on end. Oh yeah. Every day. All day. Often into the night. Once in a while they get to stop and play music. Then it's back in the bus and the return to what has now become a tedious, never-ending routine. But they suck it up and soldier on, hoping that somewhere along the road there might lay a little adventure. Invariably there does, although not always the kind they've been seeking.

DALLAS BRYANT (STREET SURVIVOR):

We've been a Lynyrd Skynyrd tribute band for eight years. Once when we were traveling from Georgia, we were pulled over in Mississippi by a sheriff's officer because we had been going eighty-five miles an hour. We'd all been consuming alcohol like fools, including Jeff, the driver. We were, to say the least, snockered. The sheriff looked us all over and told Jeff to get out of the van. He started to run him through the sobriety test. Jeff was hopping around outside while we thought stuffing all the beer can empties in pillowcases would conceal our intoxication. We watched Jeff go through test after test like a circus performer. He'd blow, and the sheriff had him do more acrobatics, and then blow and blow. Jeff honestly has a chemical imbalance. His blood alcohol level doesn't register as being drunk. Strange but true.

Two nights before, we met John Rockefeller's granddaughter. She gave us a Buddha statue and told us we would need it on our journey. While Jeff was undergoing the sobriety test, Snarley and me were rubbing the Buddha and praying. Well, the sheriff came back and shook his head and said, "I know you motherfuckers are drunk, but I can't get the proof. So get the fuck out of my county and never come back!" We surely obliged. Thanks Buddha and Jeff; without them we would have been at the parchment farm.

Another time, we stopped in Alabama at a roadside park to relieve ourselves. A big black security guard, as big and mean as Mean Joe Green, was outside the bathrooms. I visited with him and asked him why he was there. He says, "Had some, ya know, homosexual stuff going on." Well, me and Snarley and the other band members did our thing. Then Jeff and our drummer woke up and decided they had to piss. So, they jumped out of our van with their shirts off, both in their skivvies. Jeff's said "Jingle Balls" on them, and the drummer's were purple. They ran to the restroom, and when they passed us walking back to the van they started making high-pitched screaming noises. I turned and looked at the guard. His mouth was open and his eyes were bugging out as the two idiots hit the head. He followed them in and they came running out. When they got to the van, they said he had walked into the restroom and said, "Hey, we won't put up with any of that peter-puffing shit in Alabama."

There are so many stories. Like the ghost that follows us that—no shit—resembles Ronnie VanZant. We have photos. It overheats our equipment and drains our energy. There are motel stories but my God, I can't tell them. They're too nasty. Not sexual, just rotten.

There was the promoter who pulled a gun on us who we had to threaten with his life to get him to pay up; the naked tit floppers at many venues; the Louisville beer brawl where the promoting radio station advertised us for a week as Lynyrd Skynyrd without our knowing it. It was an April Fool's joke. We were barraged and beaten up with beer bottles—four hundred Kentucky mad-ass Skynyrd fans. They were throwing them from seventy yards back. Concussion city!

There was the promoter who booked us in the gay bar one night and the next night in a non-English-speaking Mexican bar in southern Texas. There were fights in Chicago. There was puking and sleeping with the homeless at the Washington Monument. There were the dwarves, one who looked like a short version of Jim Dandy who kicked me in the nuts and wanted to fight after the show in Georgia because we didn't play "Curtis Lowe," and the other in Tennessee who played the bass for the opening band who we couldn't see. There was having Kansas and Cheap Trick open—yes, open—for us at Club Lave in L.A.

And there were mosquitoes, flat tires, blown engines, and getting Leslie West water. And all the special shows with .38 Special, who are the nicest guys in the world, and Foghat and Molly Hatchet. And the drunken bastards in Chicago who opened for us as the worst Ozzy tribute, who smelled and plastered our van with ice cream. And being shook down in Arkansas by twenty highway patrolmen, ten sheriff's officers, and a SWAT team looking for drugs. We all had the flu and they made us get out of the van in a rainstorm, standing with laser beams from rifles on us while we watched them tear our van and trailer apart and then

Street Survivor. Top (left to right): Jimmy, Dustin, Orbit, Dallas, Rex. Sitting: Snarley
From the Collection of Dallas Bryant

let us go. We called the next day to complain and they had no record of any such stop or altercation.

The road is a motherfucker, and we're on it again. We'll have more stories and more great times. It's like riding a roller coaster backwards on laughing gas!

ROB SQUIRES (BIG HEAD TODD AND THE MONSTERS):

Like most great rock bands, Big Head Todd started down the musical road because it was fun. It also happened to be a great way to meet girls and get free beer. Many of our fondest moments took place in the early years, which for us began in 1986. Having tired of our crappy summer jobs, including mowing lawns, repairing bicycles, and cooking chicken for the Colonel, we decided to hit the road.

As an unknown three-piece band from Colorado, clubs and concert halls were not jumping up and down in order to provide us with work. We did, however, have a friend in Chicago who agreed to let us crash on her floor, and so the tour planning began. We planned on jumping in our van "The Colonel," a mustard-colored 1977 Plymouth, and driving to Chicago in the hopes of landing a gig.

Pulling into Chicago, we had no gigs lined up. The first gig we got was at a bar called At The Trax. We landed the coveted happy-hour gig only after massive begging of the manager, Carl, and also agreeing to play for fifty dollars.

The gig started as your basic weak happy-hour gig with a handful of people talking, not really interested in what we were up to. The longer we played, the more the bar started to fill and liven up. Before we could take too much credit for getting the party started, we realized that most of the people in the bar belonged to the improv comedy group Improv Olympic, which would be performing after us. Unbeknownst to us, Improv Olympic was a group of hysterical people, many of whom have since gone on to *Second City TV* and *Saturday Night Live* fame. About halfway through the first verse of "Beast of Burden," Chris Farley decided it was time to join the show. He ripped the mic away from Todd, and suddenly we were backing up Mick Jagger.

After begging all around town and actually landing one other lame happy-hour gig, we figured we pretty much had Chicago in our pocket. It was time to move on. Where next? Anybody ever been to New Orleans? It seems like a happening place. Surely we could get a gig there.

New Orleans was easy pickings after our street experience in Chicago. Either that or they're just more accommodating to beggars. We begged for gigs all up and down frat row at Tulane and ended up playing several parties. Didn't meet many girls, but we did get free beer. Without a friend's floor to crash on, we did the next best thing. We found an office complex that had a nice green lawn, and we threw our sleeping bags down. We're from Colorado so we know how to camp, right? Several problems. Have you ever been to New Orleans in the summer? It's hot. Even at night. So you just get rid of the sleeping bag, right? As soon as we took the bags away from our faces, the mosquitoes would attack. Also, nighttime is a good time to water that nice green grass.

We ended up abandoning our great idea and eventually we bedded down in the seats of The Colonel in a residential neighborhood. An elderly woman awakened us fairly early, knocking on the window with an inquisitive look on her face. Todd, sleeping in the driver's seat and not wanting to try and explain what we were doing or listen to a lecture, fired up the van and hauled it out of there. We'd had enough of New Orleans, but we did get a new tour strategy out of it: only go where we have friends we can stay with.

We spent the rest of the summer traveling and . . . not being able to see three feet in front of the van in a driving rainstorm while on the highest bridge we'd ever been on; blowing a water pump somewhere in the middle of nowhere in Arkansas; dodging suicidal rabbits in Big Bend National Park in Texas with Todd at the wheel after he'd lost one contact lens earlier in the day; having the accelerator cable strip out on the van and having to drive down the road manually working the carburetor; and stalling out at a tollbooth on the Bay Bridge during rush hour and almost blowing up the van by pouring starter fluid in the carb. Oh, and we did get a few more gigs along the way.

LARRY HOPPEN (ORLEANS):

I think it was in 1975 that we had a gig booked to open for Dave Mason up at the Boston Garden. We lived in Woodstock, so we drove. My brother Lance had a string of old Mercedes cars when he was in his youthful foolishness. I wound up driving him and Wells Kelly, our original drummer, up to this gig in Lance's Mercedes. I rarely drove his cars because the first time I borrowed his Mercedes, it had just come out of the body shop. It was wintertime, and a kid ran into me. Lance wasn't too happy about that.

So, I'm driving Lance's second or third Mercedes, and I went up on the Boston Pike. It's Friday rush hour. We're in the left lane doing about seventy. And this big ol' Pontiac, total jalopy, a boat of a car, comes by, and the kid who was driving it was about to sideswipe us. I was between his car and the guardrail. I put the left wheel up on the guardrail, and the next step was going over the guardrail into oncoming traffic. Well, that didn't happen. He didn't sideswipe us, and all the traffic behind us slowed down and let us get off the road. I pulled off the side at the bern [cement block at the side of the highway]. We were all just completely shaken up. There was nothing wrong with the car, except that the left front tire had blown out.

Lance was livid because this was his pride and joy. This kid gets out of his Pontiac; he's like eighteen or nineteen years old—a total hippie. Not that we weren't, but this kid was a slacker. Lance says, "Ya know, if we weren't late and going somewhere important, I would really take you to the cleaners here. But we are late and we gotta go be somewhere important, so just give me the money for

Orleans, 1975: Wells Kelly, Lance Hoppen, John Hall (rear), Larry Hoppen
Photo by Darren McGee, from the photo collection of Larry Hoppen

that Michelin tire." The kid reaches into his pocket and comes out with about $1.57 and says, "Well, that's all I got." Lance just gets more and more livid, and he's like "Jeez!" The rest of us are smoking Camels trying to calm down.

One thing leads to another, and he puts it together and figures out that we're Orleans and we're going to play at the Boston Garden. He says, "Oh man, you guys are Orleans, man. Cool! Oh, you're going to the Boston Garden! Um, can I have some tickets?" We just got back in the car, having put the stare on.

I was in Nashville a couple of weeks ago and a friend of mine was telling me that some girl backed her car into Vince Gill, hit him from the rear or something. He has a Mercedes as well. And when they got out of the car to exchange information, she gave him a tape! So, I guess people are still up to the same old thing.

JOHN STROHM (BLAKE BABIES):

When the Blake Babies first started playing shows in 1986 (all still in our late teens), none of us had ever owned a car. For our first dozen or so shows (all in the Boston area), we called for a station wagon taxicab to carry our gear to and from the club. We knew that we would eventually need to purchase a van, but our cab system served our needs well enough in the mean time.

Things happened very quickly for the band, and by early 1988 our first nationally released album hit the stores with a major press and radio campaign. We had to follow up our national exposure with a tour, which meant buying a van. We poured through the classified ads and found what we were looking for: a 1983 blue Chevy van with only 80,000 miles for less than $3,000. Juliana Hatfield came up with the funds, so she actually went and purchased the van.

It was a cargo van with no seats, so we went to the junkyard and bought a bench seat that we wedged between the two wheel wells in the back. We determined that we could pile the equipment in the space between the front seats and the wedged-in backseat. The only remaining problem that we could foresee was the lack of a tape deck, which we solved by purchasing a set of batteries for the jam box from our rehearsal space.

We set out on a full national tour two days after buying the van. The tour would take us all the way to California and back, with the final show being a triumphant return to Boston, playing at The Paradise (a plush, 1,000–capacity club) with two of our favorite bands, Yo La Tengo and Sonic Youth. The van had one of those old-fashioned odometers that flips over after 100,000 miles, and before we reached the end of the Massachusetts Turnpike we had figured out that the advertised 80,000 miles was probably fictitious. The van coughed and sputtered and emitted a strange, blue smoke. Whenever we cut off the engine, it would keep chugging away for at least a few seconds. Juliana decided that the van was possessed by Satan and that only she could be trusted to drive.

The first real breakdown occurred in Flagstaff, Arizona. We had two days to get to San Francisco, and we could barely make it up any significant incline. We took the van to a hole-in-the-wall service station next to our Motel 6, and the mechanic actually started laughing when we popped the hood. He asked when we had our last oil change, and we said, "You mean when did we last add oil?" He knew he had hooked suckers. We spent over a thousand dollars on God-knows-what. The van didn't run any better than before, and it took us over thirty hours to get to San Francisco. On the way into the city, we got pulled over. The officer said he pulled us over because he suspected us of transporting illegal immigrants.

Somehow, we managed to make it all the way down to Georgia with only a couple of minor repairs. On the way from Atlanta to Columbia, South Carolina, however, we got stuck in a traffic jam in a rainstorm on I-20. Suddenly we heard a resounding thud from beneath the van and then heard a terrible scraping sound. It turned out that a huge portion of the undercarriage had rusted out and separated from the vehicle. It took seven hours and another $1,000 to get it soldered back together, and we arrived at our Columbia show about ten minutes after our set time.

To our complete amazement, the van made it all the way back to New York City. We played a show at the Knitting Factory with our friends Tiny Lights, and we vowed to sell the van for scrap the minute we returned to Boston. It was Saturday night, and we were to play with Sonic Youth the following day.

After the Knitting Factory show (around four AM), we went to an all-night diner on the Lower East Side called Kiev with our friend Phil Morrison, who worked at our booking agency. Unbelievably, we found a parking space directly in front of Kiev. We pulled up and cut off the van, but the engine kept running. Soon the van began shaking wildly and emitting a noxious, blue-gray smoke. We tried to start the engine, but nothing happened. The van had died its final death. Various street people and late-night weirdoes had seen the spectacle of the van dying and hovered around, trying to see if we had anything worth stealing. Of course we did, so we stayed put while Phil went to try to find us a van. It seemed like a completely futile mission, but amazingly, he returned less than three hours later with a Ford Econoline with a comfy loft in the back. We loaded the new van, on loan from the band Das Damen, and high-tailed it for Boston, already in danger of missing sound check.

When we arrived behind The Paradise, Thurston Moore from Sonic Youth watched us pull up. He waved, and then went back into the club, returning with all of his bandmates. They all stared intently at the van, pointing and talking amongst themselves. When we climbed out, they said, "Hey, that's our van!" It turned out that they had recently sold their original van to Das Damen, and they were understandably amazed to see it pull up at their own show.

The following day, Phil managed to get our van out to his neighborhood in Brooklyn, where he left it for the vultures. Within a week, it had been picked apart and only the frame remained. A week after that, the only sign that the van had ever existed was a giant oil spot. We had three weeks off, during which we went to a Dodge dealer and bought a brand new Dodge Ram van, which I finally sold three years ago with over 200,000 miles on it.

We learned the most important lesson for a young touring band: the show is the easy part—the most important thing is making sure that you can get from point A to point B in one piece.

ZAK DANIELS (ZAK DANIELS AND THE ONE-EYED SNAKES):

Ah yes, the power of radio can be delicious. When small-town radio stations have been spinning your songs for three months prior to a live performance, it may sound strange, but the fans, the radio station personnel, and even the hotel employees treat you like rock royalty. When that first happened, it was a welcome change from the terminally jaded L.A. audiences we were used to playing to. Somehow, our first indie CD had two songs on the charts, and we went on tour to support it. We were hyped!

Notwithstanding the serious fun we had on that tour, it was not without its share of hellish moments. The day we were scheduled to leave, a member of our crew, who was also the owner of one of the trucks we were depending on, canceled two hours before departure time. Many frantic phone calls ensued, and we found a replacement. Although our replacement didn't have much experience, we were lucky to find anyone on such short notice. Unfortunately, he didn't have a truck. What he did have was an old beat up minivan. Let's see now, whose equipment should we leave behind? Hmmm . . .

"Is your van in good enough shape to make a 4,000-mile trip?" I asked our new recruit. "Sure, just had a tune-up. Runs great!" he replied boastfully. Although it ran okay, he had neglected to mention that his heater, windshield wipers, and defroster were completely shot. However, that didn't come into play until we were high above sea level, attempting to traverse one of North America's more impressive mountain ranges. Which (surprise, surprise) was also where we hit our first snowstorm. (Yep, the tour was off to a great start! That is, of course, if we could make it over the mountain alive and without frostbite.) Now I know what "cold as hell" and "snow blind" really mean.

Besides the shivering and uncontrollable teeth chattering, we had to stop every few miles to clean the windshield off. Every twenty minutes or so, we'd trade vans to let the "popsicle people" thaw out. By the time we made it to the other side of the mountain range, we had all experienced the joy of being "popsicle people." A wagon train would have been faster.

One of the dates scheduled was in a town in southern New Mexico. Like the other towns on this tour, the local radio station was promoting it. They had been all over the record for months, along with phone interviews and commercials for our show. The station paid for the hotel and meals, and as with most of these shows, we were to get a hundred percent of the door. The owner of the station promised me that it would be a minimum of $1,500. Not a bad deal for a new band on a shoestring promo tour.

As we were pulling into the hotel parking lot, we heard one of our songs on the radio, followed by a commercial for the show. We just sat there spellbound, with the radios in both vans blasting. It gave us all a good rush and recharged our energy. The journey's exhaustion had vanished; we were up and ready to rock!

UNDER THE WINGS OF TRANSIENT ANGELS

During a tour with Guns N' Roses, Metallica felt they needed to do something to get more attention from their audiences. They put their heads together and decided that setting off fireworks on stage might do the trick. Nice plan, but the first night, the fireworks set fire to vocalist James Hetfield.

Life on tour tends to make rockers more self-reliant than they might otherwise be as they deal with glitches with transportation, faulty equipment, unsatisfactory accomodations, and an assorted other 101 things that can go wrong on tour. While they're on the road, there's no one who has the artists' best interests at heart more so than themselves. Most of the time, things go according to plan. The basic plan isn't usually that complex, although it can take a lot of time to figure out and organize all the particulars. If they're lucky, they have a road manager or group of roadies to take care of such things because once musicians set foot on the road, their main focus is traveling and doing their musical thing. Yet, as is the case with life in general, once the musician sets foot outside his or her door, there can be snags and unexpected developments. This, that, or the other thing may occur to make them scratch their heads and wonder if, at the end of the day, it's all worth it. Sometimes they have no choice but to shrug their shoulders and throw themselves into the arms of unexpected angels. And believe me, those angels come in all shapes and forms.

NEAL CASAL (SOLO ARTIST):

There was this tour the Beachwood Sparks did with the Black Crowes a couple of years ago. I played guitar and piano with the Sparks for about six or seven months. The Black Crowes asked us to go out and open for them on what turned out to be their last tour. We thought it would be pretty cool: drive around, see the country, play in all these big places for thousands of people, maybe even make a few bucks if we got lucky. Well, I guess we didn't think it through, because in reality we didn't have nearly enough cash to survive the adventure.

We had a beat up old van that broke down all the time, a trailer that always seemed to be getting flat tires, and worst of all, we had to keep up with the Crowes with all of their big buses and semis. They could drive at least a thousand miles between shows with no problem. The drivers knocked down the miles while the band and crew slept soundly in their spacious bunks with satellite TV, DVD players, reading lights, and all the rest. We, on the other hand, did our own driving and had to cover the same miles in our dying van and trailer. We had to be on time for the five PM sound check every day, then play at seven thirty or maybe eight o'clock for the two or three hundred people who happened to have wandered in early, finding their seats, buying their beers, checking their tickets. All

Neal Casal
Photo by Laura Heffington

this was an extreme case of the good old "opening act blues." Not exactly the rock 'n' roll dream tour we had in mind.

Worst thing was that the first show was in Fargo, North Dakota. That's right, Fargo, North Dakota. We were an L.A. band. Do you know how far it is from L.A. to Fargo? It was a three-day drive just to get to the first show. Quite an exhausting way to start a two-month tour. Well, we somehow made it to Fargo and got through the first show all right. Next show was in Nampa, Idaho, which was another two-day drive from Fargo. From Nampa it was on to Eugene, Oregon, which turned into a harrowing death drive that none of us can ever forget, even if we want to.

We had to get to Eugene by five o'clock. We raced all through the night down these really steep and dangerous mountains doing eighty miles per hour or more. There were steep cliffs off each side of the road, and wave after wave of blinding fog. Our drummer was at the wheel, and at times it felt like we were on a suicide mission. Nobody slept a wink. Damn near ran out of gas at four AM. No service stations anywhere, no streetlights, nothing. By daylight, things seemed to be mellowing out a little bit. If we could just stay awake, we might actually make it to Eugene. We stopped someplace for a few quick eggs and coffee around seven AM. Everything's cool, we're still alive. Let's get back on the road.

We were still in Idaho somewhere, I think, when the van decided to quit on us. Broke down cold. Middle of nowhere. Nothing around for miles except for an irrigation ditch off in this field. Ninety-five miserable degrees outside. No cell service, hardly any cars on the highway. As you can imagine, morale was pretty low at this point, but we mustered up enough energy to climb the fence and gather around the irrigation ditch, taking our shirts off, throwing rocks in the water, telling jokes, and discussing our options. There weren't any. Got bored with that after awhile. Went back over by the van, threw some more rocks (at passing cars this time), told the last few jokes we could remember, and pulled our shirts back on as if something else just had to happen.

Well, it finally did. A big flatbed pulled up and stopped. The driver got out and asked us what the deal was. We told him we had to get to Eugene by five PM or the Black Crowes would kick us off the tour. Of course, they wouldn't have, but we were desperate. He said he felt for us, but that it was illegal for him to cross state lines while hauling another vehicle. He then said that it was illegal for us to be riding in our vehicle while being towed across state lines. He also said that it was illegal for him to tow our trailer while carrying our vehicle with us inside the vehicle across state lines. It was just plain illegal no matter how you looked at it. There was really no way around it, but he thought for a minute, and for a fee of six hundred dollars in cash, he would take the risk and make sure he got us to the show on time. He loved rock 'n' roll and if we could just get him an autographed Black Crowes T-shirt, it would really score big points with his girlfriend. She was a big Black Crowes fan from way back. She really loved the video for "Hard to Handle." So we counted all of our money, and as it turned out, we only had $470 between us. We promised we'd get him the rest of the money from the Crowes' tour manager when we got to the theater. He said he didn't like it, but we looked like we could be trusted (I do think he was half blind). Incredible, it looked like we were gonna make it after all!

So here we go. The guy drags out a long chain, pulled our van up onto the flatbed, and hooks our trailer up to his hitch. We climbed up onto the flatbed and into our van. He said that we all had to lie down on the floor 'cause if the cops saw us, we were all going to jail. So, now we were lying down on the floor of the van, using empty cups, candy wrappers, dirty socks and shirts for pillows. It was probably 110 degrees in there. The van wasn't running, so we couldn't use the A/C and it was really bumpy and strange being this high above the freeway. By some miracle, we found a bottle of Cuervo under a seat and started passing it around.

After a couple of punishing hours, the driver decided to stop for food. We all climbed down out of the van, off the flatbed, and into our second McDonalds of the day, drunk and sweating and laughing hysterically now. Quite a sight we must have been. We called ahead and explained the situation to the Crowes' tour manager. We were out here on this flatbed but we'd be on time. Meet us out front with the money and the T-shirt at five o'clock on the dot.

We climbed back up onto the flatbed and into the van with our reeking food and a little more Cuervo left in the bottle, a couple more shots until the Oregon line. Things were getting a little blurry, but I got the feeling that we were going really fast now, even faster than the eighty-five miles per hour we'd been doing in the mountains the night before. I looked out the back window to see the trailer bouncing wildly from side to side down the highway. It's hard to believe, but I thought the whole rig—flatbed, van, and trailer—was moving close to one hundred miles per hour. Tears filled my eyes, thinking our equipment would be in splinters by the time we finally dragged it out of the van. If we even made it at all.

I must have passed out cold, because the next thing I remember is waking up to the sound of a small crowd cheering. I looked at my watch: five o'clock sharp. I struggled to my knees and realized that the flatbed had come to a stop. Someone said, "I think we're in Eugene." Someone else said, "I think we're in front of the theater." And finally, "Hey, I think we made it." But where was the cheering coming from? I looked out the window and lo and behold—it was the entire Black Crowes band and crew holding "Welcome Beachwood Sparks!" signs and greeting us like astronauts or war veterans as we climbed down off the flatbed. Hugs, handshakes, and high fives all around. Signed T-shirts and posters for the driver. I'll bet he had a good time with his girlfriend that night. We paid him the rest of his money, said thanks and goodbye, stumbled into the theatre as usual, sound-checked our battered equipment, and played the show of our lives for two hundred lucky music freaks that night.

MOJO COLLINS (SOLO ARTIST):

Playing solo was fine, but I longed for another band sound. I met a bassist named Bill Ellis up in Raleigh, my hometown. A drummer percussionist named Keith Shealy had been recruited from Newport News, Virginia, and rounded out the trio. We came together in my garage in Kitty Hawk and named the band after the famous town. It wasn't long before our sound was tight enough to go on the road, so we booked a long road trip up to North Wilkesboro, North Carolina, some ten hours from the Outer Banks.

The gig was cool and we got a room, so off we went to our slumber.

The next morning after breakfast, we packed up the Monte Carlo that belonged to Keith. We were hauling a trailer full of gear and band clothes. We arrived in North Wilkesboro sometime after lunch. We managed to just get something ordered before the Holiday Inn restaurant closed.

After eating a hardy meal, we headed to the bar where we set up our show and equipment. We used what are known as flash pods to accentuate the endings of some of our rock songs. The bassist Bill Ellis, or "Daweez" as we called him, would step on a foot switch to set them off. We tested them before we left that afternoon and they seemed to be working fine.

That night at the show, after our last song, he stepped on the flash pod button and sure enough, they went off. But one malfunctioned, and when it exploded, it shot fireballs into the air instead of smoke. I was standing with my back to the pod when it went off and didn't realize what had happened until it was too late. Some of the ashes landed on my head. They burned my scalp and made for quite a large amount of applause from the audience. I guess they thought it was all part of the show, but seriously, my head was on fire. "Put it out! Put it out! Put it out!" I shouted. Daweez came running over and poured his Coke over my head, dousing the smoldering remains of the flash pod's bevy. All three of us had a big laugh along with the audience members, and it was time for the curtain for sure.

We were asked to do an encore but politely refused, and I headed for the comfort and warm shower in our motel room. After showering, everything was fine. I just left a bunch of hair conditioner on my head overnight, and the next morning it was not as bad as it had seemed to be at the time.

After completing that week, we were heading home for a much needed rest and were somewhere along the highway just outside of Greenville, North Carolina. Keith Shealy was driving while Daweez was in the backseat snoring away some z's. I was riding shotgun in the front when I thought that I smelled something burning and turned to Keith to ask him if he did also. He said "Yeah," and when we looked into the backseat, smoke was coming out from underneath it and also from the rear of the car by the right-hand taillight.

Slamming on the brakes immediately, we pulled off the road onto a median that was marked for that very reason. Coming to a stop abruptly, I turned to Daweez and shouted, "Weez, Weez! Get up and get out of the car! It's on fire!"

Well, he jumped up from a dead sleep and was out of that car in seconds, standing on the side of the highway as cars flew by us on either side at high rates of speed. Keith had gone around to the back of the car and opened the trunk, and smoke just bellowed out like crazy. Once it had cleared, we were able to see that a wire had shorted out where the trailer we were pulling had been hooked up for lights. Sparks had gotten under the back seat and started smoldering in the foam that stuffed the seat.

Keith shouted as he pulled the wires apart, "Get the backseat out of the car quick!" I got the tools out of the toolbox, and Daweez and I quickly undid the bolts holding the seat in and pulled it out onto the median. All along it was smoldering like crazy. Not having any liquids in the car at all, the three of us just looked at each other and said, "Put it out! Put it out! Put it out!" Whipping out our hoses with their little fireman's hats, we extinguished the flames and smoldering smoke within a few seconds.

Getting the seat back in the car and bolted down was easier than getting it out. It wasn't long before we were on our merry way. We started chuckling under our breaths, and then just bursting out loud with laughter at what just happened. To date, this story lingers as one of the all time great tales of my life and travels on the many highways with rock and roll bands. We were definitely being watched by angels that day.

DEBBY BOYER (AUSTIN PETTIT BAND):

I'm now fifty-three, but I've played in bands since I was sixteen. While traveling with my rock and roll band in our converted school bus through Kansas in the early seventies, a very weird thing occurred. We spent the weekend gigging out in southwestern Kansas and were headed for home, which at the time was the western Kansas town of Ft. Hays.

We were probably fifty or sixty miles southwest of Dodge City that night, and even though it was two thirty in the morning, we were wide awake and having a good time. We were all in our early twenties and used to staying up late and sleeping in. The land through which our old yellow bus traveled was very flat. One could see for many miles. Towns in the distance always seemed to float above the surface of the horizon. Everything was pastureland or planted to wheat. It was after the harvest, so stubbles remained where the wheat once grew. Buffalo grass out in the plains in the best of times is probably not over a foot high in places.

There were five of us in the band and we were laughing, partying, and carrying on in our usual way when all of us looked out of the windows and saw an old man dressed in brown khaki pants with a brownish plaid shirt, wearing a Stetson. We were probably traveling no more than forty-five or fifty miles per hour. The old man was standing close to the shoulder of the road. We drove past him maybe a couple of hundred feet and then slowed down and backed up to where we had last seen him. We thought perhaps he needed help. But he wasn't there! As I mentioned, the grass wasn't tall. Even if he had lain down, we would have been able to see him.

We didn't get out of the bus. We were spooked. We sat there for some minutes trying to figure out if we were all suffering from a group hallucination. We drove forward a bit and then backed up even more in case we'd missed the place where we thought we'd seen him standing. But he simply disappeared.

It was spooky. We all saw the same thing at the same time. There was no way he could have walked anywhere. It's flat as a pancake out there on that part of the prairie. No trees. Not even a ditch. Just endless prairie. So what happened? Why did we all see the same thing at the same time? If indeed we did conjure up the old man from thin air, then it surely was a testament to our group unity!

THE WHEELS ON THE BUS GO ROUND AND ROUND

Pearl Jam wrote their song "Dirty Frank" about their tour bus driver. They had an inside joke that the driver, whom they called "Frank Dahmer," was a serial killer in another life.

The tour bus is synonymous with being on tour. A musician who hasn't experienced "life on the bus" probably doesn't exist. If a musician is blessed with the unique success that keeps him or her playing music to interested audiences ten years or so after starting out, that musician has without a doubt spent hundreds of hours on a tour bus—the rocker's home on wheels.

TOM BRUMSHAW (GUITAR PLAYER):

When I first started with Buck Owens in 1964, we had a Dodge motor home that we toured in. Which wasn't too bad, considering that George Jones had an old flex bus that had a wood-burning stove in it for heat. On our way back from North Dakota in late '64, coming down through Montana, Don Rich spun it out on some ice and tore it up so bad we had to leave it and fly home to Bakersfield, California.

So on our next tour, Buck's dad volunteered his pick-up camper. This tour was about three weeks long and the last date was in Philadelphia, Pennsylvania. By the time we got up to Philadelphia, we were pretty beat up and tired and dreading the long trip back to Bakersfield. At this time, we had several hit records and we were headlining the show. When we arrived at the auditorium, we parked alongside of the other performers' buses. As we stepped out I heard someone say, "Who's in that thing?" I went over to the lady and introduced myself. I said we were the Buckaroos, and this is what ol' Buck gave us to travel in.

Buck was flying home after the show that night. I told Buck that I was going to stop on the way home and get a can of spray paint and paint "Buck Owens and the Buckaroos" on the side of the camper so people would know who we were. Buck didn't think that was a good idea, and we both got a little hot about it.

Usually when I would get home, Buck would call me and we would play golf all day. Well, he didn't call for three days and when he did, all he said was, "Tom, go get a bus!" The next day I was on a plane to Custom Coach in Columbus, Ohio. I put every item on that bus that was available. It was still running great when I left, five years later.

JIMMY IBBOTSON (NITTY GRITTY DIRT BAND):

I had the chance to come home for a couple of days this week. I decided to stay out as the only rider on a private coach. This tour bus is pretty crowded with the whole band and crew and our guitars and drums and amps and T-shirts and CDs, usually. But right now, driving along Yellowstone on the way from Sturgis to Sandpoint, it's pretty sweet.

We've got a refrigerator full of the Doobie Brothers' deli tray and Martina McBride's beer. We've got a satellite dish that works even when we are rolling. We have home-baked bread from the Wisconsin Valley Fair and a new toaster oven on the counter, next to the coffeemaker and under the microwave.

I made the driver check me out behind the wheel. In the old days, I used to drive the Dirt Bus after Jeff [Hanna] and the lads had fallen asleep. Sometimes they didn't get how overworked a driver can become. In the middle of the night, when he is hallucinating on speed and cactus whiskey, it's a good idea to sit up there and sing him a song or two in the catbird seat, or listen to his stories of fishing and hunting and NASCAR and all the girls he's loved before.

But sometimes you've got to take the wheel. We are always behind schedule. Every band is. Long way to go and a short time to get there. So you get good at waking out of a sound sleep and sliding in under the driver as he hands you the wheel. Cruise control has made this maneuver simpler and safer. But a strung-out driver might just get up on a straight stretch of road and walk back to the restroom to empty his bladder of a thermos of coffee and a six-pack of beer. You'll see him chopping up white crosses and snorting them off the coffee table. A good driver can take a leak and snort up a line or two of truckers' toot and not rush

Jimmy Ibbotson
Photo by Liz Treadwell,
from the photo collection
of Jimmy Ibbotson

back to the wheel until he hears the tires hit the rumble strips on the shoulder. A good driver can surf the bus from rumble strips and not wake one of us up.

This morning, when I woke up, the driver was still passed out on the couch in the front lounge, where I left him the night before. We'd driven a ways, in the midst of thousands of outlaw bikers, most of them outlaws for a couple of weeks every summer. You don't have to ride a motorcycle too far before you start to feel a little more alive than the castrati driving the minivans with their fat wives and bratty kids to and from Yellowstone. There were three-quarters-of-a-million people at this sixty-second annual event in Sturgis [the annual run for motorcyclists]. I was glad when the bikes thinned out. I didn't especially want to lose control of these ten tons of European excess and take out a knucklehead with a couple of freaks on board. I don't care how many times I am told that half of these people are doctors and lawyers. I'm scared of these guys. When I see a girl on the back of a chromed-up chopper, wearing nothing but a pair of chaps and two strips of electrician's tape, I am intimidated by the guy who's driving it. These guys are tough. But not tough enough to withstand a run-in with a VanHool 45, until recently under the control of a tie-dyed, toothless narcissist from America's oldest rock 'n' roll band.

The Blind Boys From Alabama have been singing together longer than NGDB. But they have kids playing great Otisian R&B charts behind them. They aren't a band. The Eagles are neophytes compared to Nitty Gritty Dirt Band. Two Dog Night doesn't count. The Doobie Brothers, like the Beach Boys, hire hot Nashville pickers to play drums and keys and bass. We're a band, man. We play what we wrote and recorded in the studio. We did it in the '60s, and we're doing it now.

The Dead would have had us beat, but Jerry joined Janis and Jimi and Buddy and the rest of that choir in Hillbilly Heaven. I can't believe I am not spelling Keith Moon during his bathroom breaks. We've been lucky. None of us have OD'd, or driven off a cliff, or surfed headfirst into the reef, or eaten a gun barrel or tailpipe. We never got so famous that we made so much money that it was worth fighting over anything. That's a big deal, I think. If we had sold the number of records that Fleetwood Mac sold, we could have afforded much more destructive habits. We would have been closer to more powerful lawyers. Someone would have supported us when each of us said, "I'm carrying this band on my back. They don't appreciate what I do. I deserve more money." And some sycophant would agree, and we'd set off on solo careers. Actually, a couple of us have done that a couple of times. But our solo careers meant nothing without the brand name.

Neil Young survived Springfield. Crosby survived the Byrds, but without the success. Brian Wilson crashed and burned, even though he did the lion's share of the writing and singing and playing and producing on those great Beach Boys hits. But it drove him crazy to find out that we didn't like his perfect music as much as the clatter of his brother on drums and his other brother on harmony and lead guitar. Like Fogerty's Revival, it was mostly him. But without the rest of them, the chemistry changed. Fogerty plays the Houses of Blues to 2,500 people. Creedence Clearwater Revisited plays to 60,000 at biker rallies. Go figure.

But, NGDB is egalitarian to the max. I drove this bus four hundred miles today. Fadden sets up his own drums, every day. Johnny carries his banjo with him everywhere he goes. It's with him in Hollywood, while I am with you, ten miles out of Sandpoint. We have a whole day off. And, it isn't dinnertime yet. I've got time to clean up and log on and walk the waterfront as the sun goes down.

I'll take a guitar into my room and try to remember some of the old songs that I used to sing to the drivers: "Truck Stop Girl," "Six Days on the Road," "I Took Three Bennies, Now My Semi-Truck Won't Start." I might listen to some of our old CDs and try to relearn a song or two. Who knows? The weight of my life juxtaposed to the insanity of the world as described by CNN and *USA Today* might cause me to wax rhapsodic. I may even write a new song about the teenage waitress in Sheraton, Wyoming, who almost got on the bus with us. In the song, I'll bet she chooses to leave her college-girl life behind and join the circus. It's happened before. It'll happen again.

"911"

While preparing for a tour with Limp Bizkit and Metallica in 2003, Linkin Park's singer Chester Bennington was hospitalized with intense chest and stomach pains. Doctors were unsure of the cause of the pain but thought it might be a parasite the musician had ingested when he had eaten uncooked food.

Think about waking up and knowing you've got it: the flu. Your head is pounding, you're tossing your cookies right and left, and you're giving new meaning to that descriptive phrase "the trots." Now think about having these (or other equally wonderful symptoms) while you're at work and thousands of miles away from home. Oh, what fun. Many fans (predominately female ones) would probably love to be giving TLC to the touring musician in such circumstances, but who wants to meet chicks that way? No, you're really on your own now. Well, there's your band or the other people associated with your tour. (Oh yeah, playing nurse is really the way they want to be spending their free time.) Sometimes, if you're really lucky, there's the very welcome exception and someone—sometimes the most unexpected someone—will take pity on you and make your pain just a little bit easier to bear.

BARRY MELTON (COUNTRY JOE AND THE FISH):

In late 1967 and throughout most of 1968, several San Francisco Bay Area bands were in the forefront of the rock music revolution. Big Brother, the Grateful Dead, and our band, Country Joe and the Fish, were on the road constantly. And all of those bands spent a great deal of time in New York living at the Chelsea Hotel. In fact, as well as we all knew each other from the many gigs we'd played together back home, we got to know one another a lot better when we were all living at the same address. (I should note that for whatever reason, the Jefferson Airplane always stayed at the Algonquin—but they had a hit single ["White Rabbit"] and were making a lot more money than we were at the time.)

The Chelsea Hotel was a hell of a place to stay back in those days. This was the historic and legendary New York home of Edith Piaf, Diego Rivera, and Dylan Thomas. When we were staying there in the '60s, it was inhabited by a host of extraordinary people: artist Andy Warhol lived there, as did playwright Arthur Miller, composer George Kleinsinger, folk music anthologist Harry Smith, and the rag-tag bands from San Francisco touring up and down the East Coast. Aside from its status as the legendary home of free thinkers and the avant-garde, it was also one of the cheapest "no-hassle-to-hippies" hotels in New York at the time.

As exciting as it was to be in New York with our careers on the ascendancy, it was also very lonely. We were kind of like the Indians brought from the Western plains to perform in Buffalo Bill's Wild West Show. We were from San Francisco, a city barely one-tenth the size of New York and many thousands of miles away. And we were poor and struggling, so we certainly couldn't travel with an entourage, and coast-to-coast telephone calls cost a bundle of money back in those days.

In the midst of all that confusion and the swirl of unreality, there was only one woman on the road with us and also staying at the Chelsea Hotel whom any of us knew for any length of time: Janis Joplin. Janis was like a rock for all of us. Twenty or twenty-five guys, including road crew, and one den mother—Janis.

I remember the winter of 1967, while my band was in the midst of sessions for our second album at the Vanguard Records studio just down the block from the Chelsea. I caught the worst case of the flu I've ever had in my life. My temperature shot up to above 105 degrees for days, and I couldn't get up out of bed. Nobody, and I mean nobody, from the band came by to see me during that period. Hell, they were in the middle of Manhattan, in the middle of a recording session, and I was burning up in my hotel room with the flu. And none of the guys from any of the other bands seemed all that interested in paying me a visit either. Perhaps they thought I was contagious.

I always thought of Janis as "one of the guys"—a talented singer, a friend, someone you could have a drink and a laugh with. There was never even a hint of romance between us. We were just friends who played a little music together. But when I came down with this terrible flu, every morning and every night Janis would come to my room, usually with some hot soup in hand or something else from the delicatessen on the corner of Seventh Avenue and Twenty-third Street. She'd sit by my bedside and talk, just to check in and see how I was doing or to ask if she could bring anything for me or if there was anything I needed. She'd grab a washcloth and mop my brow, tell me about her day's events, and she would always leave my room extracting the promise that I'd call her if I needed anything at all.

As the years have flown and the legend-image of Janis has developed into one of a tough, two-fisted drinker who lived and died by the blues, what I remember is the sweet, caring, and compassionate angel who took time out of every day to come by to visit and care for me when I was at the bottom. Janis was as solid as a rock and as good a friend as I've ever had. We stayed friends until the day she died, and I dearly wish she'd lived long enough to reminisce about all this stuff.

I remember a couple of years later, after Janis left Big Brother, our bands did a show together somewhere in the Midwest—I think it was at the Cleveland Municipal Auditorium. We were staying at this hotel that had a restaurant with a Revolutionary War theme—something like the "Old Colony Restaurant" or the "Thirteen Colony Restaurant," with drums, fake muskets with bayonets, and

Barry "The Fish" Melton
(Country Joe and the Fish)
*From the photo collection of
Barry Melton*

stuff like that on the walls. Anyway, Janis and I were eating breakfast together at the restaurant in the morning with another musician or two. Some guy comes over and starts hassling me (my hair was really long back then) and says stuff like, "Peace freak," "Which one is the girl?" and other such pronouncements. The guy is loud, obnoxious, and haranguing us for about half our breakfast while we continued trying to ignore him to the best of our ability.

Hippies weren't all that popular with local law enforcement in those days, so we decided to resist the temptation to go over and confront the jerk. But finally Janis had enough, and she jumped up from the table and yanked one of those fake muskets with a bayonet attached off the wall of the restaurant. With absolute resolve she walked over to the loudmouth, weapon in hand, stuck the thing about an inch from his throat, and told the guy something like, "If you want to live through the morning, you'll shut the fuck up!" Well, sure enough, the guy did shut up. In fact, I think he was so frightened he got up, hurriedly paid his bill, and ran from the restaurant in a state of absolute fear. Like I said, Janis was as solid as a rock and a good friend. And I do miss her.

ONLY YOUR DENTIST KNOWS FOR SURE

While out on tour with Aerosmith, Joe Perry's wife Elissa had a toothache and demanded to be flown back to Boston on a Lear jet to have her own dentist tend to it. While his wife slept on the plane, Perry asked the pilot to do some barrel rolls. Lots of guys might have caught hell for such a move, but Elissa woke up during the rolls, pronounced them "cool," and asked for more.

Some mega-stars might be able to interrupt their tour to return home to take care of their own or their spouse's toothache. But that takes money—usually lots of it. If you don't have cash to burn, sometimes you just have to tough it out. Being a creative person, however, can actually come in quite handy when dealing with such inconveniences on tour.

RORY BLOCK (SOLO ARTIST):

Sorry, but this story opens in a dentist's office. The depressing words "you're going to need a root canal" were still ringing in my head. The only thing I could think of saying was, "How much is that going to cost?" The answer was, "Mmm, maybe about $1,500 for the first phase." Then a bright idea dawned on me. "How much would it cost to remove the tooth," I asked. Seventy dollars sounded like a far better option, and without considering the gaping hole that would result, I triumphantly said, "Yank it out and throw it away!"

I thought I had all but beaten the system. Although the missing tooth wasn't directly in front, I hadn't considered the fact that if anything at all made me happy and I had occasion to smile, well, you could see where the missing tooth should have been. No problem, I thought. Why do I need that tooth? Couldn't it be kind of funky and bluesy-looking to have a missing tooth? Maybe I would get a gold tooth like my buddy Jorma. It could become a trademark. Then later I reasoned, I don't really have to smile. I wandered about for a while, shielding my mouth with a thoughtfully placed hand.

The first show after the extraction was the Toronto Blues Festival. As I sat there in front of all those good people in the blazing sun, I realized that everyone on earth could see the "missing tooth," so of course I made it into the most entertaining story I could muster. Quite possibly, no one was amused.

Finally, the dentist custom-made a small pop-in tooth after I flatly rejected the giant plate that had been prepared for me. With that huge piece of hardware and sculpture in my mouth it was impossible to speak, let alone sing. I think I have embraced—even celebrated—graceful aging, but sounding like the "Pepperidge Faam remembiz" man was really too much. So a little streamlined tooth was given to me, and I found myself carrying it around in my jeans' pocket and popping it in whenever I had to be presentable.

Next, we had a two-week tour of the U.K., immediately followed by a mini-concert on QVC, the world's largest shopping channel. If I ever had to look presentable, it was probably for the over seventy million viewers who would likely watch the show. Each day when we left the hotel room in England, Jordan would say to me, "Mom, do you have your tooth?" I would slap my jeans pocket and say, "Yep, got it!" One day when he asked me, I slapped the pocket and it felt flat. I checked, and yes, horror of horrors, the tooth was not there. At that point we were three hundred miles down the road and closing in on sound check. There was no going back. We called the hotel and the proprietor was exceptionally understanding. In his elegant accent, he kindly promised to have the cleaning lady check everything, right down to the dishwasher screen. Needless to say, looking for a tooth in a glass proved futile. Back to that distinctive look of character I had always dreamed of. But what about QVC? Would the viewers really understand?

We would arrive home jet-lagged late on a Sunday night. The next morning we were scheduled for a seven AM departure for QVC in Pennsylvania. Not much time to see the dentist, but there had to be a way. It's still not easy to make overseas calls from hotel rooms, but I managed to get the dentist on the phone. I explained my emergency and asked if he could create another tooth from the mold, only to learn that they don't keep those things sitting around taking up shelf space—a little tooth mold with your name and address stamped on it. What to do?

After more than one desperate call, all we could come up with was to find an edible, pliable tooth-colored substance (possibly taffy or some other kind of hard, chewy candy), and fashion a temporary tooth. It was kind of crazy, but there weren't a lot of options. Rob and I spent the morning . . . checking every grocery store in London, searching the candy counters, attempting to explain "salt water taffy." (They don't appear to have it in London; maybe it's more of a New England thing—everyone looked mystified.) We finally discovered the right texture, but it was not the right color (teeth are not really bright white). We found the right color, but it was way too soft. Then suddenly we found something that seemed right. We fashioned a lumpy tooth; it was almost right. What's this? It was melting down! What did we expect? It was made of sugar. Another desperate overseas call, and the dentist had a brilliant plan. Come by his office at seven AM Monday morning and he'd have me out of there in an hour. "Just don't eat anything until after you're off the air," he cautioned.

Airtime was five PM, and fasting never seemed so important. All the while, I was having visions of my cute little temporary acrylic tooth flying out of my mouth during a passionate moment of song in front of seventy million confused onlookers. Nonetheless, I sang my heart out (I'm not a polite player and don't think there's a way to reduce the intensity of country blues). I've long since made the decision that the best way to go down is while doing what I love. Not only did the "tooth" stay put, but it also lasted two months until a permanent replacement was finally installed. I forgot to send flowers to the dentist. It's still on my list.

KEEPING IT CLEAN

A company that offers "rock adventures" claims it will not only take fans to a London Rolling Stones concert, but also show them some favorite band-member haunts. They offer a top-drawer accommodation package, but you have to do your own laundry. Fans taking the tour shouldn't complain. One of their idols doesn't. While playing San Francisco one night, Keith Richards announced that he loved San Francisco, but didn't avail himself of the famous laundries in Chinatown—he did his own laundry.

Doing laundry is a boring task for everyone. We all usually take enough clothes on vacation so that we don't have to waste time washing, sorting, and folding. Musicians are usually out on tour for weeks and months, and taking enough clean clothes to last that whole time would be impractical, if not terribly expensive. An appointed roadie does the rock star's laundry, for the most part. But things happen—even the lucky, personally selected laundry maven gets sidetracked and the job doesn't get done. The necessity of having to deal with dirty clothes is just one more fact of life that touring musicians share with the rest of us.

GILL MANNING (FAN):

In autumn of 1984, my sister and I went to see David Essex at Birmingham Town Hall. During his usual chats with the audience, he pointed to his flapping shirt cuffs and said, "Look, no buttons. Buttons came off. No one to sew them on for you." He then lifted his trouser leg up, to the delight of his fans, and said, "Look, no socks. That's what happens when you're on tour for months. You run out of socks and there's no one to wash them for you." After tumultuous offers of "I'll do it for you" he carried on with the show and all was forgotten. Or so it seemed.

In spring of 1985, my sister and I went to see David at the Night Out in Birmingham. In between his songs, different girls were going up to give him teddy bears and roses and such when suddenly a girl walked up to him with a cardboard tray. And on this tray there must have been at least fifty or more pairs of socks in every color you could think of. Well, everyone was amazed. Most of all David. His face was a picture. He said to the girl, "Thank you very much. Someone was paying attention!"

CHECKING IN

Bob Seger seems to have had enough of sitting in hotel rooms, living life on the road. He told a reporter: "Living in hotels is a drag. I despise it." The trials and tribulations of his lifestyle affected Seger so much that he shared his discontent in his autobiographical song "Turn the Page."

There aren't too many people who can afford to live like Warren Beatty, who made the Beverly Hilton Hotel his full-time home for over a decade. Having maids and room service may seem glamorous, but when living in hotels is a regular thing, it isn't that much fun. There's no real privacy. The sameness of the rooms is boring at best. Picking up and moving nearly every day allows very little time to give your room even the semblance of a lived-in look. Then, of course, there's always the quasi-antiseptic smell of hotel and motel rooms. Probably the worst thing for the musician, however, is the constant reminder that he's everywhere but home.

In the end, at least, the weary musician has a place to lay his or her head.

Although hotels may not offer the comforts of home, some offer a more interesting night's dwelling than even the been-there-done-that rock and roller would expect.

WAYNE KRAMER (MC5):

In the early days of the MC5, in the mid-'60s, we were a bar band. At least, we tried to be a bar band. We really tried, but it was something we did under protest most of the time. We really didn't see ourselves as "nightclub entertainers." That just was too small-time for young guys as grandiose as we were. We aspired to the Big-Time, big time. But alas, we had to work, and the Big-Time wasn't calling just yet.

We would take gigs wherever we could find them, and one offer came in for a weekend at Beechers Gardens in beautiful, scenic Flint, Michigan. These weekend adventures were great fun for us. We were all in our teens, and to go out of town and stay overnight in a hotel to be in a band was as good as it gets.

Wayne Kramer (MC5)
Photo by Margaret Saadi Kramer

We drove up to Flint on Friday afternoon. We were late leaving town because we were always late leaving town. That was just the way it was. Got to the club just in time to set up and go to work. And work it was. These nights were five sets. Forty-five minutes on, fifteen minutes off. We would always run out of material, and at a certain point it would be "up-tempo blues in C" or "slow blues in G." Whatever. Just finish out the set.

Sometimes you could get a good dancing crowd in there and really have a ball, but as I remember this gig, it was more like two old Polish alkies sitting at the bar requesting "Who Stole the Kieshka?" Didn't matter. We were loving being "in the band" and "on the road."

We finished up at two AM, and, because we left Detroit so late, we didn't have time to look for a hotel before work. So, we decided let's just cruise around town and find one. The rain hit just as we left the bar, and it was really pouring. Summer rain in the Midwest can be really intense. We were in Rob Tyner's old Chevy, and the de-icer was not working too well, so it was hard to see where we were going. After driving around for what seemed like hours and not finding a place to crash, we finally spotted the friendly blinking red neon sign: "Hotel."

"Great!" we all hollered. "We're saved!" We were all laughing and happy now. It was getting a little weird driving around and around, but it would all be fine. The rain was still pouring down and we pulled up in front, grabbed our bags, and ran from the car up the sidewalk to the entrance.

As I was running with my jacket pulled over my head to stay dry, I glanced up and saw, in the windows next to the hotel front door, young black women. Young black women who were smiling and waving at me to come in. Young black women who were smiling and laughing and waving all of us to "come on in here, boys." We were in motion; there was no turning back now. There were no other hotels. We'd looked.

We got in the lobby and went up to the reception counter. A big black man was sitting behind a wire screen. He had a big grin on his face. The young women swarmed on us like bees on honey: "You lonely, Sweetcakes?" "You wanna see a girl, baby?" "I likes you, Longhair."

"You fellows need some rooms," the big man asked. "Er . . . ah . . . yes . . . sir," I said. What else could we do?

We checked in and stayed for the whole weekend, and you know what? We had a ball. The whores were cool with us. A little rough-lived for my taste, but fun nonetheless. Best of all, they had a record player down in the lobby, and they played one record all weekend. It was one of the old-fashioned types of forty-five-RPM changers that would play a record over and over. The song? "Wang Dang Doodle" by Koko Taylor.

TWENTY-FOUR/SEVEN

Stevie Nicks claims that being on the road is one of the best sources of inspiration during the writing of a song. The singer/songwriter says that meeting all those people and becoming immersed in their problems provides any number of interesting scenarios.

If life is a learning experience, living on the road has got to be a crash course on the subject. No one can prepare musicians for what they may encounter. Every tour, while steeped in both dreary routine and exhilarating rewards, is different. Every musician is different, too, so naturally, their reactions to the things that happen are varied. When it comes right down to it, though, there are some learning experiences you've just got to have for yourself.

ROBIN BROCK (SOLO ARTIST):

I was sent off to England for a whirlwind tour. I was excited and just a little bit nervous because I had a lot to prove on my first tour "across the pond." My manager and I arrived in the afternoon at Heathrow and were promised a car to pick us up when we got there. Three hours later, we found out that our ride had just been waiting right around the corner, despite the fact that we were told to wait at the main arrival gate.

We arrived at the bed and breakfast, where we had reservations, and found no one there—no message or anything—and when we called the person who was in charge of reservations, of course we only got voice mail. Jet-lagged and starving, we staggered over a few streets to the township of Windsor. We found a charming little deli and ordered some lunch and some wonderful coffee, oblivious to the fact Windsor Castle was a few blocks over. We finally got into the B&B, and I was able to slip in a few hours rest. We had dinner with the record company that evening.

Next day was rehearsal, and I also had a live phone interview with a radio station just before 11 AM, a few minutes before rehearsal. The studio was only a few blocks from the B&B, so we decided to walk over. We had driven by the day before, but walking is not quite the same. I really hadn't been paying attention, so of course we got lost. It was getting later and later, and every direction we walked got us further and further, it seemed, from where we wanted to be. After walking in circles, we finally found a pay phone and called the studio to pick us up. Time was ticking. I got to the studio, and of course I just missed the DJ's call. No one had given me a number to call her either. I am really anal about being on time and being professional, and this, to me, was just not cool. Fortunately, she called back and we had a great interview, barring my ears getting accustomed to British accents and the vast variety of them.

The next day was rehearsal—between interviews. The day after that, we were off to our first gig. I was expecting a cool club, up-to-date equipment, you know how you get these fantasies in your mind. It was a grungy, stinky hellhole, not unlike many I had played in before. The drummer looked around and said, "I think I played my first gig here, and it really didn't get a whole lot better." Oh well, they told me that the dressing room was being cleaned up and would be ready in a few minutes. Two hours later, I went up there anyway and walked into a room that hadn't been vacuumed—ever. Oh well, I can deal with this. No lock on the door, and I had three thousand dollars of stage clothes and makeup, not to mention the guys' stuff there and my mic that I carry around with me.

After returning to the club after getting something to eat, I got into the room and was thrown back by the odor of marijuana smoke. My stomach turned, and I had had enough. I went downstairs and told them that I hadn't complained when they didn't bring my water—the only thing I specifically requested—and I didn't say a word about the filthy bathrooms downstairs. I never uttered a peep about the disgusting state of the dressing room and area, either. But this, I couldn't take. I told my manager to deal with it, but there was really nothing they could do (except maybe burn the place down).

The dope was coming from the apartment next door to the dressing room. So, I locked myself in the bathroom—a three-by-four cubicle only slightly less filthy than the public washrooms downstairs—and put my makeup on by using my one-by two-inch compact mirror, trying not to get too stoned.

The show wasn't too bad. Hadn't been promoted very well, but since it was our first gig, we just pretended it was rehearsal. We had fun onstage anyway, and for the dozen or so people that stayed through two opening acts to see me, we put on a good show.

The day after was a noon performance at the BBC lounge, so I think I ended up with three hours sleep total. On the way there, we were rear-ended on the freeway (no damage fortunately). The place was packed during the show, and we were told to turn it down (I've had worse requests). It was strange doing a show in the middle of the day with our asses in the bay window of the BBC building. It was cool though, as the people walking by would stop and watch for a while. That was fun.

The next day I had interviews and another live radio appearance. On our way to our next gig we were given the wrong directions, and our driver was trying to read the map and drive at the same time, getting caught up in the roundabouts, and talking on the cell phone, getting directions. He's a man of many talents.

We played at this club down beneath a pub, kind of like a dungeon. The stage was pretty squishy, but it was intimate. Being a small—and I mean small—budget tour, we were kind of depending on the club to supply us with soundmen, and up until that time we had been plagued with the usual shitty sound. Nothing new. Until the night in the dungeon. The drummer's friend, who was hanging out with us earlier, asked, "Do you mind if I just fiddle with the sound a bit?" It couldn't be worse than usual. He took control of the soundboard, and like no one I had ever seen, fur flying, gave us in minutes the best sound we could ever possibly imagine. He was hired. All he asked for was bed and food. Sold. Again, I used the ladies room for my dressing room. I often wonder what the customers think when I drag out my suitcase and put on my leather and sparklies and start doing my face paint. I will say that the facilities were much better there. They even fed us. The turnout was a little better than the first show, we had a great time, and the sound was awesome.

The gig that followed was really important. I was opening for Ray Wilson [who fronted Genesis after the departure of Phil Collins and eventually embarked on a solo career] at the Classic Rock Society, and there were going to be some really special guests there. One of the guys from a big rock magazine who had supported me very much was going to be there. I seldom get nervous, but the CRS had been very supportive and very kind to me, and I wanted to do a good job. They laid out a whole spread of food for us, and we had wonderful hosts and hostesses. The stage was huge, and the venue was even bigger. It was making all the other crappy shows and low attendance worthwhile.

We drove on to the next gig. We arrived at two o'clock and didn't go on until eight o'clock. That was what our contract said. We got there to check in and ask where we were to unload, and the club manager told us we had been booked for two o'clock, so too bad. My manager flashed the contract in the lady's face and said sweetly, "Do you mean to tell me that we have come all this way and have a contract that is wrong, and you're telling us to go home? I don't think so. Fit us in."

So, an hour or so later we were standing on this teeny tiny stage, our asses once again in the window to a standing-room-only crowd. The only problem was when a drunken jerk got on stage with me and tried to take my mic. I tried to be nice and dance with him until he tried to take my clothes off. The soundman and the driver were ready to grab him, but I finally shoved him off, which takes coordination when you're singing.

I learned many lessons this tour: Buy a map. Bring a bigger mirror. Bring my own water. Bring my own phone. And it's okay to punch a drunk guy in the head if he's on my stage. I'm much too nice.

STRANGER THAN FICTION

Keith Moon was known to "redecorate" many, if not most, of the hotel rooms in which his band and crew stayed. He'd remove the television from its case, unscrew dresser drawers, pour ketchup in the bathtub with plastic legs sticking out of it, put itching powder in the bed, fake bugs under the pillow and faux dog shit in the sink. Ah, life on the road . . .

Another Loony Moony tale: on The Who's first U.S. tour, the band was staying in a hotel in the South. Pete Townshend asked Moon if he could use the toilet in Moon's room. Townshend should have been suspicious when Moon mysteriously smiled as he nodded assent. Townshend was out of luck. Entering the bathroom, he found nothing more than a pipe sticking out of the floor where the toilet had once been. When Townshend questioned Moon, the drummer smiled and said he had had a cherry bomb in his hand, and when it had appeared that the bomb was going to go off, he threw it in the toilet. Townshend was astonished that Moon had been handling an explosive strong enough to lay waste to a toilet. He asked Moon how many of the cherry bombs he still had. Townshend was

*horrified when Moon claimed to have 500, and then to prove it,
opened a suitcase full of them.*

While Keith Moon's behavior puts him in a league of his own, lots of the things that happen on the road could be classified as bizarre. Sometimes, people behave strangely around rockers. They are, to put it simply, "not themselves." Musicians get used to it, accepting that it comes with the territory. The fact that at least they know what to expect from their own band members can be comforting and predictable, but sometimes even *their* behavior can surprise and stun, expecially when you factor in the unpredictable effects of behavior-altering substances.

CHRIS SPEDDING (SUPER SESSION GUITARIST):

We were touring Italy with Jack Bruce's band around 1970. One venue . . . had not provided anything that we asked for in the contract. The road crew in the equipment truck said that, contractually, they were not obliged to unload the truck until our needs were met and said they were quite within their rights to drive away and not do the gig. The promoter pulled out a gun, shot the tires out, and said, "You're not going anywhere." We did the gig.

On the same tour, we played Rome. Graham Bond, our organist, was missing from the sound check. Graham was into black magic. He wore all the robes and carried a wand. I'm not sure if all this was an affectation (it *was* 1970), but he finally wandered in just before show time complaining that he'd been thrown out of St Peter's Basilica in the Vatican for laying his tarot cards out on the altar.

This black magic stuff was a little disconcerting and a little intimidating, no matter how serious he really was about it, so at a gig in Hyde Park I decided to try and break the ice with Graham. Back stage in the trailer, before we went on, I went over to his wand, which was lying on a table, and picked it up, saying rather stupidly, "What a nice wand!" Graham shouted, "YOU'VE JUST TURNED MY WAND UPSIDE DOWN! OH, MY SPELLS, ALL MY SPELLS!"

CHAPTER 2

PERFORMANCES

There's probably nothing more exhilarating for musicians than the moment when they realize they have "arrived." They've dreamed about it, set the wheels in motion to work toward it, and scratched and suffered on the way to earning that addictive acceptance by the audience.

Musicians live for performing. At least most do. Of course, there are exceptions to the rule, such as those who are in the music business for the girls and the recognition. Most rockers, though, come alive when they hit the stage. Concerts, whether they're good, bad, or mediocre, are usually entertaining in and of themselves. But the music isn't necessarily the entertainment the musicians or their fans remember about the show.

Sometimes it's almost impossible for rockers to recall their single most remarkable live experience. There are just too many that stand out in their minds. Once artists remember one off-the-wall moment, the memories of other equally weird experiences start to flow. This can be especially true when thoughts turn to that first public performance or the sometimes strange ways acts developed. The things that happen in front of an audience can certainly be unique and are definitely worth filing away to be recounted to future grandchildren.

VIOLENT JAY (INSANE CLOWN POSSE):

Maaaaan, we got enough tour stories to fill up a hundred books just like this one. The many adventures me and my clowny partner, Shaggy 2 Dope, have endured

Insane Clown Posse: Shaggy 2 Dope (Joseph Utsler), Violent Jay (Joseph Bruce)
From the photo collection of Insane Clown Posse

while out on the road over the last decade are as scary, diverse, and colorful as our own painted asses.

First, let me say this, in case you ain't heard yet: ICP knows how to put on a live show. Putting on shows is what we do, and we do it all out, from the get. You'd have to see it to believe it. We toss out, kick out, and shoot out into the crowd about three to four hundred two-liters of Faygo soda at every show. (Faygo is a Detroit brand of soda that has over thirty-something flavors and colors.) We also shoot off plenty of Faygo-filled cannons, buckets, balloons, and all that.

We bring with us monsters, dancing clowns, girls, trampolines, and pure and absolute madness to the stage. Why do we bring all of this? Because unlike most of the other rap acts out there, Shaggy and I know that without all that crazy shit going on around us, we'd just be two more idiots walking back and forth, rapping on stage. There'd probably be fifteen of our homies walking around on stage with us, too, none doing a damn thing but waving towels and drinkin' Hennessy. That's boring as hell to have to watch for an hour and a half. ICP's motto has always been "Fuck keepin' it real; we just keep it entertaining."

Live shows are the only lifeline to our band. We're an underground group, and our music is way too explicit to be played anywhere. So playing live is what we do best, y'all. It took ten years to build up a crowd that understands and appreciates our unique and bizarre musical product. You know, Horror Rap from two painted-up clowns wasn't always well received, as it still ain't. Even so, with all six of our Joker's Card albums now released, and ten years later, we're still at it.

Let me just tell you all some of our funnier tour stories. In the era of the first Joker's Card album *Carnival of Carnage,* our manager, Alex, got a phone call from some college promoter kid, and boom, it was on. We were invited to perform at a real rap show. The headliner was a local rapper named Triplex. This would be ICP's very first show ever, so nothing would stop us from making the four-hour drive halfway up to Big Rapids University in Michigan. Not even the vicious-ass snowstorm we went through on the way could stop us, though it did turn the four-hour trip into a smooth eight. Along the way, a semi-truck in front of us blew a tire. It exploded, and one of the tire pieces smashed a giant hole in our windshield. That brought the snowstorm into the car with us, but even that shit couldn't put a dent in our karma. We were ready to rock the mic for the thousands of rap fans we were expecting to see when we got there.

We finally arrived at the university, but we couldn't find where the concert was supposed to be. Finally, some kid pointed us toward a big-ass dormitory-style building. We walked in and there everybody was, about fifty college kids all standing and sitting around in a big, open room. There was some music playing, so we figured this must be it. We went into the bathroom to get dressed and painted up. We figured we were late as hell, but the show must go on.

Alex cued up our cassette tape. Once we were ready, he walked up to the stereo system and turned off the music. He turned around and made the announcement: "Attention everybody! Get ready, because here . . . live . . . from Detroit Murder City . . . It's the ICP!" Then he hit "play" on our cassette.

We came out with no microphones or nothing; we were just right up in the people's faces. Shaggy and I were just fuckin' yelling over our own cassette. The people were staring at us in amazement and bewilderment. They must have been in shock and awe. We finished our two-song set, and the crowd did nothing at all. They didn't cheer or boo. They just stood there, stunned. So we quickly ran back into the bathroom.

About thirty seconds later some dude came charging into what I figured was our dressing room and asked us, "What the hell was that?" He was a dorm security guy. We calmly explained to him that we had been booked for this event, and that he needed to basically step off. With all this taking place at a college, you can figure what happened next: we got schooled. The guy explained to us that the real show took place in the auditorium on the other side of the college about three hours ago. This place was just a dorm lounge area. We couldn't believe it.

The security monitor got a hold of the real show's promoter through his fresh walkie-talkie. When the promoter guy finally showed up in the bathroom, he just couldn't stop laughing. He told us that the real show they had earlier was off the hook and all, but they completely forgot we were even coming. Even so, he was still cool enough to give us forty dollars for gas, and I guess we gave him a funny-ass story to run and tell his boys in return. So much for ICP's first concert.

During the era of the second Joker's Card album, *The Ringmaster,* we were play-ing a sold-out gig in our hometown of Detroit at a place called the Magic Bag. Three hundred people were packed in just to see ICP. This would be our first-ever self-promoted concert.

The stage was set. Behind us was a table with a large bucket full of Faygo two-liter bottles. They were only put out there for us to drink. You see, we've always mentioned Faygo in our lyrics, so we figured that it would be cool to have some on stage with us.

This was our first sold-out show, our own show at that. This was also my and Shaggy's first time playing without ICP's original third member, who had just quit the group. We both were nervous as fuck.

The three hundred people were chanting, "What the fuck?!" because we were taking too long to get it together. Finally, we went out there and took it to 'em. It was off the hook. Things were going well, except for a pack of gangsta-lookin' thugs all flippin' us off. They were standing right in the middle of the floor, just beamin' fingers at us. I was getting pissed because it was going so well all around these haters, but they were just fuckin' up our karma.

I was taking a sip off a Faygo two-liter when I noticed them again. Fuck that; I'd had it. I chucked the full two-liter of red pop right at them. THE PLACE EXPLODED. Shaggy popped open another one and squirted it at them, too. The place was going crazy. We started spraying everybody with it. Faygo was flying everywhere.

The club-owner lady saw this shit and started having a panic attack. She ran on stage and grabbed the huge bucket of Faygo, but just then our manager, Alex, ran out to stop her. She was trying to pull the bucket off the stage, but Alex was pulling it on. It was like a tug-of-war over the Faygo bucket. The whole time,

Shaggy and I were grabbing the Faygo, kickin' them, and straight up realizing our dream.

Suddenly, just like that, "Juggalos" were born. Faygo showers, stage diving, and pure insanity quickly became our trademark at shows. Juggalos grew in number and the shows were packed. Before long, we gained much love in Detroit and nearby Toledo and Flint. We could fill any thousand-seat venue in those three cities. We called them our Clown Towns. Back then, our tours would be only three cities long.

One night in Toledo, I tried to do one of my trademark backwards moonsault flips off the speaker stack. This was the second night of two back-to-back sold-out shows. The night before I had been moonsaulting back, flipping off everything all night. This time, for whatever reason, something went wrong. I slipped up there, and fell straight down on my head. I was knocked out cold. Shaggy took to the stage and announced the show had to be stopped, obviously, but then he screamed the line that would become infamous for ICP: "The Wicked Clowns will never die!"

The thing that sucked the worst was that while I was knocked the fuck out, the ambulance people cut my shirt off in front of the whole crowd. I'm a fat kid, and fat kids hate taking off their shits. One thousand-plus Juggalos all saw me shirtless and knocked out cold.

The next thing I remember was being at the hospital. They told me I broke my collarbone in four places and slapped my dome with a fat-ass concussion. So what? Give me some Vicodins and a Play Station—six weeks later I was back at it again.

Did I say Juggalos were born? Not everywhere, they weren't. This was 19-fuckin'-95, the era of the third Joker's Card album, *The Riddlebox*. We had yet to take our Carnival wagons cross-country, but we were ready for the world. We went out on our first national tour as the opening act for the rap groups Onyx and Das EFX.

The first show was in New London, Connecticut. I'll never forget it. The place was about half full. Maybe four or five hundred people. The whole crowd all looked like some no bullshit, diehard, New York–style rap fans. They all had on the big-ass boots and puffy coats. We were peepin' out from behind the curtain like, "Daaaaaaaaaamn."

It was on, and it was amazing. The very second our show tape started, the people started booing. Shaggy and I looked at each other like, "Huh? We ain't even out there yet, and they're already booing our fuckin' intro! So fuckin' what? Let's go!" We walked out there painted up and rappin' our wicked shit. When they first saw us, the whole place erupted with laughter at first, and then boos, and finally laughing-boos. Once we broke out with the Faygo it got really ugly. There was so much shit flying at us, we felt like we were being stoned to death. With the strange and horrible sound of 500 people laugh-booing, and all that shit flying at us, I thought a tornado was coming. We just kept rappin' though it all, like, "Fuck it. Maybe they'll come around." They never did come around, but some chairs did. We left when they started throwing chairs at us, about ten minutes into our set.

The next night in Jersey was the same shit. Just an insane barrage of boos and laughter as soon as we stepped out. What made it worse that night, though, was this fat chick who was sitting on the stage with her back to us, flipping us off in protest or whatever. We didn't change our shit for nothing. We started squirtin' and chuckin' Faygos back at the people who were throwing shit at us. All of this while we were rapping and dodging other shit.

Finally, some dudes from the rear threw a big-ass table at the stage. It missed us, but hit the fat chick. She got hurt and fell to the floor. They made a huge circle around her while they tended to her injuries that were intended for us. The crowd suddenly got really pissed and rushed the stage. It was a full-on riot: everybody versus us. We were all swingin' and punchin' back at puffy jackets everywhere. Finally, Billy Bill pulled us out from underneath about thirty stomping pairs of big-ass boots and off to safety. That shit had to be the craziest show.

We got violently booed off the stage every night on that tour. We even went up to Montreal, Quebec, and they booed us off in French. We thought for sure the Frenchies would dig the clown shit, but nope. By the looks of that crowd, you would've thought we were playing Brooklyn.

We were so frustrated that night that afterwards we ate and left out for the next city so fast that we forgot Shaggy, who was still in the pizza place bathroom. He was stranded in Quebec. The pizza place closed, and he had to walk around with no money, in the blizzard, for three hours until we returned and rescued his ass. By the time we finally found him, he had on a New York–style puffy coat, he was two thirds frozen, and was speaking completely in French.

When the tour finally came to Detroit, Toledo, and Flint, though, both Onyx and Das EFX had to open up for us, because the hometown Juggalo power was too powerful. After that, we dropped off the tour and went home. We only stayed on the tour as long as we did so that we could come to our hometown with Onyx and them on a national tour and look like big shots. Nobody at home knew it was a near-death experience for us everywhere else on that tour.

The era of the fourth Joker's Card album, *The Great Milenko,* resulted in our first platinum album. That's thanks mostly to Disney for pulling our record from stores, because after they did that, a giant wave of controversy ensued, and Shaggy and I were finally introduced everywhere. No need to open for anybody else's crowd anymore because we now had our own Juggalos pretty much everywhere.

One time on our "House of Horrors Tour" in '98, we played a big huge-ass outdoor place deep within Texas. The police showed up and informed us that we couldn't cuss too much over the mics because local residents who live near the venue could hear it. If we cussed too much, they'd unplug the whole show. Man, there had to be about 2,000 Juggalos there that night, too. How the fuck is ICP not gonna cuss a lot at an ICP show? We knew we wouldn't last long out there, but we went on nonetheless.

Billy Bill argued with the cops and stalled them for as long as he could, but about a half hour into our set everything went black. The mics went dead, and that was that. The fuckin' cops actually did it; they pulled the plug on us and the 2,000 Juggalos.

In my opinion, what happened next made up for it. In our eyes, that show made history that night, because suddenly everybody in my road crew came out there on stage with us, and we all just started booting two-liters of Faygo. Kicking them up and out into the night sky over the sea of Juggalos. You had to have seen it. It was unreal. For about twenty minutes, we practically emptied our semi-truck of Faygo. Crates and crates of Faygo all flew through the sky and dumped onto them Texas Juggalos, falling like cluster bombs of various colors and flavors. The place was outdoors, so the fuckin' Faygos were soaring high as hell that summer night. Hundreds of them. Everybody just kept kicking out two-liters. Everybody—I even think the fuckin' cops might have been out there bootin' off a few. Billy Bill and them just kept bringing out more and more crates from the truck.

What made this long strange moment of Faygo rain so completely eerie and surreal was that the stage was so dark and silent. All you could hear was the punting sound of wet Faygos. All you could see was a dark stage full of figures launching hundreds of two-liter bottles. They were splashing and raining down severywhere. When it finally stopped, the place just cheered for another twenty minutes in the dark. It was one of our favorite nights.

Some Juggalos really became down-with-the-clown during those days, too. One time, we didn't even know it, but there was a kid riding on the roof of our tour bus from New York City all the way until about halfway to Baltimore. We finally discovered him when Billy Bill seen him climbing down off the bus when we stopped at a truck stop. The kid had both pissed and shit his pants while he was riding up there. Crazy-ass Juggalos, I tell ya.

In the era of the fifth Joker's Card album, *The Amazing Jeckel Brothers,* we went to Europe. We never really did very well in Europe, except for in London. We could sell out some big shit there, but everywhere else it was like starting all over again. The thing that made the Europe tours so crazy was their strange Faygo bottles. See, they weren't really Faygo; it was more like Fake-O. It was impossible for us to bring all that Faygo through customs without a sales permit visa because they refused to believe that we were just throwing it all on crowds and not actually selling all those crates of Faygo. So instead, our affiliate European record company purchased mad amounts of some other soda and stuck these ICP Faygo stickers over them.

The craziness was this: they were not the regular two-liter bottles we're used to; they were some other amount, I guess. Like maybe one-and-a-half-liter bottles. Over there, they make their plastic bottles taller and thinner. Fair enough I guess, but the only problem with that is when you're doing what we do with them—that makes a world of difference. Them fuckin' Euro bottles rocket off twice as hard and fast! Them crazy-ass-shaped pop bottles made like Scud missiles.

One time, at some place in England, I rocketed one of them bottles off my foot and that motherfucker shot straight up and out like a guided Patriot missile, right towards the disco ball high above the crowd. BLAM! The bottle nailed the disco ball, and the fuckin' thing came falling down, right—BLAP!—on top of some English kid's head. I was like, "Whoa!"

What could we do? We just kept rappin' and doing the show. Then about fifteen minutes later, I saw the same kid back out there, standing in the same spot, only now he had his fuckin' head all taped up and he was still dancing around. We must've knocked fifteen or twenty people flat-out cold on that tour, shootin' off them crazy-ass shaped rocket bottles. Shaggy and I both had black eyes and several injuries and bruises ourselves from them things hittin' us.

We got to Rennes, France, and it was time to play the biggest show on the tour. It was some crazy-ass huge concert. The night's lineup was the Foo Fighters, Corner Shop, and ICP. I don't know, but if you ask me, Corner Shop and ICP together sound about as good as water and cereal. Eight thousand fans were up in that bitch. The fresh-ass arena was sold clean out. The Foo Fighters were the absolute stars of the house. It was their night. I don't even know what the fuck we were doing there, but we were glad to be, I'll tell you that. The only bad news was that because of the mess that our show makes on stage, we had to go on last. "Last? Who the fuck is going to stick around to see us after Foo Fighters play?" I thought.

Oh well, we've seen it all before, anyway. We hung out with the Foo Fighters all night backstage, which was the shit to us. They rocked the 8,000 French fans half to death. Dave Grohl kept saying, "Stick around, everybody; we got ICP comin' up next." He must've plugged us five times throughout their devastating set. That was so fuckin' fresh to us. As soon as they finished their set, though, that place cleared out like somebody farted anthrax. Man, them 8,000 screaming fans turned into 6,000, then 40,00, then 1,000, all the way down to about one hundred people left standing around a big-ass empty arena, waiting for us to go on. I'm guessing those one hundred people were only still there because their rides probably weren't showing up until later.

This was the only show on that whole European tour where them crazy Euro missile two-liter bottles came in handy. You could peg somebody off with one in the upper balcony, or way in the back, by the bathrooms. the Foo Fighters watched from the side of the stage while Shaggy and I played to an empty arena and pegged off each and every one of the hundred or so remaining patrons with our Faygo missiles. Everybody who stayed got wet, got pissed, and then left. I don't know what value we added to that show, if any, as ICP, but as Joe and Joey, meeting the Foo Fighters and hangin' out like that was the shit.

We also played Woodstock in 1999. We knew that tickets were hella expensive, and we were getting hella paid to be there, so we thought we should give something back. We brought along these big beach balls. We announced to the crowd that they each had a hundred dollars taped to them, and then we proceeded to kick about thirty of them into the crowd. Then we rolled out these bigger giant-ass beach balls and announced, "These ones have five hundred bucks taped to them!" We booted a gang of them out into the human sea. That shit was great. I also was riding a scooter around in the backstage area, and I faked like I lost control for a second. I crashed into Sheryl Crow and grabbed her ass. That's a whole other story.

Now is the era of the sixth and final Joker's Card album, *The Wraith: Shangri-La*. Right now we're out on tour. I'm sitting in the tour bus. Insane Clown Posse's niche is pretty much carved in stone here in the U.S. now. Only Juggalos come to the shows. These days we pretty much only play for Juggalos. We're still growing and climbing, though. It don't stop; it won't stop. Come see the insanity for yourself one day.

FIRST IMPRESSIONS

During KISS' debut show, Gene Simmons attempted to breathe fire. Instead, he caught fire to his hair.

First appearances at important shows are the stuff of which musicians' dreams are made. When they finally get the call to participate in something big before thousands of fans who might not otherwise be exposed to their music, it's an awesome thrill. It's one thing to have new listeners sit up and take notice, but it's an even greater satisfaction to have musical peers recognize a musician as one of their own. That's assuming that they *are* recognized. Touring musicians can sometimes be in a world of their own and not necessarily aware of who else is sharing the stage.

BRIAN HYLAND (SOLO ARTIST):

It was the winter of 1962, and I was doing two shows: first in Montgomery, Alabama, and then in Jacksonville, Florida, for my first wild WAPE Radio sponsored "Rock & Roll Shows." I arrived backstage at the Coliseum by the Gator Bowl in Jacksonville, Florida. At this time, if you were on the charts and on the radio, they wanted you on the show without regard to music categories. I was excited to be on the show with Bobby Bare, Marty Robbins, Bobby Darin, and Chris Montez, as well as Roger McGuinn (pre-Byrds), who was playing guitar for Bobby Darin.

The usual backstage confusion reached a crescendo when the stage manager discovered the stage crew has set up the stage, risers and all, backwards! Standing around like sidewalk supervisors, I heard Bobby Darin suggest that they set up huge mirrors behind the stage, and we could all just perform facing the other way! We all cracked up, but the stage manager wasn't buying it, and the crew wasn't laughing.

Brian Hyland
*From the photo collection
of Brian Hyland*

So, the mad scramble began. With the usual time to kill, I went outside for a smoke. The fans began to gather, and I realized it was time to get back inside. This was pre–backstage pass days, and as I was struggling to get through the crowd I was relieved to see another performer. Quickly introducing myself to Marty Robbins, I told him I was a huge fan. His friendly response was, "Yeah, you go to school around here kid?" "No!" I told him. "I'm on the Show with ya!"

Later that evening, I was thrilled to hear the booming ovation as I started singing my latest hit record, "Sealed With A Kiss." I was later brought back to earth again when my guitar player at the time, Tommy Boyce, a songwriter and future producer of The Monkees and later of the recording duo Boyce & Hart, enthusiastically advised me that the ovation was for the dramatic blue spotlight that hit me on the intro! So much for rock and roll smoke and mirrors.

SHIT HAPPENS

At an outdoor concert with the Patti Smith Group in Florida, Tom Petty was knocked unconscious when he grabbed hold of a microphone. Some say lightening was to blame; some say faulty wiring was the culprit.

Petty wasn't the first rock star to be the victim of some sort of natural disaster or equipment malfunction, and he likely won't be the last. In 1990, Curtis Mayfield was paralyzed when a lighting rig collapsed onto the stage. Several shows along the Justin Timberlake/Christina Aguilera tour were postponed when the same thing happened in 2003. It's not as uncommon as you might think for musicians to occasionally get a buzz from a live wire.

While anyone getting hurt on stage, seriously or otherwise, is indeed a serious concern, it is usually the smaller, more personal, mishaps that bring unwanted attention. Avril Lavigne once "pretended" to knee a fan in the groin during a number, but the fan evidently moved during the sight gag and experienced the real thing. No matter how well planned the production or the performance, shit happens.

LEE DORMAN (IRON BUTTERFLY):

Winter '69. Philadelphia Spectrum. Blinding snowstorm. Sold out Theatre in the Round. I was wearing a pair of paisley drapery material pants held up by elastic.

As we started "Vida," the elastic broke, and the pants headed for the floor. It was the '60s. No underwear. I never got exposed, but had to grab the pants and go back to my amp and sit down, still playing until the drum solo. Then I ran to the dressing room and changed my pants and returned before I had to play again. Upon returning there was a great round of applause, as several hundred fans saw my plight!

THE UNINVITED

In 1998, while Bob Dylan performed his song "Love Sick" at the Grammy Awards, a man named Michael Portnoy somehow got on the stage with the words "Soy Bomb" painted on his bare torso and performed an animated dance behind the music icon. When Dylan pointedly ignored the self-proclaimed "multi-genre mastermind artist," many in the audience—both in the theater and at home— thought the strange choreography was part of the act. It wasn't. Portnoy later explained that "soy bomb" referred to "sort of life and death and explosions." All-righty, then . . .

Almost any rowdy rock and roll show will have someone in the audience—male or female—attempt to get on the stage with his or her heroes. Guys have been known to jump onstage for some air guitar pantomime with their six-string idols. Girls once content to toss their panties at Elvis now demand steamy embraces and deep kisses from the rockers at whom they throw themselves.

Unwelcome guests on stage aren't always human. Travis Tritt had to fend off the coins thrown onstage by fans when he performed "Here's a Quarter, Call Someone Who Cares." The Beatles were once bombarded with jelly beans. Lynyrd Skynyrd found themselves pelted with bullets by fans who misinterpreted their song "Gimme Back My Bullets."

And then there are the unwanted intrusions of a more "natural" variety.

KEN SKAGGS (GLEN CAMPBELL BAND):

We were in Crystal River, Florida. The sky had slipped from burnt amber to indigo as the stage lights began to summon the insects of the night. The show was without incident until about halfway through the "William Tell Overture," when I witnessed a three-inch praying mantis launch an airborne assault on T. J. Kuenster from two o'clock. T. J. was intently focused on his keyboard at the time, but suddenly became shaken by the situation. In self-defense, he began waving his arms about and dancing a jig, trying to repel the invader. A challenging piece of music under the best of conditions, the "Overture" demands total concentration from the performer.

About this time, Russ [Skaggs] and I started laughing. T. J. managed to knock the invader to the ground, whereupon it crawled over to and onto his shoe and began to ascend his leg. As I watched the upward progress of the mantis on T. J.'s leg, my vision became impaired by tears of laughter. Once again the insect's progress was interrupted by the hand of T. J. as he knocked it to the ground. This time though, our raptorial predator decided to fly to and land on top of Russ's stage monitor. It then got into position facing T. J. and swayed back and forth with the music for some time.

T. J. continued to play with one eye on the attacker until the mantis flew off in search of smaller prey. My sides were aching, and I couldn't stop laughing for ten minutes. Glen and the rest of the band were completely unaware of T. J.'s experience that evening; however, at least one audience member wrote me to inquire about the source of our antics that evening.

DIFFERENT IS NOT NECESSARILY BAD

Back in the day, audiences had to have a strong stomach to attend a performance by Iggy Pop. And performance is the key word. In addition to his music, Iggy was known for entertaining his fans by throwing the microphone into his teeth and bleeding on the people in the front row, picking his nose, dripping candle wax over his bare chest, and removing imaginary hairs from his ass.

We've all seen shows where the artists have held us spellbound. We've also seen shows where the act had no business being on the stage, be it because they were too wasted to play, displayed absolutely no talent or simply didn't have their head in the music. It's a wonder that rockers give what they do and present good, if not outstanding, shows more often than not. Coupled with the exhaustion of the road and the repetition of the music (although some actually do change their act from night to night), they can't be blamed for sometimes breaking up the boredom of both of those negatives to have a little fun.

LEE UNDERWOOD (GUITARIST):

One of the greatest gigs we ever had took place in March 1969 at the Philharmonic Hall, Lincoln Center, in New York City. Those words sparkle in my memory. This was the concert for which Tim Buckley missed the afternoon sound check. It turns out he took his clothes to the laundromat, instead of showing up for the pre-concert run-through. It soothed his nerves to watch shirts and socks spinning around in the dryer all afternoon. It never occurred to me at the time that he might be nervous about that evening's show, and so, like some old lady, I was upset with him for standing us up.

He may have missed the sound check, but he arrived on stage—and in great shape.

Back stage, vibraphonist David Friedman played piano and John Miller played bass while Tim warmed up by singing excerpts from a few great standards, including "Angel Eyes," "September Song," "That Old Feeling," "What's New" and "One for My Baby (One More for the Road)." Then he leaned over the piano in a vampy chanteuse pose, bent his wrist, clouded his eyes, smiled, and swished through "Mad about the Boy." Hilarious. And musically excellent. Eyes bright and happy, he pulled the guitar strap over his shoulder, cinched up his guitar,

Lee Underwood
Photo by Jay Crutcher, from the photo collection of Lee Underwood

and chortled that old Judy Garland line, "Hey, ya babies! Get ready for the dream sequence! Show time!"

What a surprise. I didn't know he knew those tunes (rather like his son, Jeff, who also knew the words of songs perhaps generations old, even tunes he might have heard only a time or two). In the years since then, of course, Linda Ronstadt, Willie Nelson, Michael Bolton, and others released albums of classic jazz standards. They were good. But Tim was great. He would have blown all the pups away. And that was just a backstage warm-up.

When Tim, Friedman, Miller, and I walked on stage, people cheered and rushed the footlights. Girls tossed bouquets of flowers, passed paper valentines and notes up to him, squealed with delight. A tall blonde stood up and handed him a single red rose (not a carnation as reported elsewhere). Tim graciously accepted it, smiled at the girl, stuck the flower in his mouth, and chewed it up! Spitting the crunched petals out, he said, "Yeow—that really tastes terrible!"

Later, he told me he had met Salvador Dalí in an elevator that afternoon. Tim mentioned the concert coming up that evening, and Salvador attended. From the stage, Tim saw him sitting in the audience. "What could I do that would be audacious enough to get a laugh from a master comedian like him? I ate the flower!" We played well, the crowd loved us, reviews were good, and we stood on top of the world.

It was a glorious shining moment.

ED KING (STRAWBERRY ALARM CLOCK):

One night after one of the Buffalo Springfield shows with the Beach Boys, a roadie was loading guitars into the luggage compartment of the bus. A couple of guys in a station wagon pulled up real fast, took two guitars (one of which was Stephen Stills' prize possession, his '59 Les Paul Custom), threw them into the car, and sped off. But Dewey Martin and Stills were running after them, and they *caught them,* dragged them out of the car, and stomped them real good.

The Springfield closed their shows with "Bluebird" and quite a lengthy jam at the end of it every night. One time, at the end, Stills bent the Bigsby bar *all the way back* and, with his Marshall cranked up all the way, you could hear the strings bust one by one: PANG! PING! WHAM! PONG! BOING!

Afterwards, in the dressing room, I commented to him I'd never seen *that* lick before. He said, "Yeah . . . but didn't it make the *neatest* noise?"

BUT IT CAN BE . . .

KAYT E. WOLF-STRONG (SOLO ARTIST):

I spent an entire year (or two) reading the autobiographies and biographies of famous performers in a scientific study to determine what universal actions each artist took in order to succeed. I kept reading about singers driving back and forth across the country crammed in old station wagons, sedans, vans, and buses, and singers who were sleeping in trains and airplanes. This is where I got the idea that if I kept in constant motion, I would eventually cause a commotion. It didn't take long though, before I found myself in a situation where I was in way over my head.

I began working with the top agent who booked outdoor street performances, and like every other hungry musician, I trusted in her judgment and guidance and would have done anything, yes anything, she asked me to do just to get in her good graces. I had six festival performances with her under my belt and was beginning to develop a feel for and confidence in the venues. So, when this agent called me with a gig performing on the streets of New York City, I was all-confident and all-knowing, and, unfortunately, all-naive; I was my usual fearless self. I'd been to the Big Apple once before, so I was vaguely familiar with the city. Basking in a false sense of security, I packed my anvil cases complete with one mixing board, one amplifier, one keyboard, a dolly, and lots of CDs to sell. In my purse, I had a single piece of paper with details on where the hotel was and where the gig was. I had a stack of maxed-out credit cards and a couple hundred dollars cash in my wallet.

I boarded the plane at LAX airport. I was immediately shocked by the poor condition the airplane was in (I normally travel on Southwest, so you know where my standards are). Seats were stained, the lights on the aisle-ways were broken, the doors to some of the bathrooms were taped with *x*'s to keep people out of them, and my seat came with a barf bag that had already performed its function. The coffee machine in the galley was out of order, and the flight began with an irate passenger being escorted against his will off the plane in front of the few others on the plane with me (all the while screaming about how [he] really *did* pay for the ticket). The one remaining operational lavatory had a nasty habit of not letting you out once you were inside, so that's probably how all of the other doors were broken on the other bathrooms. Okay, so it was a cheap flight. Next time,

I'd remind the agent *not* to use this airline. No, I won't state the name of the operation, but let's just say it starts with a *t* for *terrible*.

Five long hours later, we landed in Newark, New Jersey. I couldn't get a single cabby who wanted to shove two large eighty-pound flight cases in the backseat, let alone help me lift them into the trunk. But there are always those scab cabbies, the illegal ones, hovering around the terminal, and they would do the undoable, so I went with an unlicensed cab driver. This driver drove me all over the place, acting as unfamiliar with the area as I was. The fare was almost sixty bucks plus tips for the heavy luggage. Oh well, I got to the hotel in one piece. It's only money.

The hotel was just outside the Holland Tunnel. A congested, noisy stream of anxious drivers merging into two lanes was the ambient sonic backdrop in the "lobby," where you communicated to the "concierge" through a hole in the several sheets of bulletproof glass behind which he sat. I looked around to see two old plastic chairs, and a host of very strange and colorful characters that were renting rooms by the hour, not by the night. Some of them were BYOB-ing in the halls, while others were getting down to some other Serious Business. I checked in, and asked if there was an elevator. First law of the Big City: there are no elevators where you need them. There was no handicap access (aren't there any handicapped pimps and hos?) where I might carry my eighty-pound bags through and down to the basement, where my room was. So I left my equipment unattended in the "lobby" while lugging each heavy box down a flight of stairs and into my tiny room, all the while thinking how fun it would be to drag them all upstairs early the next morning. I closed the door, locked it immediately, and drew in a deep breath of relief. To the gentle sounds of honking horns and blaring car radios outside my hotel window, I drifted off into a blissful hotel sleep.

The cabby who picked me up in the morning exclaimed loudly how I was not gonna "scratch his leather seats with those cases" (do cabs have leather seats?) and I proceeded to cover the seats with blankets I had brought from the hotel and nurse them gently into the cab, all the while assuring the cabby that he'd get a nice tip for this inconvenience. Once we had arrived at Lincoln Center, the cabby told me how he had to add another fifty bucks to the fare for crossing the state line into New York and six bucks for the tunnel fare, in addition to the regular fare. It was almost a hundred bucks by the time I had tipped him. I was getting the idea that using a taxi in New York City to transport large anvil cases was not only a stupid idea, but also a costly one.

But here I was; I had made it to one of the most important places in the city,

PERFORMANCES

Lincoln Center. All my friends back home were *so* impressed, mainly because they thought I was playing *in* Lincoln Center, not in front of it. (I was not going to burst their bubble, not just yet. Maybe they still think I played there.)

I was carefully positioned outside the box office in the square where I could look up at the tall building and, framed in a humid blue-and-gray sky, the tall white clouds peeking through the skyscrapers. I set up my keyboard and amplifiers, plugged in to a small electrical socket in the granite stairwell next to me, and at the stroke of twelve noon, I sang out onto the courtyard. The people stopped and turned and gathered around me and my little card table of CDs. I began to take their money without stopping the performance, one hand on the keys and the other giving them change. And then, at exactly 12:10 PM, I felt a single raindrop on my face, and I looked up to see a thunderhead and its trail of rain heading right for me.

But I needed the money! I was going to keep on playing, even if it rained! However, the audience wasn't interested in wet CDs and my solo performance of "Singing in the Rain." They ran away. As I looked down upon my wet electronics and the growing puddle of water I was standing in, I had a vision of my next song being "You Light Up My Life" with me as the lightbulb.

There was a group of people watching me with obvious concern from the sheltered box office entryway not ten feet away. And as I started to rip apart my gear and hustle the equipment piece by piece to the entryway, a few blessed souls offered to help me escape the torrential downpour. When all was in a safe place, one man looked at the dripping wet electronics and astutely asked, "Will your equipment be okay?" to which I cheerfully replied, "Oh, yes, I covered it with a blanket as soon as I could" (albeit a blanket wet with rain).

A half an hour later, the squall had passed. The warm, moist pavement was steaming in the humid June summer. The sky was once again a bright blue, with little, puffy, white cotton ball clouds darting behind and above skyscrapers. Was it okay to set up again? I eagerly reconstructed my one-woman street show and switched on the power. A nasty crackling like television static blared out of the speakers, and then the mixer went down with a big *pop.* Now I'd done it! I had ruined my setup, and worst of all, I didn't have the fare to get back to the hotel. I counted with shaking hands four twenties and several five-dollar bills, and with a flood of tears, grasped the reality of my situation: I had to get a new mixing board, *now,* or I was in deep, deep trouble. All I had was a checkbook, six over-the-limit credit cards, ninety bucks, and a phone.

First, I called the Musician's Union to ask if they could help me out. No help there. I called several instrument rental companies, all of which declined to rent me anything for use in the out-of-doors (wow, they would have rented gear to *me*??). I then called a local music store, which didn't have the mixer I needed but recommended that I call the Sam Ash music store next door. They had the very mixer I needed for $320. I didn't have that much money, I didn't know how to get there, but I'd be damned if I wasn't gonna find a way to get that mixer.

So, I asked a security guard what subway to take, begged him to watch my remaining equipment, and minutes later I located the Sam Ash music store. They had the unit, but they would not take my personal check. Nor would any of my credit cards run. That is, until after my pitiful crying in front of the register persuaded the clerk to run small amounts of money on each of my six cards (charges of less than fifty dollars go unverified by Sam Ash as to account status—please don't try this yourself—I love Sam Ash). With some additional cash out of my pocket, I raced out the door with a renewed sense of accomplishment. I was back in business!

But as I watched the unfamiliar numbers and letters whiz by through the subway train's windows, no one looked familiar anymore. What had I done? I thought I had retraced my steps—normally I'm pretty good about that—but somehow I was far away from where I'd been and was getting farther by the minute. I was headed towards the Bronx, somewhere on the Upper East Side, totally lost. I can't believe I did this, after all of the effort now I can't find the gig. So I got off the train, started asking for directions, and then headed back the way I came. Three hours after I had purchased the mixer, I returned to my pile of equipment sitting out in the open—unprotected and unwatched but luckily untouched—on the Lincoln Center Plaza and began setting up.

I was in the home stretch. I powered up the P.A. and began to sing. And the people reappeared, gathered around me and my little display of CDs. I began taking money, and just as I finished the second song, looked up into a huge black thunderhead that greeted me with a few fat raindrops. I grabbed the mixing board and ripped the cables from it, and with Herculean speed and Amazonian strength threw the various pieces of electronics into the shelter beneath the awnings in front of the Lincoln Center. And it was here I sat, until one of the employees of the Lincoln Center came out to inform me that I could not store my belongings there. That is when I started bawling. The employee went away.

The rain was so heavy and the wind so strong that some of the rain found its way to me, huddled under the large awning with forty or fifty other New Yorkers waiting out the storm. If I could have located an electrical outlet, I would have considered playing a few songs for the poor people trapped with me. I continued to cry to myself. The rain hid my tears.

It was around six PM when the rain stopped. I moved back out on the plaza, set up again, and by seven o'clock I was making music again. There were few people passing by, as the festival was over in one hour. I was getting a few people to listen, mostly those on their way to a show somewhere in the Center's complex of theaters. So, when it came to closing time, I just kept on singing, loudly and desperately trying to make the taxi fare I would need to go to and from the hotel.

All of a sudden the festival promoter yelled out to me: "The festival's over! Go home! They can hear clear inside the halls of the Lincoln Center where there is a show going on!" Just as my friends believed back home, I was entertaining (at least some) of the audience in the Lincoln Center. In fact, it was intermission and many of the patrons were out on the balcony one story up listening to me; watching, I waved, and some of them waved back. "Thank you and goodnight!" I called out to them.

Reaching in my pockets, I counted several hundred dollars, enough to return tomorrow. The next day I was back, it was five minutes before noon, and I was seated in front of my keyboard, adjusting the microphone, checking my sound. Curious people stood around me waiting to see what kind of strange thing I was to do. The weather forecast had not changed in the past twenty-four hours; the prediction had been for more of the same unpredictable, humid summer sun, wind, and rain. I saw ominous cloud shapes in the distance and was filled with dread. So, with all of my heart and faith, I said a prayer that I might be able to get home from this impossible gig in this unforgiving city. Please God, don't let me go home broke. Please, no more. I began to sing.

A large monarch butterfly circled just above me, then landed gently on the upper right corner of my keyboard. His wings slowly unfolded, folded, then unfolded again. I kept playing and singing, exchanging CDs for cash. The line of people grew and grew until it must have been sixty people deep. I was so busy I was unable to perform, and just played my music on a Walkman while selling CD after CD. All the time, the butterfly flexed his fiery black, yellow, and orange wings in a lazy rhythm to the music. He was unafraid of me. And my fear of the city and what might have happened today left me. Amazingly, the bank of thunderclouds went from left to right across the sky, circling the city but never coming close.

The frenzied people were buying an album that I had never sold, or sung before the public. That album to this day is one of my best sellers: "Four Roses." I couldn't believe the reaction; everyone loved it. How fortunate I was to debut this album here, and now.

I have never seen a butterfly stay in one place so close to me for so long. He stayed all afternoon, amid the crowds. When it was time to leave the show, the butterfly left, taking the crowd with him.

I zipped up my pockets, which were full of twenty-dollar bills. I was too afraid to sort and count the money out on the street, so I went to a booth in a ladies' room in the lobby of a four-star hotel across from the Center. I counted over twenty-five hundred dollars. I had never seen this much money come to me from performing, and all in a matter of hours. Even though the little monarch butterfly had flown away, a butterfly went back to the Lincoln Center Plaza to pack up the music equipment, hail a taxi, having learned a lesson or two about the road.

What I learned:

- Always carry adequate cash.
- Always have a credit card with lots of room on it.
- Bring two of everything. Two mixers, two keyboards, etc.
- Bring a tent in case of rain.
- Always have a "Plan B" for every "Plan A."
- Expect to get lost. That's how you get to know each city. You are never alone. Murphy loves to join you on the road. Anticipate the worst, but enjoy and expect miracles, too.
- And never, never give up.

BOBBY BERGE (GUITARIST):

I had forgotten about this until Mark Craney, a fellow Sioux Falls native and a great drummer, reminded me of it when I visited him at his home. I guess around 1969, he came to see me play when I was with The Chateau, a three-man power group, which was kind of like Blue Cheer, I guess. It was at some dinky little town ballroom and not too far from where I live now.

Anyway, he comes in the place and notices a crowd gathered around in front

Bobby Berge (Cherokee Studio, 1976, Tommy Brolin "Private Eyes" session)
From the photo collection of Bobby Berge

of the stage. Curious, Mark works his way up to the front to see what was goin' on. Well, there I am lying on my back with my legs spread, lighting farts for an amazed group of onlookers! That Katawba wine made me do some crazy shit! And that was when I was young and before I developed a serious drinking problem! I guess Mark mentioned this story in an interview, and I just wanted to confirm that unfortunately, yes, it is true!

SHARING THE STAGE

John Cale's performances were always out of the ordinary. Sometimes the performers, who were mostly unknown to the audience, would play and hold only one chord for up to forty-five minutes. One noted performance consisted of one of Cale's cohorts screaming at a plant, with the intention of having the audience watch it die. It didn't.

Musicians who have been fortunate enough to take the stage with some of rock's icons offer a variety of stories about their experiences. Sometimes the artist, as in Cale's case, will allow the unbridled participation of the guest musicians. These guest stars, whether they are known or unknown to the audience, become part of the act. Other times, they are asked to serve only as backing players or singers. In cases such as these, it might not matter to the particular musician who has been allowed to join the performance. Sometimes just being on stage with your musical hero, whether or not you are a key element of the show, is a dream come true.

LEE DORMAN (IRON BUTTERFLY):

It was the summer of '68 at the Rock Factory in Old Town by the river. A local band, Chuck Berry, and Iron Butterfly were on the same bill. Chuck Berry came to town with no band, so he used the opening act for backup. They were all young kids, so they had no clue.

Ron Bushy and I were sitting in the wings wishing we had known, as we both knew his songs by heart and would have gladly sat in for the honor of doing it. Chuck did a monologue with guitar only about his life as a musician. It was so intense it brought a tear to my eye. I've never forgotten it.

SCREAMIN' SCOTT SIMON (SHA NA NA):

Chuck Berry is the first true rock writer/performer. Starting as a blues guitar singer, he branched out with the "Chuck Berry Beat" to write literally dozens of rock and roll classics. In live performances, his "duck walk" became his signature move on stage, profiling to the audience with one leg straight out as he crouches balanced on the other and hops across the stage.

He remains notorious for never traveling with a back-up band of his own. Each promoter must provide a band that knows the Berry songbook, and then Chuck strolls in to play his show while they try to keep up. In the film of his six-tieth birthday party *Hail! Hail! Rock 'N' Roll* [1987], you can watch Keith Richards of the Rolling Stones try to put together a band for Chuck and note his frustrations in dealing with the man.

Working with Mr. Berry live is a lesson in the predictably unpredictable. Over the years, I have had the opportunity at least a dozen times of observing the Chuck Berry "show" as a fellow performer. His appearance invariably begins by him pulling up in a Cadillac rental about five minutes before the show is sched-uled to start. Now we're already in a gray area, for an eight o'clock show may mean that Sha Na Na is scheduled to go on for an hour, and then Chuck goes on at nine o'clock or so. But if Chuck shows up at 7:55 and shows the promoter a contract that says the show starts at eight o'clock, he may insist that HIS show starts at eight o'clock, and that all the equipment set up for our show be torn down and his equipment put up. He may also add that he has a plane to catch later that night, and that he's paid to perform one hour, beginning at eight o'clock. And the clock is already ticking on his hour's worth.

It's worth noting that Chuck, as all artists do, demands payment in full before going on stage. The only slight glitch with Chuck is that he demands payment in cash. For numbers as big as Chuck's fee, this becomes a very large roll of bills, which he counts and pockets. So now he's been paid, and the question becomes, when will he go on stage?

There have been times when he is supposed to on before us, as well as the other way around. Either way, Chuck has the buyer's cash in his pocket and may not be moved by the promoters saying that Chuck should close the show because, after all, he is the true "King of Rock and Roll." Wreaking havoc with the buyer's head seems to be Chuck's main concern. Here's a specific example of what happens to the show by the time Chuck has played out his game.

The scene is a sold-out coliseum in Denver in 1972. The opening act, pushing their very first record, is the then-unknown Steely Dan, fronted vocally by a friend of ours from L.A. named David Palmer. They go on at eight P.M., and do forty-five minutes or so. At 8:55 P.M. Mr. Berry's Cadillac appears in the loading dock, and he strolls in to tell the promoter that he must go on at nine. He has a plane to catch out that night. "But Chuck, you're the headliner," implores the buyer. "Now or never," replies Mr. Berry. He seems to mean it, having pocketed his cash, so now all of our equipment has to be struck from the stage and Chuck's stuff set up. He demands and gets very specific amplifiers for his guitar, which is all he brings. He doesn't even bring extra strings in case his break mid-show.

Back to the show. It's now 9:40, and the double changeover is almost done. We have nothing to do but cool our heels, knowing that his set will probably be over in short order because he has a flight to catch. In the meantime, the audience is waiting out this unexplained one-hour intermission, and is wondering when they are going to ROCK AND ROLL.

By the time Chuck finally hits the stage, after some last-minute concerns that maybe he doesn't have the right amplifier, the mood in the arena picks up. The centerpiece of Chuck's show at this time is a very long sing-along version of "My Ding A Ling," including "Louis Louie"—it's probably the filthiest song ever to get to the top of the charts. So Chuck is playing and playing and apparently unconcerned about missing his late-night flight. He doesn't give up the stage until eleven thirty PM. The promoter goes into "Golden Time" with the union hands at midnight, the audience is worn out, and we haven't even gotten on stage yet. Chuck waves goodnight on his way out the door: "Good night gentlemen." By the time we actually get on stage, only the hardcore audience is left.

The tenth anniversary of Disney World show provides a variation on the theme. There are mobs of people in the park and three different stages set up in different areas: one with The Four Tops and The Temptations, one with Frankie and Annette, and the third Sha Na Na/Chuck Berry stage. We are to do alternating half-hour sets, with both bands having their equipment on the large porta-stage to make the transitions seamless. Sha Na Na has nine people onstage, with a myriad of wardrobe changes to make throughout the show. We are given three dressing rooms in the wings of the stage. Chuck is to use a large motor home parked just behind the stage. We are finishing our opening set when Chuck pulls up in his Caddy to announce that his dressing room is unacceptable to him, as it is too far from the stage for his taste. The Disney producers, who by this time have paid Chuck his cash, ask us if we are willing to vacate our dressing rooms and move all our wardrobe into the motor home to placate Chuck. "Sure," we say, knowing that it is senseless to challenge the needs of Mr. Berry. He, in the meantime, goes on stage to play his first set as he always arrives—in his flamboyant shirt and the double-knit slacks, ready to go on. We finish moving our stuff into the motor home as he finishes up his half hour. Two wary (and beefy) security guys flank Chuck as he leaves the stage, concerned that he has the money but may threaten to bolt without finishing his second set. We go up for OUR second set, and Chuck sits at the side of the stage, still flanked by these two guys, for our entire set. We finish up, and then without ever having set foot into the three dressing rooms he had us vacate, he goes on for his final set. When he's through, he waves good-bye to us as he passes the motor home: "Good evening, gentlemen." And we close the show.

While the portrait of Mr. Berry painted here is one of a professional nightmare, on a personal basis, Chuck Berry has always been cordial. After a show in Birmingham, he took me aside for a moment and said, "You've still got it," which is as fine a compliment as one can get. During our show that night, he did watch, and I noticed him watching. At Disney World he also sat on the side and watched. At the most recent show we did with him for a hospital benefit in Orange Country, California, his demeanor back stage was devilish in that he had everyone so cowed in advance by his reputation for trouble that all he did was keep his friendly glint in his eye, as if to say, "You know how bad I can be; I just have to decide if I want to go to all that trouble this fine afternoon." Mr. Johnny B. Goode, Chuck Berry.

STAGE MANAGER TO THE RESCUE

Rock and Roll Hall of Fame DJ Red Robinson tells a story about when the Beatles played Empire Stadium in Vancouver, Canada. The crowd of young teenagers in attendance pushed toward the stage until it got to the point that the police had to inform Robinson, who was acting as MC, that he needed to interrupt the show and tell the kids to back off before someone got hurt. Robinson tried to explain to the police officer that musical acts don't like to be interrupted while on stage, but the Beatles' manager, Brian Epstein, told him it would be okay for him to intercede at the end of the song. Robinson walked up to the microphone as the crowd roared their appreciation for the just-completed song. He was startled when John Lennon demanded, "What the fuck are you doing on a Beatles stage?!" Photographs and concert footage show Lennon wiping his forehead while addressing Robinson out of the corner of his mouth. But Lennon understood Robinson's explanation, and the DJ did what he had to do.

The stage manager is a jack-of-all-trades when it comes to making sure that the presentation of the musical act is all it can be. Some stage managers are better than others. The good ones, though, are worth their weight in gold. They work with the musicians, the soundmen, the lighting guys, security, and the myriad and sundry backstage "guests." They have a lot of responsibilities and are present from the beginning to the end of the performance. Actually, they are present *past* the end of the performance. In some cases, one of the more appreciated parts of their job is helping the artist actually *leave* the venue.

CAROL KAYE (SESSION PLAYER):

I have a live-concert story about playing at the Shrine Auditorium, Los Angeles, with three acts live: jazz guitar with the Jimmy Smith Jazz Trio, jazz guitar with the great Oliver Nelson big band, and electric bass with "Little Stevie Wonder." It was probably about late 1965.

I had been recording guitar in the L.A. recording studios since 1957 on electric bass, but by 1965 I was missing all the jazz gigs I used to play around L.A. and Hollywood. So this was going to be fun to play live again. I was getting a little tired of recording day and night in the L.A. studios and thought it would be fun to do this special concert. Since I was recording some at that time for Little Stevie Wonder too, it felt good to play bass live for him.

The Shrine was packed and the audience just was the greatest, tons of applause. Stevie was the last act and the audience just went crazy. They were so excited.

We were happy the show was a smash as we headed afterwards to the back exit to go out to our cars. All the musicians and H. B. Barnum, the conductor, waited to get out the backstage entrance. Someone went out with my amp first and came right back in with his sleeve torn off. The audience was evidently "after us," or more probably after Stevie Wonder. Anyway, it didn't help to have H. B. Barnum on the inside yelling through the back door, "Wilson Pickett!" You heard a big roar from the outside: "Yaaaaah!!!" He was inciting them.

The man with my amp tried to get out again, but came back in fast, saying it was "too dangerous out there." The stage manager got us through the secret back exit door, and we all ran for our lives to our cars, with the huge mob of people running like crazy after us. We all barely made it out of the parking lot okay.

Needless to say, I was very happy never to play a live concert again for a long time after that, being very happy to just do studio work for years to come. No, thank you, too wild for me. I did do some memorable jazz concerts in the mid-'70s with the great jazz pianist Hampton Hawes. It was very "civil" compared to that wild Shrine concert.

UNEXPECTED RECEPTIONS

While most musicians live for the minutes when they perform their music, just getting to the actual venue at which they're supposed to be playing can sometimes be an effort. According to one story, Ry Cooder once had an extremely difficult time getting Captain Beefheart to a gig. Cooder arrived to find Beefheart still in bed.

When the guitar player urged the performer to get up so that they could get to the show, Beefheart stalled, saying he had to take a shower first. After a very long shower, Beefheart put his clothes on without toweling off, and later in the car complained that he couldn't perform because he felt clammy. Cooder reminded Beefheart that he hadn't dried himself off, which Beefheart proceeded to do in the car, then announcing that he felt better. Yet, once introduced to the waiting audience, Beefheart clutched his chest, claiming he had a pain in his heart. He left the stage, then the backstage area, and that was the end of the gig. Some days you just don't want to go to work.

Most music fans have a favorite concert or performance that stands out in their minds. Some fans even have a show that, for one reason or another, had a terrific impact on their lives. Knowing that the acts have been traveling the country performing their songs night after night, we might not think of the musicians themselves as having reciprocal experiences. Because they usually do their sets nightly, over long periods of time, sometimes things happen that make an evening special in some way. When you're on the road as much as a rock and roll act is, you'll welcome anything out of the norm that may happen to you at a particular stop if it breaks up the same-old, same-old. Sometimes it might even inspire a song.

GRAHAM PARKER (GRAHAM PARKER AND THE RUMOURS):

When my agent called to inform me that two promoters, one in Orlando and one in St. Petersburg, had made decent offers for a couple of shows, I was at first reluctant. Florida was way off my circuit, and I was not likely to do well there. After a bit a cajoling on his behalf, however, I decided to agree. The money was okay, cheap flights were available, and the mileage between the two towns reasonable. I could fly to Tampa, drive across the bridge into St. Petersburg, do the gig, have the next day off, and cruise up to Orlando the following day. Piece of cake. Music for money. In and out.

About a month before the trip, my agent called again and told me that some guy in Jacksonville had made an offer to play a club called the Milk Bar; this would be on Saturday night, the day in between St. Petersburg and Orlando. The money was lousy, but seeing as I was going all that way, why spend money on a hotel when I could at least be making a few bucks instead of doing nothing? It was the weekend, the place might get packed regardless, and the deal was structured allowing me lots of "back end" and "overages," along with other agent terms that I've never understood and have rarely seen materialize in my long career. Whatever, I said. Let's do it. How bad could it be?

And so on September 26, 1997, I landed in Tampa, fully expecting bright Florida sunshine and oranges literally rolling down the streets. As I made my way across the parking lot to my rental car, however, the rain was coming down so hard I was soaked through within minutes. We're talking rain of biblical proportions here, hardly the Sunshine State.

As I staggered across the parking lot in torrential rain, up to my shins in water, my mood—not exactly sprightly after hours in a stifling tube full of old people—dipped a few more degrees.

"You can't drive over the bridge!" yelled the man at the parking lot gate as I handed him my rental agreement. "It's flooded."

"I've gotta get to St. Petersburg!" I yelled back through the pounding rain. "I've got a gig to do."

He shrugged, raised the barrier, and off I went, wipers on high speed as I practically pressed my nose to the window in order to see through the onslaught. It turned out that although the airport parking lot was deluged, the bridge was fine, and within minutes I was in St. Petersburg at the hotel desk checking in before setting off for the gig.

The theater I was scheduled to perform in was a crumbling monolithic joint and seemed far too big for any audience I was likely to pull. After sound check and a meal, I sat around morosely in the dressing room, carefully placing both my guitar and myself in the two spots that were not receiving liberal soakings from the rainwater that leaked in through the roof.

Amazingly, the crowd that evening wasn't as small as expected and seemed well versed in my material, so I set off with more hope the next day for the hastily conceived Jacksonville show. The rain had let up a bit, although abundant signs of flooding were evident in the fields surrounding I-95. I'd picked up a local newspaper that morning and read with horror how the previous day's rains had claimed the life of a thirteen-year-old girl who'd been swept down a storm drain. A twenty-two-year-old lady had been similarly dragged off, only to pop up eleven blocks later, shaken but unharmed.

As I arrived in Jacksonville, the rain picked up again with a vengeance, sweeping off overpasses in waterfalls, pummeling my rental car, and almost forcing me to pull over more than once.

After checking into a very decent hotel, I made my way down to the fiendishly named Milk Bar for sound check. The club was located on a nondescript street. I found the unassuming entrance and inched carefully down a steep flight of spiral stairs, loaded with two guitars and a bag containing effects pedals and other gear. The room I entered was huge, low-ceilinged and decorated in a way that suggested grunge and heavy metal bands were its specialties, not solo singer/songwriters. On the grim, low stage at the back of the cavernous club stood a band with their gear all set up. No one else seemed to be around, so I introduced myself to a very young man who informed me that I could borrow his amp for the night. When I do solo gigs, I use both acoustic and electric guitars, and therefore have it in my contract that the promoter must provide an amplifier. Obviously, the skinflint Jacksonville promoter had conned the band into lending me an amp so that he could save a few bucks on the rental fee. Not a good sign.

The kid offering me the amp also mentioned that their outfit was not the only opening act that night, and that a solo performer would go on after them. Another bad sign. These people were probably not even getting paid, but merely offered a gig with the "legendary" Graham Parker and perhaps given the illusion that I would actually pack the place. This promoter was turning out to be a right piece of work, and I doubted I'd ever meet him. "Two opening acts?" I said to myself. Opening acts are a waste of time, in my opinion, and two is just plain pointless.

After some pleasantries with the band's apparent leader and amp lender, a guy with a fine mullet haircut and very few teeth slunk out of the shadows and introduced himself as the club's soundman. He then returned to the darkness and came back a few minutes later only to announce that the closet that held the microphones and other necessary items was locked and that he would have to drive off to the promoter's place to get the key. I sat around the gloomy hall for an hour awaiting his return as a few guys arrived and messed about in the bar area, each one fairly similar in appearance to our Joe Dirt look-alike soundperson.

At last the man returned, and with a semblance of a sound check completed, I got out of there and drove through a wickedly brutal rainstorm to a nearby sushi joint for some dinner.

You can tell if a gig is a stiff from a mile away, and as I approached the Milk Bar later that evening, I could see this one was going to be a stinker. The street was deserted, not a soul lingered at the club's entrance, and no cars were parked nearby. I gritted my teeth as I swung down the ominously quiet spiral stairway.

My mood was not much improved as I entered the club to the sight of some enormous bald bastard up on stage, playing to about thirty people. I stood unnoticed at the back of the room and checked out his act, which consisted of songs that appeared to be an unholy cross between Neil Young and Johnny Rotten. He'd be singing verses in that thin, lonesome Neil Young way, then when he reached the chorus, the entire song would change—rhythm, speed, key, and all—into something resembling "Anarchy in the UK," complete with braying English accent. Just as suddenly, he'd be back to old Neil again, whining on about Ontario or something. The audience, thankfully sitting around the stage on chairs that someone had placed there, seemed to be enjoying this nonsense immensely and cheered encouragement after each travesty as if it were the work of someone with talent.

Instead of this spectacle further depressing me, I foolishly decided—perhaps in some kind of anti-suicidal delusional self-defense reaction—that this was a good sign, and that if they liked this rubbish, then they'd surely love me. Yes, by Jove, I'd show 'em a thing or two and have them grooving out of their minds in five minutes flat!

The giant bald singer finally disappeared, and at ten past midnight I took to the stage and struck into my first song. As I hit the final chord and waited for a surge of enthusiastic applause, I realized that this was going to be a very long hour and a half. Tepid might be the word to describe the crowd's reaction. Almost complete disinterest would be closer to the truth. They were so unimpressed, you'd have thought that I was the opening act, and a bad one at that. Normally, I do three tunes in quick succession before I say anything, but right then, after that first number and the terrible lack of response it received, I decided that not a single word of greeting would cross my lips until I had either turned these people on to my act or turned them away. At that point, I was so incensed, so crushed, so mad at myself for accepting this gig and peeved at the audience for being idiots, that the latter seemed like my best (and most likely) hope.

And so it was that after four or five relentlessly intense songs, the audience—whose applause had grown even less after each tune—began to drift away until I was suddenly left with two couples out there in the darkness surrounded by a sea of very black, very empty chairs.

Not a word would I utter throughout the entire performance; not a "Hello, how ya doin'?" or "This one's from *Howlin' Wind*"—nothing. I would act as if I expected to play to an empty house. I would not acknowledge their presence even if you put a gun to my head and told me to do so. This petulance, of course, was not really fair to the two couples who bravely stuck it out. They were probably fans (one bloke even requested a song), and were at least not complete fools like the fans of the bald giant. But I'd made my mind up and was too depressed to stand there and be pleasant.

Song after song I belted out, changing from acoustic to electric guitar in record time, the better to lessen the effect of the complete silence after a mere four pairs of hands had offered their rather embarrassed applause. Then suddenly, another person appeared from the gloaming in the back of the room. A thinning-haired, scruffy-looking fellow was shuffling around behind the seats. Gradually, he made his way into the group of black fold-out chairs and planted himself in front of one of the couples. He then began to stare down at the legs of the female partner. He stared in a weird, spaced-out-looking way before wandering off, only to return a few minutes later to repeat this strange stunt. He was obviously mentally challenged, and my heart cheered at the thought of an incident occurring. Perhaps he'd set fire to the place; perhaps he'd pull out a gun and shoot the five of us, or hopefully just me—that would at least be preferable to completing my contractual agreement and having to carry on playing for another hour. Unfortunately, he didn't go quite that far, but after a few more return visits to the lady's legs, her partner could take it no more: he got to his feet, grabbed the nutter by the lapels, and head-butted him!

Ah, joy! Anything to take the enormous weight of embarrassment off my weary shoulders. A most pleasant distraction indeed.

So, there are five people in the audience in Jacksonville that night, *and there is a fight!* Marvelous stuff, and I continued my show with renewed vigor and vitality, even after the two barmen had removed the mentally challenged gentleman from the premises and I was back again to an audience of four.

There is a postscript to this story. A year or so after the Milk Bar debacle, I wrote a song called "I'll Never Play Jacksonville Again," which was included on my 2001 release *Deep Cut To Nowhere.* It's all in there: the floods, the girls swept down the culverts, my feelings of uselessness, the Jägermeister that the young barmen who worked the club cheered me up with after the show (*they* paid me: the promoter never showed his face).

Just recently, a reporter from a St. Petersburg newspaper called me requesting an interview. He wanted to know about the song. I described the events as best I could, warning him that accuracy in songwriting is not a given, and that I could have dreamed up the whole thing about the girls going down the storm drains (the song starts with the lyric "Two young girls were swept down/the culverts in the rain/St. Petersburg was flooded again").

As we were talking, he searched online for records of these events. Sure enough, the reports were there, almost exactly as I'd remembered and described them. For his article, he took things a step further. He found the twenty-two-year-old lady who had survived and he interviewed her, and also the parents of the young girl who had died. The survivor, it turns out, is a troubled young lady ("slow" is how her mother described her) with a history of drug abuse and shoplifting, among other things. He played her my tune. She thought it was "a nice song."

The mother of the kid who perished warmed to the song because she felt it brought her daughter back in some small way, but she couldn't understand why I started singing about the accident, then almost immediately went on and on about other things—myself, mostly. The father was very distraught, understandably, and very mad that the authorities had done nothing about the storm drains to this day. He was given a copy of the song. When the reporter called him back sometime later and asked for his opinion, he said that he hadn't listened to it. But he'd finally had enough of the inaction concerning the drains and was getting quotes on having warning signs put up, regardless of the authorities.

All of this made me feel very weird indeed. I felt bad that I'd so casually thrown a reference to a child's death into what is basically a frivolous, albeit angry, song. Who the hell am I to play around with stuff like that, just to get a couple of good rhymes in order to complete my own selfish agenda? I'll think more carefully about the power of a song in the future and how things can come back to haunt you.

THE VALUE OF THE LIVE SHOW

One of Elton John's tours featured porn star Linda Lovelace, as well as people posing as the Queen of England, the Beatles, and Batman.

The diversity of rock and roll styles is one of the great appeals of the genre. Just as each act presents its music a little (or, many times, a lot) differently than the next band, the style each act uses to obtain a following differs. People think that once an artist has an album deal, they've got it made. But if no one hears their music, no one will buy that album, and the act will soon be dropped from its label. Thus, acts take to the road to find audiences who will support them through sales and concert attendance.

Occasionally, an act focuses its energy on its performances rather than its album sales. The albums become a second thought. While this is not the usual way most artists go about making themselves star attractions, it has worked very successfully for some.

MITCH LOPATE (JOURNALIST):

I came to the South, I saw a show, and I was conquered—thanks to the power and persona of The Georgia Songbird Ms. E. G. Kight and her band.

With a voice that has the power of a brass horn in the hands of a virtuoso, E. G. knocks the daylights out of a range of songs that cross back and forth from tearful blues to steamy sensuality. Do you remember how Dizzy Gillespie looked when he was letting loose those gale force winds through his trumpet's mouthpiece? Well, that sound has taken human form. It's no secret where she gets her influence: a good friend like Koko Taylor is worth every second of E. G.'s onstage persona, and this talent is too bright to hide. Her sound is a cross between Phoebe Snow's fragility and Janis Joplin's anguish, but E. G. is really carrying on the work of the blues as her voice shimmers and radiates. If Janis's sound was "Southern Comfort," then E. G. is cognac—and her voice is not alcohol-influenced. "Crossroads" scorches our ears, and Eric Clapton's vocals could not match this on the Fahrenheit scale.

On stage, she's absolutely in her element: the quiet, modest country girl is now shaking her hips, singing á la Elvis, and picking away with absolute conviction on a blue-and-mother-of-pearl Fender Stratocaster. This is why she's the consummate musical field general: there's no choice but to follow the burning intensity of the music. Her supporting band is a variation of veteran warhorses and young rising stars (just wait till you see her lead guitar players). Even the audience gets involved: friend and fellow singer/songwriter/guitarist Tom Horner helps out with two ferocious, shaking versions for "Stagger Lee" and "I've Got News for You."

The obvious question is this: how on earth can someone so volcanic be kept in the dark? Yes, E. G. is as sweet off stage as spun cotton candy, and as refined and respectful as any gentle Southern belle. If there were ever a reason for a seismographic warning about a pending earthquake, the music world at large in this country needs to tie down and brace up for one hell of a show when E. G. fires up. The Richter scale also recognizes little tremblers, and when she's in the mood ("Blue Dawn," cowritten with Horner), the only thing that's quivering are the tears in your eyes. She's also a knockout composer in her own right, as testimony will endorse in full measure on her latest release, the incendiary *Trouble* CD (that carried me away with the first bars of the title song).

E. G.'s country roots are neatly mixed into her set, too. "Angel from Montgomery" is rocked slowly in its cradle, darling, with wavering bottleneck, and Dusty Springfield's hit "Son of a Preacher Man" leaves you gasping for breath. But it's "Somewhere in Atlanta" that E. G. stakes out as her fortress (cowritten with friend Sunny Stephens), and there's no doubting why so many bands have honored this wonderful city. Speaking of places, her encore could level the walls of Jericho. She steals a heart-melting version of "I've Been Loving You Too Long (To Stop Now)" from the immortal Otis Redding. As I recall, the only other woman to righteously take a song from Otis and claim it with her own signature is Aretha Franklin. On her second CD, *Come Into the Blues,* she closed with this one, and it demands replay after replay (a half hour would be a suitable beginning; this one song was worth my trip south on I-75). That isn't enough: she and her bandmates one-upped The Killer, Jerry Lee, with an explosive rendition of "Great Balls of Fire," and the chicken in the fryer never crackled so much as the boogie-jazz of "First in Line." (That's where I am for the next show, and E. G. plays a three-part, five-hour set. How lucky can I be?) I'm not asking to be rescued. It's a lot easier for me this way to see E. G. perform, and if that means that I break the lease and let the landlord chase me, it's okay. Maybe I'll buy him a ticket and get a full refund for the rent—because I'm staying if E. G.'s playing. Forward my mail!

JOCKO MARCELLINO (SHA NA NA):

We're a funny animal. We've had several gold albums of our own and the double-live *Golden Age of Rock and Roll.* Then, of course, we were involved in *Grease* and *Woodstock* [the legendary concert and the film about it]. So we've had record success. But more than that, we've had success in other media.

Most of the acts—99 percent of the acts—have to depend on their record success. They have a career. We do not have to rely on records. We go the other way. We look at records as a promotion of our live show. Everything is ancillary to the marketing of the live show. And luckily, we've had some nice pieces of marketing. One, we're at and in *Woodstock,* the biggest documentary ever. Two we're in *Grease.* We had more songs in *Grease* than any other artist as Johnny Casino and the Gamblers. The biggest musical ever. And then we had the first TV show in syndication, in television history. First-run syndication. We had NBC O-and-Os (owned and operated). There were only seven at the time. Then they syndicated it first-run, and we had almost two hundred markets. For a couple of years. It was amazing. And then we had another three years after that, stripped, five days a week. So the power of the medium is ridiculous.

And all of this goes into that live show, which is always the bread and butter. The music we celebrate has become America's folk music. I don't mean with acoustic guitars, but the folk music. Word of mouth, pass it on. The music that we most have in common as three generations of a family. On your AM radio dial, every city has one or two oldies stations. You'll find a family, and the only station they might listen together to, if they're three generations, is the oldies stations. They're not going to listen to the hip hop together; they're not going to listen to classical music together—they're going to listen to the oldies stations. It's a remarkable music. Of course, I didn't write these songs, but I feel we truly are the neoclassicists of the era. We brought it around more than anyone else. We do it with great joy, and that's why we still enjoy doing it.

NEWS OF THE DAY

Rocker Patti Smith is often booed when she performs her song "Boy Cried Wolf" about John Walker Lindh. Smith feels strongly enough about asking for leniency for the suspected Taliban–influenced expatriate that she doesn't care about audience reaction and performs the song anyway.

Because an act is on the road so much throughout the year, there are bound to be times when its concert coincides with some major news event. Just because they are living a unique lifestyle doesn't mean they have removed themselves from society. The rocker is as susceptible to news-related emotions as the next guy. Rockers pay attention to what's going on in the world, even as they attempt to go on with their business as usual.

KEN SKAGGS (GLEN CAMPBELL BAND):

September 11, Branson, Missouri: That Tuesday morning, I had risen early for no reason other than that my brain was running with ideas and I couldn't sleep. Not being a TV watcher, I turned on the local NPR radio station in time to hear that an airplane had crashed into the World Trade Towers. I immediately turned on CNN and watched United Flight #175 fly into the second tower, creating another inferno. I continued watching in disbelief as another airplane crashed into the Pentagon and another crashed in western Pennsylvania. I had this feeling that things were never going to be the same.

As the old show business axiom says, "The show must go on." Nowhere is this more a truism than in Branson, Missouri. So I took the stage that afternoon stunned, with images of the morning playing and rewinding over and over in my mind. That was the first time I've ever cried on stage during a performance. I cried for the victims, but also for my country, the victim of a callous, senseless act. When Glen sang "God Bless the U.S.A." to close the show, every cheek bore a trail of tears.

Over the course of the next week, as many of you probably did, I spent every waking hour that wasn't occupied by work or sleep in front of the tube. I couldn't get enough. I wanted answers, and I wanted resolution. I was angry, thinking that if they'd let me back in the Army I'd be on a plane tomorrow. It took a week for the devastation to sink in. Never had there been an attack of this nature on American soil.

The shows go on, the leaves are turning, and the squirrels are burying acorns beneath the oak trees behind my condo. It's been nice not rushing around airports, instead only having to drive three miles to the theater each day. Another week, and that will change as we're back to the skies again: Phoenix, Florida, New Jersey, Nevada, California, Phoenix, and Nebraska. I'm not afraid to fly, but I'm not looking forward to the new climate of flying. Maybe those tour buses aren't so bad after all.

CHAPTER 3

IN THE STUDIO AND SPECIAL PERFORMANCES

While musicians live to perform, without that intricate, ball-busting time in the recording studio, there would be few people to hear those performances. Recording is a difficult process, involving everything from composing and charting to take after take of vocals and instruments.

Recording studios used to be little holes in the wall where the musicians would be called in for an hour or two to do their thing and be gone. With the advent of longer single releases, concept albums, and hefty recording contracts that allow artists leeway for experimentation and perfecting tracks, that has all changed. Recording studios now become a temporary home away from home, offering food, relaxation devices, and assorted services. Many sessions can be difficult and painful, while others can be rewarding and even enjoyable. But, when all is said and done, most musicians remember each and every one of their recording sessions, painful or not.

MICHAEL "SUPE" GRANDA (OZARK MOUNTAIN DAREDEVILS):

I don't remember what it was I was dreaming about, but I do remember how I was awakened. It was not a rude awakening. A loud, spontaneous thunderclap of laughter ripped through the air. It became apparent quite quickly that I, still quite spaced out, was the focus of the merriment. As the cobwebs began to clear, it became obvious that no one was laughing *at* me but at what had just happened *to* me.

Supe Granda (Ozark Mountain Daredevils)
From the photo collection of Michael Supe Granda

The sign in the reception area of London's AIR Recording Studios read: "Studio A: Ozarks; Studio B: (blank); Studio C: Pistols." Everyone entering AIR must pass through a common reception area before heading to their respective studios. It was in this reception area that I had fallen asleep. It was here that I was awakened by the guffawing of the handful of Englishmen who were also using said reception area to sit around between overdubs, read magazines, take naps, etc. And it was here that I first met "him."

Well, to be perfectly honest, I didn't actually *meet* him. By the time I'd come out of the fog, Sid Vicious had already yanked on my beard (which I wore quite long) and run down the hallway into the sanctuary of Studio C.

"You're going after him, aren't you mate?" "You're not going to let the bloke get away with that, are you?" "He's an arsehole."

Groggily, I strolled down the long hallway past Studios B and C on my way to the bathroom, which just happened to be located at the end of the same "hallinary" cul-de-sac. As I passed by the door to Studio C, I was tempted to enter.

The door was tightly shut. I didn't knock. Judging by the racket coming from within, they wouldn't have been able to hear a knock on the door anyway. I knew the Sex Pistols would be in Studio C for the entire week.

And what a week it was. Elvis Presley had just died, and Elvis Costello's first record had just come out. While we were comfortably nestled in the studio, record companies were in a feeding frenzy on the street. The media were maniacally elbowing each other, trying to cover this crazy little thing called "punk rock." England was definitely swinging.

It wasn't until early the next afternoon that I actually met him. Once again, it was in the hallway. The same hallway where, just moments earlier, I'd run into Sir George Martin on his way back into Studio B. We both held cups of coffee in our hands. Being the proprietor of AIR, Sir George was aware of our band, our music, and our presence in Studio A. After a warm introductory handshake, he asked if I had a minute to spare. Of course I did, and we ducked into Studio B where he was mixing Paul McCartney's latest record (thus explaining the blank space behind Studio B on the sign in the reception area).

After a brief social visit, he asked if I'd be interested in listening to the song he'd been working on that morning. He also asked if I thought the guitars were too loud in the mix. During the playback, I couldn't believe my eyes, my ears, or any other part of my absurd life. THE George Martin, asking me if Paul McCartney's guitars were too loud. Of course they were sparkling. And mixed perfectly, an opinion I expressed with a series of stammers and stutters. He thanked me, told me to stop by any time, and I continued on my merry way to the restroom.

Leaving the cozy confines of Studio B, where I'd just been face to face with the quintessential English gentleman, I hit the hallway where I stood face to face with Sid Vicious. Can you say "dichotomy"?

Sid and an equally strange friend of his had emerged from Studio C, and they began walking up the hall toward me. I had no intention of bringing up yesterday's antics, but sure enough, when we got close enough to each other, some strange urge overtook him. His hand went right for the bottom half of my face. It was not a punch, but merely another frontal assault on my facial hair.

This time I was awake and grabbed his hand before he could grab my beard. He tried to pull away, but even though I am not a big, burly guy, the firmness of my grip was too overpowering for him. He was helpless until I decided to let loose of his hand. The conversation, if you can call it that, did not last very long. It didn't take a rocket scientist to figure out that Sid could not comprehend what I was saying. Nor could he talk (grunt is a better word for what he did).

Had I had my wits about me, I could've (and should've) gone nationwide, making the front pages of music tabloids everywhere with headlines like "Country Rocker Pummels Punk Vicious" or "Rival Bassists Square Off in REAL Battle of the Bands." I just held onto my handshake grip until he looked me in the eyes and got my unspoken message. Then I let go of his hand and chuckled as I watched the two of them make a mad dash up the hall and around the corner.

George Martin and Sid Vicious in the same breath. I told you my life was absurd. AIR Studios is located on the third floor of a beautifully ornate building, directly overlooking Oxford Circus. Right outside the aforementioned reception area stands the elevator that transports passengers from the tranquil quiet of the recording studio to the hustle and bustle of downtown London. I had already pushed the "down" button when I heard that familiar grunting coming up the hall and out the door. He was alone this time, and we immediately became just two guys waiting for the elevator.

No big deal, you say? Not when you're waiting for an elevator with Sid Vicious. There was, once again, no real communication between us. Just my eyes keeping an eye on his hands and my amusement gland holding its side.

Eventually, the elevator cometh. A handful of people already occupied the car as we got on. I immediately blended in and became the "normal" guy as Sid grunted, sniffled, flung his head and shoulders about, and in general took up more than his share of space. Eventually we reached the ground floor. I don't think Sid liked elevators much, for as soon as the doors opened he rushed out as if he were escaping a burning building. I was in no big hurry, so I decided to follow Mr. Vicious just to see what he was going to do once he hit Oxford Circus.

He stumbled through the lobby and out the door as I inconspicuously trailed him. He bought an ice cream cone from a sidewalk vendor and caromed off into the crowd. I was disappointed.

It was back upstairs into Studio A and the work continued. Later that same afternoon, during a lull in the action, I took the opportunity to quietly daydream out the window at the rush hour scene and the ant-sized people below. My trance was interrupted when a startling flash of "viciousness" flew through my field of vision. There was my friend Sid, running around right before my very eyes. He had climbed out of a window in Studio C and was running along a narrow catwalk that encircles the entire third floor of this grand old building.

I rubbed my eyes, for I couldn't believe what I was seeing. Yes, he was out on that ledge and out of his mind. When I turned my gaze back towards the control room, the rest of my bandmates were beside themselves with laughter. Pete Henderson, our English engineer, was not amused by his fellow countryman.

That was the last time I saw my old friend Sid. He laid down his bass parts (or so rumor has it) and split. I heard their record. I love their record. I bought their record. Every well-rounded record collection has a copy of *Never Mind the Bollocks, Here's The Sex Pistols* in its midst. I also recognize its place in history as not only one of the greatest rock 'n' roll recordings made, but also one of the greatest rock 'n' roll swindles of all time. Because A&M Records, one of their victims, was also our record company, Sid and I were label mates for literally hours. They followed their record with a tour of the United States, but I was not interested. I had been friends with Sid for only one week, and that was more than enough. They'd swindled hundreds of thousands of dollars from several record companies. They weren't going to swindle me out of five bucks. I knew it was a hoax. I saw it firsthand. I loved every second of it. I have a very healthy amusement gland.

Yeah, Johnny Rotten was there at AIR, too. He was a good guy and sharp as a tack. He could, at least, hold a conversation. We talked about Elvis as we sat around, passing the time between overdubs.

KNOW THY INSTRUMENT

Rolling Stones founding father Brian Jones was possibly the first mainstream rocker identified with the harmonica. Jones didn't particularly like to play the harmonica during performances because it obscured his face—another facet of an ongoing battle to keep Mick and Keith from taking the lion's share of attention in the band he formed.

Brian Jones was an extremely talented musician. In addition to guitar and harmonica, he contributed a variety of obscure instruments to the Stones' tracks, including organ, dulcimer, marimbas, harpsichord, glockenspiel, piano, accordion, banjoele, recorder, saxophone, trombone, sitar, and other complicated conduits of music. Jones prided himself in learning new instruments and was a talented enough artist to play each one well. But sometimes, being in the studio teaches a musician that he or she should just stick to doing what he or she does best.

DAVE ANDERSON (FRIEND OF LYNYRD SKYNYRD'S FOUNDING DRUMMER BOB BURNS):

During rehearsals at Hell House, Bob said that Ronnie VanZant had taken the notion to try to play harmonica on certain songs they were working up. Bob's exact words were, "Ronnie never sucked at anything he put his mind to do. The harmonica was his musical Waterloo." Ronnie was so bad at the mouth harp that whenever the band would let out from practice, they would hide Ronnie's harmonicas in the back of the P.A. columns, in the back of their guitar amps, in the kick drums, anywhere they could hide them.

After twenty-seven or so harmonicas disappeared mysteriously, Ronnie had enough. He walked into rehearsal one day, ripped off his shirt (in typical Ronnie fashion) and proceeded to tell them all they were in for an ass kicking if the harmonica abductions continued. After much discussion, Ronnie was finally convinced that he should lay down the instrument and concentrate on vocals. Bob said the band was grateful.

OPPORTUNITIES TO LEARN

Mike Love, singer with the Beach Boys, has never been one to hold back his feelings. During the band's induction into the Rock and Roll Hall of Fame, Love taunted other mega-name bands, at one point saying, "I know Mick Jagger won't be here tonight. He's gonna have to stay in England. He's always been too chickenshit to share the stage with the Beach Boys!"

Some musicians are so caught up in their own "artistry" they have little or no respect for the music of others. But it isn't unusual for a musician to find someone in the studio whom they greatly admire as they define their artistry. The act an artist watched as a teenager just might be the same musician who eventually helps form his or her career.

FRANKIE FORD (SOLO ARTIST):

Although I'd been to New York in 1952, to appear on the Ted Mack Amateur Hour at age twelve, I was too young to observe the politics and continuity of the entertainment business. (What is good for the show is not necessarily what is good for the artist.)

In 1958, with a regional hit in "Cheatin' Woman," I was summoned to Philadelphia by George Woods ("the man with the goods") to appear at the Uptown Theater. Such acts as Jerry Butler & The Impressions, The Dells, The Dubs, The Spaniels, The Isley Brothers, Little Anthony & The Imperials, Ann Cole, and Doc Bagby's large orchestra were on the show.

On the afternoon of the first show, I arrived and sat in the theater awaiting rehearsal. When my name was called by Georgie, I ascended the stage to hand out to the orchestra my thirty-five-dollar-apiece arrangements. With a look of disbelief on his face, George declared, "Oh my God! You're white!" No pictures had been published of me to date, so he had no clue. After a little convincing he allowed me to rehearse.

I stayed for the ten days duration of the show. During that time, I also made my first appearance on Dick Clark's *American Bandstand.* In later years, it is always a big laugh when the other acts and I get together and say, "Remember the Uptown Theater?"

Upon my return to New Orleans from Philadelphia early Monday morning, sleeping in my own bed was a luxury. That afternoon when the phone rang, I was called to Cosimo Matassa's recording studio for the evening. When I arrived at the studio they played tracks for me—with only the music and no vocals—which I'd never heard before. There has been some confusion about Bobby Marchan's vocals being on the track I heard. That is definitely not the case, as Huey Smith sat at the piano with me, teaching me the words, which I wrote down on my high school three-ring loose-leaf paper. After thirteen takes, they called it a wrap on "Sea Cruise."

At the time, Huey "Piano" Smith & The Clowns were riding high on the national charts with "Don't You Just Know It." Johnny Vincent (president and owner of Ace Records) and Joe Caronna (my manager at the time) suggested that "Sea Cruise" should be released under my name, therefore creating another act for Huey to produce. He agreed, and the record was released in February 1959. The rest is widely known to all.

After sixty years in the business (I was onstage when I was five years old!) I'd like to thank everyone involved. It's been a great ride with, God willing, many more years to come.

RICK ROSE (SOLO ARTIST):

As a kid growing up in Niagara Falls, Canada, we frequently went to see concerts in New York at the Niagara Falls Convention Center and the Buffalo Auditorium. We spent many nights studying our *Circus* magazines and the linear notes in our albums. One of my biggest heroes growing up was producer/ guitarist Mick Ronson. His influence, his image, his guitar playing was what we all wanted to be.

I met Mick in 1982 in Connecticut. My band Lennex opened up for his band. He heard one of my demos and offered to work with me. A year later he came to

Rick Rose
From the photo collection of Rick Rose

Toronto and helped me launch my first record deal. We remained friends till his passing nine years ago. Mick went from being a hero to a great friend and believer. The music business sometimes rewards you in peculiar ways!

ON THE RADIO

One of the most infamous television appearances by a rock act is that of the Doors on the **Ed Sullivan Show.** *The band was told during rehearsal that Jim Morrison would not be allowed to sing the words, "Girl, we couldn't get much higher" when he performed "Light My Fire." The producers were somewhat surprised when the band agreed. They should have known better. When the show aired live, the always controversial Morrison sang the words anyway. He said later that he "forgot" about the agreement. The Doors were banned for life from the popular television show.*

Promotion is much more than a slick guy in a Corvette tooling from city to city, glad-handing radio station programmers and on-air personalities. That may have worked back at the beginning of rock and roll—we won't go into the whole payola dynamic—but with the advent of national television and radio programming, promoting an act became much more complex. It is essential these days that musicians appear in person on radio and television in order to elevate their name to that plateau needed to break a song or CD.

The age of the super or shock jock has provided a natural radio format for rock musicians. The media frenzy surrounding acts is such that it is almost impossible to be overexposed. Sometimes that means musicians putting themselves at the mercy of someone with whom they might otherwise not be talking. If they're media-savy enough, they can turn an uncomfortable situation into a great opportunity for the listening audience to get to know them—and their music— better.

JANIS IAN (SOLO ARTIST):

I did Howard Stern and joined the ranks of the politically incorrect. I love doing Howard (as it were). I've done his morning radio show, his E! television show,

Janis Ian
From the photo collection of
Janis Ian

and his disgusting New Year's Eve special. I like Howard. He treats me with courtesy, and he recognizes my personal relationship as valid. In fact, he tried *very* hard to find an appropriate term for introducing my partner. After rejecting "Mr. Ian," "Mrs. Ian," and "Her Better Half," he finally settled on "Mr. Lesbian," a term we find appallingly funny and poignantly correct.

When Stern ran for governor of New York, he received a great number of votes. Why? Because he touches people, although by his own admission his penis is too small to touch much, which is another reason to like him. Who was the last man *you* heard admit to that? Howard operates from the theater of honesty in a way very few performers dare. He says things I'm afraid to say, and admits to feelings I've overheard on tour buses and in men's locker rooms when no one thinks I'm listening. He's thoroughly uncomfortable with gay male sexuality, but he also excoriates anyone who would deny anyone's right to consensual sex. As performers, Howard Stern and I attempt to do exactly the same thing—to break down the stereotypes.

The fallout of doing Howard has been both educational and frightening. People writing to my fan club who identify themselves as politically correct are horrified and furious that I find any common ground with him. The hate mail contingent seems to mistake theater for reality, and their own bigotry for enlightenment, threatening us both with "dire consequences." I'm at a loss as to why they find the friendship so dangerous. Howard's *Lesbo Dial-A-Date* is one of the hottest shows on radio; during it he treats us *exactly* like he treats his hetero-sexual female guests—snidely, with double entendres flailing.

My mail assumes that because many of the guests on *Dial-A-Date* are women with big hair and harsh rural accents—I consider a heavy Brooklyn accent rural—who strip/spank/tease with gleeful abandon, he's "victimizing the lower econom-ic strata, who can least defend themselves." Excuse me? Does that mean if you have a sixth grade education you're less capable of deciding what to do with your body than a Ph.D.? I find that attitude incredibly patronizing, and demeaning to *all* women. Why is it so odd to see Janis Ian laughing with Howard Stern? When he says, "Oh Janis, if you'd only slept with the right man you'd be straight," and I reply, "Oh Howard, if you'd only slept with the right man you'd be gay"—and he agrees that there's always the possibility—it sends a message to his core demo-graphic of white fifteen-to-twenty-five-year-old males that they get from no one else on radio.

That message is tolerance and acceptance. I've had earnest boys in full hetero drag appear back stage to say that their evening's choice was "between you and Alice In Chains, but you were on Howard so we came here." I've watched an audience comprised mainly of heterosexual couples interact with me, a gay woman, in a positive way. Remember, these are the kids who think all lesbians are fat, ugly, man-haters who want penises for Christmas, and all queer men are sissies who couldn't get a girl.

I spent a good part of the '80s trying to get a record deal because no record company at the time would take a chance on a gay forty-year-old female who'd already had two careers. My partner and I mortgaged our home so I could make the album *Breaking Silence*. Howard Stern and singer/songwriter John Mellencamp, both dismissed in a recent article I read as "misogynistic breeders," were the *only* performers to back me with airtime and money before my record broke.

I thought being politically correct was about integrity and acceptance. If that's so, Howard is as P.C. as they come. The Federal Communications Commission are always trying to close down Howard Stern's show for "obscenity," and I know part of the obscenity they refer to is people like me. My demands for equality. My insistence on parity. My very *being*.

I do Howard because he's good. Because he has wonderful eyes. Because he treats my relationship as normal. Because he thinks rapists should be cemented over, child molesters should be shot, and road crews should only work at night. I agree. But even if I didn't, I'd support his right to use the airwaves, and my right to join him. Or as Mr. Lesbian says, "Honey, you go right on doing Howard. I'll do his wife." And that about sums it up.

THE ART OF THE TELEVISION APPEARANCE

No one act was better fodder for the press than the Sex Pistols. The proper and straight-laced BBC was aghast when the band appeared drunk and disorderly on the popular Today with Bill Grundy in 1976. Grundy was having the time of his life, encouraging the Pistols to be as outlandish as they possibly could. Grundy encouraged the band to "say something outrageous" in the final minutes of their interview. Steve Jones' ensuing "You bastard!" created a country-wide gasp and gave the Pistols exactly what they wanted— public recognition.

Elvis on the *Steve Allen Show* singing "Hound Dog" to a live Basset Hound. The Beatles on *Ed Sullivan,* hardly being heard over the screams of the teenyboppers in the audience. John and Yoko appearing as cohosts on the *Mike Douglas Show* for a week. Eric Clapton performing *MTV Unplugged.* Lynyrd Skynyrd on *Live with Regis and Kelly.* Rock and roll is here to stay on mainstream television programming.

Appearing on one of the seemingly thousands of VH1 "list" programs, or at the equally numbered MTV award or video shows, is all in a day's work for the rock musician. But it wasn't always that way. While Elvis and the Beatles were making their historic appearances in American homes, no one seemed as out of place in that market as the rock act. Watching Jefferson Airplane or Cream on television shows in the '60s was almost painful. Acts such as these were formed to entertain at marijuana–laden halls and auditoriums, not in front of your mom and dad.

Many musicians look forward to appearing on television as something akin to a trip to the dentist for a root canal. Others shrug it off as an opportunity to promote themselves, regardless of how uncomfortable they might be performing in an unnatural environment. As they say in show business, "You gotta have fun with it."

LEE UNDERWOOD (GUITARIST):

For a while, Tim [Buckley's] merry band of Starsailors didn't feel the least bit merry. Some people responded well to the new music. But too many others didn't. The East Coast lay dark and dreary in the dead of winter—ice, snow, gray skies, barren trees, brown grass. But not everything was bleak. With loving warmth in his eyes, John Balkin, Tim's bassist at the time, recalled a very special incident.

"Tim and I got up at five in the morning, while everybody else slept. It was cold, so I bundled him up with his coat and scarf. We were like two kids getting up and going out and playing in winter's first snow when nobody else has seen it. We had to drive ninety miles into Philadelphia for a TV show. It was a very personal thing, being together in the car, making that drive in the predawn winter morning. While we drove, we decided what to do on the show. We had a cassette tape of the backdrop of 'Starsailor,' without Tim's verbal overlay.

"When we hit the studio, we both felt the vibes of those lobotomized assholes. It was six or seven in the morning, and already the producers and technicians were getting juiced on wine. Philadelphia housewives sat out front. Backstage, all these television slickos were getting bombed, sitting there drinking cheap white wine.

"It was almost like we weren't there. They didn't even relate to us. We could have walked in naked and it wouldn't have made any difference. They didn't even *see* us, you know? We just sailed through the whole thing, carrying our roles off without plotting them.

"My role was to walk coolly into the control room and hand the cassette to the engineer. He said, 'What is Tim going to do?' I said, 'He's going to do something from his latest album, and this is the background tape to be played under what he will be saying.'

"Tim walked out into the spotlight, didn't take his coat off, and didn't even take his scarf off. It was an old black-and-white tweed coat. He walked out in front of the housewives, who sat in tiers, maybe sixty tiers.

"We cut through the whole thing. We cut through the stoned TV executives. We cut through the stoned cats in the control booth that were drinking a cheaper grade of wine than the executives—they were deciding who's gonna bring the wine next week. We cut through the guy who said, 'Well, time to go tame the animals,' talking about the housewives.

"They put the tape on. The engineer looked at me as if it was running backwards. I said, 'No, let it go, it's okay. It's not running backwards. Just let it go.'

"Tim took out a piece of crumpled paper from his coat—an envelope with lyrics scratched on it—and proceeded to read it and improvise on it, with the housewives screaming and chortling, not laughing, but having fun listening to this ragamuffin they were told was a star.

"Nobody listened to the music. Nobody listened to Tim. Everybody back stage was ready for the entrance of the next act. He was just out there. He did his shtick, they gave me the cassette back, and nobody said a word. We turned around, walked to the elevator, didn't say anything, got out in the parking lot, and just looked at each other and broke up laughing at the absurdity of it. 'Wow! Where the fuck have we just been!'

"It was an *out-front* experience. It wasn't the 'image' Tim Buckley. It was just two guys doing a thing together."

UNWANTED GUESTS

Eagle Bernie Leadon claimed he had finally had enough of the dominance of Glenn Frey and Don Henley. In a hotel while on tour, Leadon walked over to Frey, poured a beer over his head, and quit the band. Being cooped up in a hotel doesn't ease the tension of the road. But ya gotta have a place to sleep.

Several hotels that cater to rock musicians have earned the reputation for "party central," with good cause. The infamous "Riot House" on the Sunset Strip earned it's status in the '60s and '70s not so much because of its location on the Sunset Strip, as the fact that the nickname of the Hyatt House was synonymous with the outlandish acts of the rockers who stayed there. Off-the-wall "jokes" such as chucking the television set out the window, throwing various room items into the pool, riding motorcycles through the hallways, and entertaining assemblies of groupies and hangers-on in a variety of adventurous ways was the norm while the groups were in temporary residence. This behavior spread so rampantly throughout the years, that it wasn't long before rock musicians weren't always welcomed guests in hotels. If the acts were grudgingly allowed to book into a decent hotel, it was not without a substantial deposit.

Some of the first unwanted rock guests weren't necessarily those who caused the damage themselves, but those whose fans were likely to wreak havoc on the premises during their attempts to somehow get closer to their heroes. Yeah, it started with the Beatles.

JOHNNY CHESTER (SOLO ARTIST):

We all have stories about hotels and motels that were concerned about having rock and roll bands staying in their establishments during the '60s. Here in Australia, we had our share of incidents, too. During my Australian and New Zealand tour with the Beatles, we were informed that the leading hotel in Sydney at the time,

Johnny Chester (in the 1960s)
From the photo collection of Johnny Chester

The Chevron, would not allow the Beatles and their touring entourage to stay there. The hotel was apparently worried about the effect hundreds of teenagers staying overnight on their front steps would have on the other guests. So, they said no.

This was a pretty brave economic decision, too, as the Beatles entourage, including press and support acts, was fairly large and we were in Sydney for three or four days. But the decision was made, and so the promoter took the show and all who were a part of it and booked us into The Sheraton hotel, which was straight across the road from The Chevron. The show, I seem to remember, took up almost the whole hotel.

We arrived to be greeted by literally hundreds of teenagers. The kids stood on the footpath outside the hotel and waited to get a glimpse of the Beatles, who would come out of the balcony of their rooms from time to time and wave to the kids.

It soon became apparent, however, that because the hotel was built right on the footpath, it was very difficult to see the Beatles when they did appear. There was a much better spot to see them from right across the road: in front of The Chevron.

So, over the kids went and stayed for the whole time we were there. They were singing, calling out, and generally having a wonderful time. At the same time, they were driving the folk at The Chevron nuts. The Chevron not only missed out on the money that was generated by having the show stay there, but they missed out on some great publicity. They had the kids all over the front of their hotel anyway. Sometimes you just can't win!

FESTIVAL ROCK

At Woodstock '94, script was issued for change in lieu of actual money with the hope that the event would be so historic that concertgoers would take the script home as souvenirs, and the promoters would make money from the uncashed chits. Limp Bizkit front man Fred Durst had a problem with that premise, and encouraged the mass of young people who attended to set fire to the concession stands. Many of them complied.

There's a lot to be said for being in the right place at the right time. Coincidences such as a dearth of slow songs when a ballad is released, the overexposure of one particular artist that clears the way for someone new, and having a hot single or captivating act at the time a major arena show or movie soundtrack is being arranged can be greatly beneficial to musical acts. If they've good fortune, some little thing about their music or performance may catch the right person's attention and result in a career-altering appearance somewhere important, or maybe even historic.

JOCKO MARCELLINO (SHA NA NA):

We were the second-to-last act to get on [the bill at Woodstock.]. We kept getting pushed back and pushed back. 'Cause we were nobody. We were just brand new, but we made a little buzz at a place called the Steve Paul Scene downtown, which was really in Hell's Kitchen in New York. But they were lining up around the block to see us. This is how we got the gig. Hendrix was there to see us one night, Janis Joplin came in, and some of Led Zeppelin, Frank Zappa came in. I was meeting all these stars—my heroes. And then this guy came in and said, "Listen. I got this Woodstock thing. Do you want to be on the bill?" I grabbed my manager and I said, "Yes, we do. Go over and say yes!"

We got paid $350. And the check bounced. We signed off to be in the movie, the Michael Wadleigh film. Interestingly, the director of photography was Martin Scorsese. Anyway, we signed off to be in it for a dollar. And I'm not sure we got that dollar. But it was amazing to be there. First of all, to be there as an eighteen-year-old American. And then to be there as a performer.

The first night we had a hotel room at the Holiday Inn. The rest of it I stayed out there. I just wandered around like everybody else. We kept checking back in, but they didn't put us on till much later. We kept thinking Saturday night. But we didn't get on.

We got on second to last, before Jimi Hendrix. The place was half empty. Everybody had either been wasted or gone back to their jobs or whatever they were doing. 'Cause it looked like a refugee camp.

But, luckily, they were getting ready to shoot Hendrix and everyone waking up, and they caught about twenty minutes of our show, including "At the Hop," which made the film. We were so visually and musically combined—had a good combination of those two things that worked for the right medium. So it *looked* like we were at the top of Saturday night. From what I heard, the film was way too long—three hours or something—and they were trying to cut things out. But we got standing ovations at previews in L.A. and New York, so we made it! It really kicked off our career.

It was an interesting time, just wandering around there, because I know at one point, I was taking some sort of hallucinogen or something and I decided that I wanted to be alone. You know, this was like Saturday night sometime. But there was a small problem. There were a half million people there. So it was an interesting time.

I remember the group that got me back in the groove was Creedence Clearwater. I sorta dug 'em, but that night they were really vibing and they sounded great. A lot of people don't know that Creedence Clearwater was there. There were a lot of groups, like Blood, Sweat and Tears. They didn't sign that waiver—that dollar. So, they didn't get in the film. Some of them didn't need it. The Grateful Dead said it was one of the worst shows they ever did, and they didn't want to be involved. But, we were perfect for the medium and were the neo-classicists. We, historically, said there's a beginning to this thing. Here we were "At the Hop," but, instead, we're on Max Yasgur's farm with half a million people.

Of course, that's one of the important moments in rock and roll history. It was a mind-blowing event for me in so many ways. When we returned, we were the act in *Woodstock* singing "At the Hop."

JUSTIN SENKER (ATLANTA RHYTHM SECTION):

My ten-plus years as the bass player for Atlanta Rhythm Section have all but blurred into one grand experience. However, my first year with the band, we performed at a show that truly stands out for me and to this day is my most memorable concert with the band. It was the first of three Georgia Jams I would play with ARS, and was actually one of the first handfuls of shows I had ever played with the band. Up to that point in my career, I had performed many times with other bands, but never to a crowd of more than a few hundred. I was about to perform with a legendary band, with which I had never had a full-band rehearsal, in front of nearly twenty thousand hometown fans. Did I mention I had an abscessed tooth?

If you grew up in Atlanta during the '70s and '80s, as I did, you grew up with the Atlanta Rhythm Section. Their music was on the radio all the time and you would hear tales of someone seeing a member in a grocery store or at a gas sta-

Atlanta Rhythm Section
(Justin Senker, on right)
*From the photo collection
of Justin Senker*

tion driving a big Cadillac. You certainly either had yourself, or knew someone
who had, attended one of the famed "Champagne Jam" festivals of the late '70s,
which was produced by legendary local concert promoter Alex Cooley. You'd
never hear from a fellow Georgia native how good Heart, Aerosmith, or any of
the other bands that appeared at those shows were. It was always how great ARS
played and how Paul Goddard's bass solo stole the show. Little did I know those
were shoes I'd have to try and fill.

In the early '90s, Alex was behind another series of festivals in Atlanta called
the "Georgia Jams," which were sort of the rebel little brother to the earlier
shows. These were held at the Lakewood Amphitheater, a typical "shed" with several thousand reserved seats under a large roof and acres of grassy general admission seating extending up a slope behind the seats. The first Georgia Jam I was
involved with was headlined by a recently re-formed Lynyrd Skynyrd. This was
their first Atlanta performance since Johnny VanZant had joined the band,

replacing his brother, Ronnie. The venue was sold out, and it was reported that as many as a thousand ticketless fans jumped the gates to witness the historic reunion. The place was packed.

The Georgia Jams featured more Southern-flavored fare than its sibling [the Champagne Jams]. Lynyrd Skynyrd, .38 Special, The Georgia Satellites, Wet Willie, and Mother's Finest were typical of the artists to appear. However, the common thread to both jams was the Atlanta Rhythm Section. I remember I spoke with a longtime Atlanta radio personality, Willard, at one of the Georgia Jams, and I mentioned what a great crowd I thought the headliner had attracted. He looked at me and said, "Hey man, a lot of these people are here to see ARS." And I know he was right.

When a band is onstage in thousands of watts of stage lighting, it is nearly impossible to see the audience when the venue is dark. Beyond the first several rows, the crowd quickly fades into the darkness out of the reach of the stage's glow. This, however, is not an issue when the show is outside during the day. We had the middle slot on that first Georgia Jam, putting us onstage well before nightfall. It felt like I was able to see every single person in the capacity crowd, most of whom were having a great time basking in the light of a bright Georgia sun. This was the first time I actually experienced my knees knocking, and I wondered at one point if I could even keep on my feet for the whole show, much less play Paul Goddard's famous bass solo during the song "Champagne Jam."

Of the thousands in attendance that day, one man should have garnered more of my concern than all the rest put together, but fortunately, at the time I didn't know any better. The man behind the Atlanta Rhythm Section, manager Buddy Buie, made a rare appearance at a live show to see the band and check out the new bass player. Living in Atlanta and being involved in music for as long as I had been, I had certainly heard his name before. But at that time I didn't realize how important he was to the success of ARS and so many other acts from the Southeast. I didn't know what a successful songwriter and producer he was beyond his work with ARS. I'm also glad I didn't realize at the time that if he didn't like me, it might not only have been one of my first ARS shows, but one of my last!

Despite my case of nerves, the band played great, based on the crowd's enthusiastic response. Performing with such an incredibly talented group of musicians makes it almost too easy for a bass player to sound great. I did end up muffing a note during the "Champagne Jam" bass solo, as our drummer kept pointing out over the next few months, but I was able to stay upright. I was far too nervous to truly appreciate that time onstage, literally stunned by the sea of people in front of me. Afterward, I recall Buddy telling me with a smile that he liked my "funky" look. With that note of approval and the "attaboys" I got around the backstage area after the show, I was overcome with relief, and the thought of my impending emergency root canal never crossed my mind.

Over ten years later, I'm still playing with the band, unlike that drummer. We've had a few personnel changes, but Barry Bailey and Dean Daughtry—the two original members to have never left the band at any time—still love performing and are fantastic musicians. And the rest of us, a couple of whom have been involved with the band for over fifteen years, feel honored to be included in such a great band. I've had a number of great experiences with ARS: having the opportunity to stand on stage beside a legend—singer/songwriter Ronnie Hammond, record bass tracks with Buddy Buie and producer Rodney Mills, play at Dick Clark's Olympic Flag Jam at The Georgia Dome, and perform alongside all the original members of ARS when the band was inducted into the Georgia Music Hall of Fame. I sometimes have to pinch myself to realize I've done all these things. But that first Georgia Jam still sticks with me. If a musician can have a home-field advantage like a baseball player, I know I had it that day. A few thousand fans carried this rookie through that set. That's for sure.

MAY I SHAKE YOUR HAND

Some years back, Sheryl Crow was called on stage to sing "Honky Tonk Women" at a small club in Las Vegas with Mick Jagger and Keith Richards. Crow commented later, "Someone sent me a picture. I still look at it and think, 'God, was I superimposed'?"

Even big stars have music heroes. They listened to the radio and shelled out bucks for records, CDs, and concerts just as we did. A handful of recording stars has usually influenced each individual musician as he or she was learning the craft. The devotee may not sound exactly like the hero, but the hero's music has usually shaped the new artist's music in some way. Rock and roll is music with deep roots in rhythm and blues, and almost everything you hear played today can be traced back to the beginning of the genre.

Playing on stage with an artist you admired growing up, whose career and music you have watched closely over the years, has got to be a huge rush for a professional musician. The actual experience of meeting and playing music with your hero may not actually go down as you have dreamed it, but the fact that it has happened at all is cause enough for celebration. For some, the opportunity can be a validating experience. Others may wish they had never set foot on stage. Regardless, you've got to hope it goes down well, because one way or another, it's going to be a defining moment in your career.

SCREAMIN' SCOTT SIMON (SHA NA NA):

In the pantheon of rock and roll royalty, John Lennon has to be in the first rank. In 1973, there was a benefit show for the Willowbrook State School [an institution for people with developmental disabilities] in Madison Square Garden. Willowbrook came into the New York spotlight when a young investigative reporter, Geraldo Rivera, brought its primitive conditions to the public's attention. John and Yoko felt they could do something substantive both financially and in raising public consciousness by arranging two shows in one day. John's song "Imagine" was a monster hit at that time, and this would give him an opportunity to perform live in his adopted city with his Greenwich Village backup band, Elephant's Memory.

Phil Spector, reclusive rock producer, would be in a truck parked outside the Garden to record the audio, and ABC cameras would shoot the video for a special to be aired later in the year. The Lennons wanted three other acts on the bill: Stevie Wonder, whose "Superstition" was everyplace, Roberta Flack, to add a touch of class, and Sha Na Na, for the rock and roll party-animal aspect. We were, of course, honored to be included in such select company.

The afternoon show was kind of a rehearsal for the evening one because neither the audience nor the performers were used to being at their peak energies at four PM. After our set, Phil Spector actually fought his way past security to get to our dressing room to tell us we were playing everything too fast, too raggedy. (The security guards questioned Phil's nonexistent credentials, and Phil exploded in the "Do you know who I am?" mode. Fortunately, our sax player, Lennie Baker, did know who Phil was, and explained to security that this guy could go anywhere he wanted.) Little did Phil know that playing fast and raggedy was our trademark. Our choreography looked best when the tempos were just below completely frantic. But we appreciated his suggestions and tried to play with more precision for the evening show.

The big moment of the entire show came when John sat down at one of the side-by-side Wurlitzer electronic pianos placed downstage left, and in a pin-spot played and sang "Imagine." I was able to post myself just inside the speaker column of that side of the stage during the evening show, having scoped it out during the early show. And there, not six feet away, sat John Lennon playing that little lick that begins the song to the quietest 16,000 people in New York City.

The blowout close of the second show came during the encore. All of the acts were invited to come back and jam on Lennon's favorite Elvis number, "Hound Dog." The guy you see in the photos from the Beatles' Hamburg days, the one in the "Black Leather Jacket," resurfaced that night singing in that voice that made "Twist and Shout" such a signature song for his old group. The idea for the jam had come up after the first show, when the whole thing had happened sponta-neously but more than a little tentatively. By the second show, it was definite: rush the stage when "Hound Dog" starts.

There's only one Stevie Wonder, one Roberta Flack, but at the time there were ten guys in Sha Na Na. I had set my sights on "sitting in" at the Wurlitzer which John had played on during "Imagine." Yoko is at the Wurlitzer on its right, with her stylish pant-suited legs propped up on either side of the keyboard like a rag doll, her hands flailing away at the keyboard in what appears and sounds to be an extremely random fashion. Although her volume is up in the monitor, I wonder whether it is being mixed into the house. I figure the Wurlitzer John had played on surely is in the house, so I crank it up and start playing. So there we flail, the greaser and the performance artist.

Soon enough, it seems that Yoko has had enough of her random banging away on her keyboard, and in the middle of a measure gets her legs under her and makes her way off stage and into the back of the American-made suburban-looking station wagon that the Lennons employed to travel unobtrusively in around the city. John is playing guitar stage right across the large Garden stage, while I am all the way stage left at the Wurlitzer next to the now vacant Yoko Wurlitzer.

I am looking his way, taking this whole scene in—Stevie and Roberta with arms around each other; Sha Na Na guys grabbing tambourines and generally shame-lessly finding a spot on the stage; Elephant's Memory laying down the heavy beat;

John Lennon laying back playing rhythm guitar—when I realize John is talking to me from all the way across the stage. He has to say it (mouth it, the music is throbbing at this point) twice before I get it. "Where's YO-KO?" I give him the international symbol for someone being gone, the right thumb extended, the raised fist moving backward toward the shoulder as I say/mouth "she's OUTTA HERE." The minute he gets it, he takes his guitar and gives it to a roadie, and is off the stage and in the back seat of the car. They roll out the door before any-one knows he's gone. It was a great night.

TONY FRANKLIN (THE FIRM):

In April 1985, Jimmy Page, Paul Rodgers, Chris Slade, and myself (collectively known as The Firm), were camped out at the elegant Le Parker Meridien Hotel in bustling New York City. Manhattan was our hub for two weeks as we flew or drove in and out of the neighboring cities and states, performing large sellout shows and then traveling "home" to midtown Manhattan.

It was a somewhat surreal existence. We had our own plane, with The Firm logo painted on the side. We had our own limos, we had the best rooms in all the hotels, and we were played constantly on the radio and MTV. We were treated like royalty; whatever we wanted was available, and I loved every minute of it!

We had recently performed a sellout show at Madison Square Garden, which for me was a dream come true. For ten minutes of that evening I was alone on the stage, standing before a wild, loud audience as I went through my "moves"— my riffs, my chops, my crowd-pleasing fretless bass growls, slaps and harmonics, my vaudeville-inspired dance moves, oh, and my hair, let's not forget my hair— something like a teddy bear with it's paws in the plug socket!

On one of our days off, I scanned the gig listings in the local paper (some-thing I rarely did), and noticed that Jaco Pastorius was playing at a place called the Lone Star Café that night! I couldn't believe it. Jaco was my all time bass hero, and he was the reason I played fretless bass in the first place. I had to go. I called some of the other guys to see if they were interested. In the end, Jimmy Page and Chris Slade joined me, and we headed off with our security guy to the Café.

Some moments stay in your memory forever. I can still see the sign outside of the Lone Star: "Tonight, Jaco Pastorius." I was surprised to walk into a near empty, tiny bar. We were chaperoned to a cozy little table on the upstairs balcony with a great view of the stage. This didn't seem like the kind of place my larger-than-life, legendary bass hero would play, but on the stage were his bass and his rig, primed and loaded, ready for action. I had no idea what to expect.

Someone told us that Jaco would be playing two sets, the first with his trio and the second with a full band. At some point, Jaco ambled onto the stage, casually checking a few things, tinkling on the piano, strumming a few bass notes, and wondering if his two other trio band members were going to show up. I was transfixed. To me, in my youthful impressionability, he was somewhere between Elvis and Jimi Hendrix. I guess the set started (without the two other guys) when he played for more than a minute on one of the instruments. It was either the bass or the keys, or a combination of the two. He was doodling. Sketching little musical ditties comprised of snippets from his past works, and wherever his free-form musical-genius mind wanted to take him. Time stood still.

There was still no sign of the other players. At one point, when Jaco was ad-libbing on the keyboards, Chris Slade (The Firm's drummer), went up to the stage, looked at Jaco, and pointed at the drums. Jaco nodded his head and Chris jumped up and started giving it his best jazz-rock-Slade chops. Jaco's bass was propped up against his amp, and I was chomping at the bit to get up there and jam! I finally plucked up the courage to walk up to the stage, got Jaco's attention, and motioned for me to pick up the bass and play. He looked at me, shook his head, and said, "No, no man, next set." Fair enough.

I don't know how long the first set was or for how long Chris played. It was long enough for everyone to get into a "happy space" though. The drinks were flowing, and the Café was filling up. Then Jaco took a break. We were told that we could meet Jaco on the roof of the club, where the halftime party was happening! We were lead upstairs to an area that was busier than the Café itself. It was buzzing up there, in more ways than one!

After a short time, I was introduced to Jaco. I shook his massive right hand, a hand that dwarfed my not-so-small bass player's hands! Starstruck and bewildered, I said probably one of the stupidest things I've ever said in my life: "Hi Jaco. Good to meet you. Uhhh, what kind of strings do you use?" Jaco just said, "Uhhh, I don't know man." And that was the extent of my conversation with Jaco Pastorius! I didn't mind though. My only regret is that I didn't have a camera with me.

Jaco was urging Jimmy to get up in the next set and jam with the band. Pagey was hesitant. He could hold his own of course, but this was a jazz gig. "We'll just play a blues," said Jaco. "All right," said Jimmy, "but none of those fancy jazz chords." A deal was struck. And with the prospect of me possibly getting up to jam also, the second set promised to be a good one!

The rest of the band arrived. I couldn't tell you who they were, for Jaco was the only one I was watching. They all played well, and Jaco looked like he was having a great time. After a while, they called for Jimmy to join them on the stage, which he did. Shortly afterwards, they kicked into a mid/up-tempo twelve-bar blues shuffle. This was the first time I'd actually stood back and watched Jimmy Page play while I wasn't playing at the same time. Jimmy smoked! He was playing someone else's guitar, through someone else's amp, and he was magnificent. He launched into the most smoldering blues licks, and just when you thought the round was done, he'd raise the intensity and the excitement level with another blistering riff. The crowd was going nuts, and Jaco was jamming! Jimmy stole the moment, and my respect for him rose up to another level.

The set was over all too soon, even though it probably went for a couple of hours. I never did play, but in hindsight I'm glad. We left shortly afterwards, without saying our good-byes to Jaco. Security and safety was becoming an issue for Jimmy, so we had to make a swift exit.

The next night we were off to another big sell-out Firm show. I don't know where. Whatever followed from there, we all knew our lives had been illumined by the bright talented light of Jaco Pastorius. Less than three years later, I heard about the tragic death of Jaco. It didn't hit me immediately. Sometime afterwards, I was dining at a restaurant and just started sobbing. The light was gone. Thankfully, Jaco left some incredible recordings and some beautiful compositions. Thankfully, I was able to meet him, see him play, and tell him something stupid! God bless you, Jaco!

HOLLYWOOD KNOCKING

Most know Sting as a talented singer and songwriter, but he also made his mark as an actor in the 1982 film Brimstone & Treacle. Sting portrayed a creepy con man named Martin Taylor in the film. Sting liked portraying Taylor because the drifter shifted from religious to demonic, in Sting's words a "much more interesting [person] than the average cinema character."

everal musicians have found their way into acting in films, for example, Kris Kristofferson in *A Star is Born,* James Taylor and Dennis Wilson in *Two-Lane Blacktop,* Bob Dylan in *Pat Garrett & Billy the Kid,* and Mick Jagger in *Performance* are among the more notable rock stars who have had the opportunity to attempt another form of artistic expression. And, of course, there was Elvis and all those movies, some of which were entertaining and good, and some of which were boring and just bad. And don't forget Madonna in . . . let's not go there. (It seems a tenet of show business that actors want to be rock stars and rock stars want to be actors.)

While some musicians are asked to participate in a film through traditional music channels such as soundtracks and theme songs, others are able to realize their fantasy by actually appearing on screen. Either way, it's usually an entertaining and unique experience, and yet another opportunity for the musician to spread his or her artistic wings.

RICK ROSE (SOLO ARTIST):

Film producer Aaron Russo, who managed Bette Midler and produced films such as *Trading Places, The Rose,* and *Teachers,* asked me to write a theme song for his Orion film *Rude Awakening.* Some weird telepathy that took place: while I was reading The Doors biography, I got a call from Paul A. Rothchild [The Door's record producer], who was the music co-coordinator for Aaron's new film. He sent me the script and asked if I could write a theme song. I wrote a song, and I knew I had it 'cause it was just something very magical.

I went to New York City and met with my manager, Dee Anthony. We went to see Paul and Aaron and they listened to my demo of the song. John Sebastian was in the room at the time. Aaron looked over and said, "Great song. We'll call you if it's the one."

Two weeks went by, and they called and said, "Your song is the theme song for the movie, but we are gonna go with a different vocalist. Someone who has more of a status right now." Roger Daltrey at first confirmed to record the song, but had to back out of it 'cause Peter Townshend put The Who back out on the road. So in came Bill Medley to sing my song.

When the song got confirmed by Paul, he said, "Come to New York City, and we'll work on a bridge for the song." Knowing what style song I wrote, I started listening to Jim Steinman songs to get inspired. The next thing I know, Jim Steinman was called in to produce the song!

CELEBRATING THE MOMENT

During a match with Malcolm Monroe, wrestler Bloody Bill Scullion was clocked with a padlock. After the match, Bill threw a bandage on his head and went to a club with Zakk Wyld [guitar player in Ozzy Osbourne's band] and a handful of Zakk's friends. Scullion knew the rockers' reputations as hardcore partiers and didn't want to be perceived as a wuss. His plan worked, until his eyeballs started turning black and blood started to pour from his head where he had been hit earlier. His evening was cut short by a trip to the emergency room. This hardly fazed the rockers, and they stayed to "party on."

Usually the post-premier parties in Hollywood are kind of boring and predictable, with the assembled stars making a cursory appearance, talking to the press and splitting early. Of course, that would be out of character for a movie with the title and theme of *Rock Star*. Those who attended the party after the screening got just about what they might have expected. Rock stars like it loud and spontaneous, and any excuse to party is, well, *an excuse to party.*

RALPH SAENZ (METAL SHOP/ATOMIC PUNKS):

I had a small part in the movie *Rock Star*. I had the chance on the set to meet Zakk Wyld from Ozzy's band. He and I hit it off from the gate. Fast forward to the movie premier at the House of Blues in Hollywood. Full star-studded event: Brad and Jennifer Pitt, Fred Durst, Nikki Sixx, Mark Wahlberg, and the list goes on.

Our band was hired to play that night. We had LL Cool J come up and rap some heavy metal Van Halen with us. Fred Durst requested some Def Leppard. I thought, "Hey man, let's ask Zakk to come up and jam some Ozzy with us." I called him out by saying, "Everyone, let's give it up for Zakk Wyld from Ozzy!" The crowd went crazy.

Everyone knows Zakk and Ozzy. He came up on the stage, and we went to hand him a guitar. He refused it. He grabbed the mic out of my hand and told the crowd, "Fuck off. I'm going to sing." I didn't realize it, but Zakk was completely wasted. When I say wasted, I mean he didn't even remember me and we spent a week on a movie set together.

Ralph Saenz (Metal Shop/Atomic Punks)
From the photo collection of Ralph Saenz

Zakk told my guitar player Russ to back "War Pigs." Russ said to Zakk, "Hey man. We don't know that one. Let's do 'Crazy Train.'" Zakk lost his mind and said, "If you don't play that song, I'm gonna kick your fuckin' ass." He threw a full beer bottle toward the front of the stage, and it shattered. After that he began to sing. Well, not really. He was yelling. He destroyed the mic stand and the drum set. Our bass player hid behind his bass amp in fear of his life. Zakk would not leave the stage. Remember "War Pigs" is a seven-minute song. Zakk's version was going on twelve minutes.

Zakk managed to clear the whole room. I mean the whole room. Six hundred to eight hundred people.

I will never forget that night. I saw Zakk again. He joined us at another show, almost sober, last weekend. He played the guitar on "Crazy Train" and ruled! I talked to him back stage after the show, and he didn't even remember that other night. He invited me to the studio to hear his new record for his band Black Label Society. By the way, it was amazing. He told me stories about Ozzy. I went to bed at six AM. Now that's rock and roll.

CHAPTER 4

BEHIND THE SCENES

Okay, so after hours and hours on the road, they've finally arrived at their destination. They are ready for the show, but somebody has to check in with the person putting *on* the show: the promoter. The promoter is the one who takes the risk. Promoters have to sell the tickets, so they want to be sure that the band they are putting on their stage is exciting enough to bring in the type of crowd they want—and need—to show a profit.

The band and the promoter usually want the same thing: a successful show. For their part, the band wants to make sure the proper equipment has been organized for them, they'll want to check on the advertising, promotion, and the number of tickets sold. They'll check on the time they have been scheduled to go on, and whether there will be food later or maybe a party after the gig. Of course, the bottom line is actually getting paid for the show.

JOHN MCKUEN (NITTY GRITTY DIRT BAND):

We were booked to play a Missouri farm in 1975, which was the Mud Festival Era. Here we were in the middle of another muddy field, in the middle of the '70s, in the middle of a set, in the middle of not getting paid. I saw our agent walking toward the stage, happy, through the mud-covered throngs that made up the audience. Usually, contracts were signed by a promoter and sent back with a 50 percent deposit weeks prior to the show, the balance to be picked up before the show. Only this time, a deposit never arrived, and there was nothing to pick up when we got there. Lance Smith, our great agent who put us out there on the road, deserved to be here. The opposite of the apex of gigs, below the curve, off the scale, the antithesis of a career high point—and one of his bookings.

The people were there, some of them anyway. Diehard Dirtheads, who had come to see us with the Earl Scruggs Revue and a few other acts in that Missouri heat/humidity one could only find there or in Vietnam. This was fitting, since we were just a few miles from where the Marines trained for their ongoing combat thousands of miles from our "battleground."

I had called Lance at nine AM because he could get there from Denver in time to maybe force payment, and I could tell the promoter was a flake. We were to go on about eight o'clock PM, but we couldn't seem to get paid as required by contract prior to the show. Though I had already decided we'd play without it: the people were there, we were there, the P.A. was set up, and there was nothing else to do (this was pre-cable TV). Lance wanted us to get paid.

It was under these conditions he headed east for the combat zone. Although it seemed a bit far from Denver, after one flight and a two-hour drive he arrived there, at this guy's delicatessen/farm/festival site, ready to earn his 10 percent. There was a little store on the edge of an open field on the edge of the Ozarks. This promoter was over the edge and, apparently, the stereotype of a "hillbilly" for the Ozarks, as Lance found out. Lance showed up, went to the promoter and said, "Gimme my band's money. All of it. Now!" He received the reply, "Haven't got any money. Not enough people showed up."

Well, Lance knew there were enough people for enough money to pay us and continued to press on. He'd come all the way from Denver to show his clout and didn't want to lose our dough, his integrity, this battle, or his commission. But I don't think it had that much to do with getting his cut on this booking when he finally offered to kill the promoter, and not without reason.

All through his "negotiation," the promoter's thirteen-year-old daughter sat on a filing cabinet, watching the grown men arguing about the day's business. It was obvious Lance would not give up, and the guy would not give in. It was not in Lance's duck-hunter nature to call off the hunt, but he didn't expect the promoter's counteroffer. The promoter stepped back so he could give the proper, sweeping, grandiose (a word he probably didn't know) motion with his arm, and pointed at the young girl he professed to be his daughter: "Take her. She's all yours. I guarantee you'll have more fun with her than you could with the money anyway. She's yours. Take her home and keep her. You'll have a good time with her."

Not appreciative of this offer to participate in the white slave trade, at this point Lance stood up to his full six-foot four-inch—plus a few boot-heel inches— height, picked up the promoter by the shirt, lifted him to his bulging eye level, and screamed: "Give me my band's money, you bastard, or I'll kill you! Right now!"

Summertime livin' in Missouri, veins a poppin', sweat runnin' free! Right after that is when I saw Lance walking through the crowd with his clout intact and the biggest bulge in his pants that any man's woman could ask for. It wasn't because of the daughter. He got the money. We were in the middle of another frenzied set, and all was good in the land.

THE *BEATLES* NEVER ASKED FOR M&Ms

While playing in Hamburg, Germany, the Beatles pelted local nuns with condoms filled with water calling them "raindrops from heaven."

In the early days of rock and roll, before the infamous riders where the act could dictate—down to the sandwich meat, beer label, and color of M&M—what he wanted for his show and dressing room, the promoter held the key to the sound and light equipment. Many bands have had to use the equipment provided by the venue or the promoter. Obviously, such equipment is adequate at best or we wouldn't have so many rock acts spending millions to cart their own amps, soundboards, microphones, and the like around the country. The consolation to not having a big enough name to call the shots on such matters is realizing that most rock and rollers have, at one time or another, been in exactly the same shoes.

NIGEL OLSSON (DRUMMER):

While rehearsing for a show at Madison Square Garden in New York with John Lennon in 1974, John stood next to me in awe of my massive drum set (thirteen drums at the time). John asked, "How many microphones do you have up there Nige?"

I replied, "Sixteen or eighteen."

Nigel Olsson
Photo by Susan Myers

In astonishment he said, "Fuck me! We were lucky to get three for the vocals when we were on."

A GOOD ROADIE IS LIKE A MELODY

Legendary Allman Brothers Band roadie "Red Dog" Campbell so impressed up-and-coming journalist Cameron Crowe that when Crowe made it big as a film writer/director, he put the Dog in a movie. Not only is a character in Almost Famous based on Campbell, the character's name is . . . Red Dog.

While roadies seem to get the short end of the stick when it comes to respect, a good roadie is indispensable. It is true that many roadies get treated as second-rate citizens on some star tours, with their long hours and minimal pay, but there is nothing more valuable than a roadie who is made to feel like an integral part of the production. These loyal members of the traveling carnival get the equipment to the venue, set it up, and get it ready to be used with regularity, precision, and timeliness, just the way the act or the band wants and expects it to be done. All the artist has to do is plug in and perform.

Some roadies follow the letter of the law when it comes to their employment contracts. They do only what they are specifically assigned to do. Others, especially those who sign on for long tours or repeated employment, are treated as members of a tight-knit clan. Those who are embraced as family often find themselves in the position of protecting their artists and the integrity of the show. It's not what they necessarily get paid for, but the crew is certainly an asset when situations get sticky.

BARRY HAY (GOLDEN EARRING):

After the incredible success of our album *Moontan,* featuring "Radar Love," we went back home to Holland and started working on a project called *Switch.* The production was all artsy-fartsy shit, including a shiny white stage floor, a life-size dummy hanging from the rig and extra musicians, which included a horn section and a famous Dutch friend called Robert Jan Stips on keyboards. We were really confident about the whole thing and returned to the States in '76.

I remember playing this venue in Kansas City. The support act was a band called KISS. No one had ever heard of them before. The local promoter said they were from L.A. and put on quite a crazy show. I heard them jamming in their dressing room and thought they sounded pretty damn good.

Anyway, we did our sound check and went back to the hotel for a nap and dinner. When we returned to the gig, we found our crew in an uproar. These KISS faggots had puked blood all over our impeccably white floor and they had burnt the dummy with their pyrotechnics. Our guys were beyond anger. KISS had left the building without undoing the damage, and our crew was running around like a bunch of hysterical housewives mopping up all the blood and gore. They threw a fit when they heard that KISS was going to be with us for another two gigs.

Our stage manager stood firm: no more blood and no more bombs. FUCK YOU!! The funny thing was that we had never seen the band. We had no idea what they looked like on stage 'cause we always arrived thirty minutes before our own show, and they had usually disappeared by then. Well, the rest is history, I guess. KISS hit the big time with their circus act and that was that.

Golden Earring in the '70s; Barry Hay in front jumping
From the photo collection of Barry Hay

Anyway, two years later we were touring with Aerosmith. This was their dark period, when things were out of hand dope- and booze-wise. We were in this big auditorium in Washington, D.C., really cooking and playing a fantastic show. Aerosmith came on after us and really sucked. Tyler and Perry didn't know where they were. I could only watch for so long and went back to the hotel with mixed emotions.

The next morning I was having breakfast. A guy I knew from Sha Na Na called "Denny the Bodyguard" walked up to my table and said, "There's someone who would like to meet you. Would you like to come over to his table and join him for breakfast?" Now, nobody says no to Denny.

"Meet Gene Simmons." Big guy. I didn't recognize him without the makeup. "So you're the guy that wouldn't let me spit blood on his stage, huh?" he said. I told him he could spit blood on my stage anytime he felt the urge, and after that we had a nice big cowboy breakfast.

IN THE WINGS

According to legend, during a lull in activity, The Who's John Entwistle was thinking of forming a new band with Keith Moon. One night, Entwistle sat down with Moon and their chauffeur Richard Cole to think of a name for the entity. "Led Zeppelin" was floated as a possibility, along with images of the first album cover, which would be a zeppelin going down in flames. Entwistle ended up sticking with The Who, but when Cole went to work for Jimmy Page as a roadie, he evidently remembered that night. The rest, as they say, is history.

One of the first things a musician does when he gets together with his compadres of the road is to share the triumphs and horrors that have brought him to where he is today. When musicians talk to their fans, they don't always share the intricacies of performing and touring. (One exceptional case would be Jackson Browne's revealing behind-the-scenes *Running On Empty* album.) But the roadie, always present in the best and worst of times, sees and hears it all. What goes on in the wings off stage can sometimes be more entertaining than the show itself.

JAMES BLESIUS (ROADIE):

I was working as a stagehand at the Aragon Ballroom in Chicago in 1974. On the bill were Hall & Oates, Dr. John, and Lou Reed (this was back in the day when it was common to have two or three touring acts on the same show).

Hall & Oates were the opening act. They were touring in support of the *War Babies* album (which was produced by Todd Rundgren). They were dressed in the space-age/glitter/glam outfits that were popular at the time. They seemed very nervous backstage before going on. I thought they put on a pretty good show, but much of the audience was mystified. This show was quite a departure from the R&B and soul music of their previous two albums. Hall & Oates didn't seem too pleased when they came off the stage and engaged in a heated discussion on the way to the dressing room.

At about that time, Todd Rundgren and Bebe Buell arrived. Todd had played the night before at the auditorium theater. They looked like the most perfectly matched couple imaginable. Bebe was dressed in a white floor-length dress. She was absolutely radiant, as if there were a glowing light around her. Todd was dressed in a white suit, blue shirt (no tie) with matching blue lipstick, and eye shadow. Everyone back stage just stared at them, slack jawed.

Hall & Oates's manager showed up and asked Todd to come to the dressing room. Todd told Bebe to wait there. She protested. He said, "It won't take long." Todd went off with the manager. Bebe looked very apprehensive and the backstage crew was still mesmerized. The stage manager asked everyone to get back to work (taking down Hall & Oates's gear and putting up Dr. John's). The stage manager then asked Bebe if she would like anything. She asked for a glass of water. The stage manager turned to the first nearby person (me!) and said, "Get this lady a glass of water." "Yes sir!" I replied, and off I went. I returned with the water, and at that point I figured it was my duty to keep her company. She was polite but not too talkative. I tried to remain cool and say knowledgeable things like, "Watch that electrical cable," and, "Maybe we should stand back here out of the way."

About fifteen minutes later, Todd came back. He was very pleasant and easy-going. I told him how much I enjoyed his show the night before. He responded that they were still working the kinks out and that there were a number of technical problems to overcome. Bebe was ready to go, but Todd said he wanted to check out some of Dr. John's show.

Dr. John came out in full "Night Tripper" regalia: feathers, boa, glitter, and walking stick. He stopped and said hello to every person back stage. He was a very cool guy. He spent a couple of minutes talking to Todd, and then took the stage. He had a big band—five to six musicians, plus three female vocalists. He put on a spirited show. The crowd loved him. Todd and Bebe enjoyed the show. I stood next to them, grooving to the music like we were all old pals hanging out together. About two-thirds of the way through the set, they left. I shook hands with Todd; he waved to the rest of the people assembled back stage, and out they go.

The strangest part of the night was yet to come. After Lou Reed's equipment was set up, the stage manager told everyone to leave the backstage area. This was very curious, since the stagehands and roadies had been back stage (where you would expect them to be) all night. While most everyone left the backstage area heading for the floor area, I just stood behind a post. A few minutes later, the back entrance door opened and in came Lou Reed, with a guy under each arm propping him up. Lou was holding a half bottle of Jack Daniels, but seemed to be passed out (he was wearing dark glasses, so it was hard to tell.) They brought him to the back of the stage. His band was playing the instrumental intro to "Sweet Jane." One of his handlers took the bottle of Jack away from Lou, pointed him in the direction of the microphone, and gave him a gentle push. Lou slowly made his way to the mic stand, which he held onto the entire set. The show rocked. Lou appeared to be in total control. After the last song, he walked off the stage where he fell into the waiting arms of his handlers. One guy gave him his bottle of Jack, and they dragged him out the door and into his limo.

Wow, what a night. By the way, I never did see Hall & Oates emerge from the dressing room.

NOT JUST MUSCLE AND SCOWLS

One night before a gig at The Starwood in Hollywood, an obviously inebriated Delaney Bramlett asked Sons of Chaplin front man Bill Chaplin if he could jam with the band. Chaplin didn't usually like to have people up on stage with him, but wanted to be polite. He hemmed, hawed, and finally muttered, "Okay." Bramlett understood. He laughed and said, "Why don't you just tell me that I'm drunk and you don't want me to screw up your act?"

Concert security: you know them well. While it may appear to the audience that they are there to show their muscle, look menacing, and stop people from having a good time, they are actually necessary for keeping shows safe. The bottom line is that more often than not, they stop people from throwing themselves on stage to give their favorite artists a hug of camaraderie, or they grab the idiot in the second row before he's able to launch that half-empty bottle of Jack onto the stage. It's a fine line between what security should allow to happen for the sake of the show and whom they should even let near the band. But as careful as they are about protecting the best interests of their charges, sometimes there's nothing even security can do to stop mayhem.

WILLIE OLMSTEAD (LED ZEPPELIN SECURITY):

My short time with Led Zep as security has a great Keith Moon invasion story. When I was stationed on the back of the stage next to John Bonham, Keith Moon climbed up the back. I started to stop him, but then recognized him and let him on the stage. Plant, who was singing at the time, said, "Keith Moon! Keith Moon!"

Moon started banging on Bonham's drums. He knocked a symbol down and cut the big drum's skin in half. He walked off laughing. Did I mention that he was drunk? Bonham could have killed him. I scurried with another guy to get the drum refitted as soon as possible.

INSTRUMENT REPS

In July 2003, French arts employees went on strike over their government's plans to reduce their benefits. Ninety roadies on the Rolling Stones' tour stopped working and were replaced by the Stones' secretaries, security staff, assistants, and volunteers.

It takes a village to raise a show. The roadies, security, sound, and light men are indispensable. But without instruments, the show would be kind of boring. Even further behind the scenes than the roadies and security staff is the instrument rep. Ever wonder how a particular artist came to own so many guitars or why he favored one over the other? How did he know that a particular instrument was even out there? The instrument rep has been doing his job.

Instrument reps introduce artists to the latest and greatest that their employers, the instrument companies, have to offer. A good representative will provide musicians with additional means to stun and impress their audiences, and the artists appreciate it (particularly when those reps have a cutting-edge or unique instrument.) The musicians have many ways of showing their appreciation, but nothing beats tickets and a backstage pass. Armed with goodies such as these, the instrument rep can become the most popular player in his personal posse.

ED PREMAN (GRETSCH REPRESENTATIVE):

While in my mid-twenties, I spent a lot of time on the road as a traveling sales professional. When I worked for companies that made mundane products such as copy machines or scientific equipment, many of the phone calls I received at home while I was away were work related, but boring at best. They were an inconvenience to my roommates, who labored over the phone messages I would receive while out "on the road." Everything changed when I switched employers.

When I sold guitars and drums for the "Gretsch Guitar & Drum Company," the phone calls got a little more interesting. Gretsch in the '60s and '70s was one of a handful of companies that still handcrafted fine wood instruments. They were sold with high sticker prices and had a rabid cult following. Gretsch was owned by the Baldwin Piano Company, and so we also had a close-knit relationship to those who arrived at music's upper echelon through manipulation of a keyboard such as Elton John and Liberace. My list of business friends and contacts was starting to become a little more impressive.

The phone calls I received took on a more entertaining demeanor. When I was the "Gretsch Man," my roommates anxiously awaited my departure and remained near the phone to answer calls, in the hopes that they would be for me *and would be work related.* You see, big-time musicians typically use a guitar or drum set that they really like. As they move up the "ladder of success," they're able to afford the better quality instruments and are treated like royalty by the manufacturers of their favorite instruments. Consequently, individual artists and their road management keep an up-to-date directory of manufacturer's reps for the musical instrument industry.

A major responsibility of mine as regional sales manager and assistant national marketing director was to use whatever resources I could muster to meet as many well-known players and drummers as possible. It was my job to entice them into using Gretsch equipment, get them some new equipment at seriously discounted prices, and get a signed endorsement from them for use in our marketing and advertising programs.

I was very successful in obtaining backstage passes to the Philly-area concert rooms, including the Spectrum, which was originally built for ice hockey but was also considered one of the best venues by the epic rock tours of the '70s. I managed to not only befriend the players in groups like Poco, America, Average White Band, Fleetwood Mac, and Dave Mason, but I also worked my way into the fabric of the road managers, who jumped from tour to tour and usually worked at the Spectrum fairly regularly. They knew to call and invite me (and an assorted four to ten friends, preferably lovely young women) whenever they were coming to the area. When I was out of town, the roomies took the calls.

Upon my return from a few days on the road, the messages would read: "Elton John called. Wants to invite you to the banquet before the show on Saturday; Paul Cotton from Poco called. Needs some guitar accessories and invited you to the

Spectrum next Thursday. They're opening for the Doobies with Bachman Turner Overdrive. Bring some soft pretzels; Ray Charles called. His guitar player is interested in an endorsement. Can he get a good deal on a couple vintage Chet Atkins models? He left six will-call VIP backstage passes for Wednesday night at the Latin Casino; America called; Dave Mason called." And the list went on and on after each trip.

Needless to say, I always went to these shows using my VIP passes, took my roommates and "the girls" that kept in real close touch with me, and my social life was definitely second to none. Unfortunately, the company fell on hard times and ultimately failed (not my fault). I've had to rely on my keen memory for the occasional trips back to the "good old days."

DISRESPECT . . . AND FISTS

Oasis front man Liam Gallagher is well known for his volatile temper. In a fight with a group of Italians in a Munich disco, Gallagher got several broken teeth, while two of his security guards (who were attempting to help the singer) got sent to the hospital. The band cancelled performances for two days. Gallagher would live to fight another day.

It's a popular myth that rock musicians always get treated like royalty. That may be the case once they achieve enough status to receive obscene amounts of attention and financial reward, but the way to the top is usually a long and difficult struggle, in more ways than one. Trying to achieve success as a rock and roller brings new meaning to the phrase "paying your dues."

While one artist is earning respect in the business, it's not uncommon for fellow artists to become jealous or resentful of the attention being paid to someone other than themselves. This response can be manifested in a variety of ways, most of them unwelcome. Sometimes, remarkable ways that result in "remember-the-time-when" stories.

GLORIA GAYNOR (SOLO ARTIST):

Fudgy's was a club we liked in Scarsdale. It was very important to the owner, Fudgy himself, that his clientele liked the band he hired for the week. If the new band didn't go over well the first night, they'd be replaced by a band he knew they *did* like on the second night: City Life, featuring G.G.

During weekends at Fudgy's, the floor would be so crowded with people dancing, just standing, or talking that I used to marvel at the waitresses as they served them all and never seem to lose a payment, a drink, or a customer. One night was the exception. It seemed to happen in slow motion: a guy appeared to be lifted by invisible hands out, up, then back over his chair. The glasses, table, and chair all went in different directions. People moved away as he sprawled out flat on the floor under a table. The man responsible slipped quietly out through the crowd. It all happened so fast we wondered if it really happened at all. I can't even remember now what the papers said it had been all about.

We were involved in an adventure of our own after a show at another club near Fudgy's. The show had gone really well and Billy [Civitella] and I had gone out back to sit in our van. We listened to the recording we'd made of the show. Tony, the bass player, was still in the club milling around. A girl came up to him to say how much she had enjoyed the show. Then a huge guy came up, pushed Tony, and said, "Why are you talking to my girl? Come outside. I want to talk to you." This man was really big. He must have weighed over three hundred pounds. Tony weighed only 140 pounds soaking wet. Tony tried to explain that he hadn't really been talking to the girl, but this man wasn't having it and insisted they step outside.

From where I sat in the car I noticed two men arguing under the street lamp. Then the very big man punched the little man, who went down like a sack of potatoes. By the light of the streetlamp I could see it was Tony. I jumped out of the van, ran up to the two of them and punched the big guy. Tony jumped up from the ground and ran off down the road. The man ignored me completely and took off after Tony. I ran after him, calling after Tony, "Don't go down there alone. Come back this way."

Tony heard me call him and veered around a parked car. He started running back toward me, but he stumbled over his platform shoes and fell. The fat man pounced on top of him. Billy and I, joined now by our lead guitar player Clay, jumped on top of the man to try to pull him off Tony. It took all three of us to get him off. Clay took off with Tony, and they both ran around to the front door of the club. But the door to the club wouldn't open. They ran back around the back door with this man hot on their heels because Billy and I hadn't been able to hold him down. As we rounded the corner we saw Tony running toward the stairs that lead to the club door. I screamed, "No! Tony, the door might be locked. Run around the van!"

So Tony started running around the van with the man still chasing him. I ran up the stairs to check the door. Billy was close behind me. I got the door open, and Billy and I stood aside to let Tony run through. Billy tried to hold the man back but the big guy tossed him out of the way by throwing him over the side of the stairs. Then the big man knocked me aside and charged in after Tony.

We ran in to see if we could stop him from killing Tony. He rampaged through the club but he couldn't find Tony. Finally the club bouncers came along and got him out. After he was gone, Tony came crawling out from under a table where four or five girls were sitting. We went back to the dressing room, where we sat panting and trying to get our breath back. We were trying to figure out what on earth Tony had done to make this man so mad. One of the bouncers came back and said the police were outside and wanted to talk to Tony. We all went to the door with Tony.

The big man had an even bigger friend with him outside now, and they stood right in front of the door. The police were a few yards away. As soon as Tony appeared, the fat man became like a giant monster trying to get at him. Tony ran back in, and I slammed the door after him. The big man was yelling through the door, "Come out and fight like a man!" I was dancing up and down, screaming, "Fight like a man? He doesn't even know what you're fighting about!" The man hollered in, "Who the hell are you? Your kind are not even suppose to be here." "Your kind" meant I was black. The band was white, and most of the town was white, but I was black. I didn't care anymore that he was a 300-pound gorilla and I weighed no more than 130 pounds. I was *mad*. I put my fists up and lunged at him, shouting, "If you don't like me being here, try and put me out!" He lunged back at me but because he was drunk and off balance I was easily able to shove him aside. He fell into the hedges. The band laughed and started calling him Mohammad Ali.

He was just a drunk bully. The police came up and grabbed him and his friend. Then they advised us to get out of town. They said, "We can't hold them, and you can bet they'll come back—with guns."

We gathered up all our gear and took off in the van. Tony was nursing his bruises and I said, "If I ever make a movie of my life, this has got to be in it."

DO YOU KNOW WHO I AM?

Michael Jackson made a trip to Krinjabo, on the Ivory Coast, where he was dubbed the "King of Sanwis." He spent the entire trip holding his nose. Guess this was another of his disguises. Or not. With Michael Jackson, who knows? Jackson remains the King of Disguises. Jackson is known to wear surgical masks, hats, sunglasses, capes, and anything else he can find to maintain his distance from fans. About the only things these disguises accomplish is to make the fans aware that he is . . . Michael Jackson. Excuse me?

When thousands of people have seen their shows, and know their faces, musicians may think that they're invincible. With that sense of adulation and isolation, it's not hard to fall under such a false assumption. The reality is that for every person they think might know them, there are thousands more who've never heard of them. Sometimes, the rock stars can get away with looking like everybody else. It's great that they can assimilate into the masses once in a while, but that might not always be a good thing.

PANAMA RED (NEW RIDERS OF THE PURPLE SAGE):

[Singer] Marcia Routh cared so much for me that on a winter night in 1973, she followed the police car they had me in and accompanied me into the Nashville Police Department downtown without even pausing to think if it was the thing to do. Before I had even snapped to the fact that in my circumstances then—that is, under suspicion of rape—a visit to the Nashville Police Department might not be a cakewalk.

Marcia attached herself to my captors blithely. Hey, coupla young cops, here's this pretty babe. She did this so as to be a friendly advocate (or otherwise, if need be).

All that afternoon I had been sittin' in Mack's Restaurant writing a ten-page letter home. I didn't think anybody who had seen me was gonna be easy to turn up at ten PM, I replied, when the young cops asked me for witnesses at the bar that night. Thus I had gotten myself smoothly caught up in a dragnet tossed across Music Mecca lookin' for a redheaded guy who had either successfully raped or attempted to rape someone. I never did learn the specifics.

But anyway, during the process of them takin' my Polaroid and me waitin' around, Marcia made herself a pleasant and yet persistent presence in the police station. And while they were runnin' the pictures over to the hospital so the victim could say yea or nay, a bullet-headed iron-gray flattop-hair dude did come in and snarl at me a little, BUT ONLY after he had gotten up the actual balls to dis-attach this, as I say, pleasant but persistent human limpet from my side. I think he was jealous of Marcia's relationship with the young, good-looking cops who had netted me.

Anyway he made Marcia leave the room and told me, "Just sit in that chair," (like there was anything else to do in this little room with the window, where on the other side Marcia was watchin' over me).

It never dawned on Country Me that I was in any kinda trouble because, heyyyyy, I'm an innocent man. Somehow, when they came back with the victim's response, Marcia was right back there in the room with us, too. The victim, a real existing person with kinfolks and a name, deserving of respect, of course, and whose life had come into such tangential and fleeting contact with mine, had said, "Nope." I've often wondered what would have happened if she'd said, "Yes, that's the guy." But she didn't.

The cop who snarled didn't apologize. He just said, "Well, if you're even thinking about being a pervert, you better think again, because this is what'll happen to you. Yeah. Beat it, see?" Really, he did, he talked like that.

And Marcia Routh took me back to the bar at the end of this outré event and got me drunk. Marcia Routh was a friend of mine. I slept on her couch many cold nights in Nashville. She valued me, and now that I'm older I think I agree, but that's another story. I knew Marcia through one ex-husband and several boyfriends. Marcia was Sam Routh's ex, and she kept his name when they split. They had a daughter who lived with Marcia. She was someone who took care of me during times I didn't even realize I needed taking care of.

Marcia was a working singer here in Nashville back in the day. You can look up her work just by typing in her name at Google.com. She sang on Crystal Gayle, Michael Nesmith, Doc Watson records, among numerous others. She had a great alto. She passed away some years back; I think I heard it was cancer. But I didn't learn she'd died until about five years ago.

I thank the Lord for Marcia Routh, because on a November night in 1973 she advanced with me into the maw of the metro machine, and we stuck like glue until we came out together.

She was the best of pals.

CHAPTER 5

SEX, DRUGS, AND ROCK AND ROLL

M usic is music, but is it *rock and roll* without the sex and drugs? Rarely. The gypsy lifestyles of rockers put them in contact with people from all walks of life. Sex and drugs are sometimes too common a commodity—and too frequently available—to resist. Many fans and hangers-on seem to think that the way to rockers' hearts (or at least the way to hang with them back stage) is to offer freebies, be they an assortment of drugs, a quick slug of alcohol from a shared bottle, or sexual favors. The freebie method frequently works. But as we've all seen on VH1's *Behind the Music,* the consequences for those who indulge are sometimes dire. Still, the refrain "sex, drugs, and rock and roll" is grounded in reality when applied to the rock and roller lifestyle.

The "Riot House" of the Sunset Strip is one well known stop on the party on wheels that musicians experience on tour. There is usually one hotel at each major tour stop that serves as party central for rock and rollers. At other times, that "rented room" might be the emergency room at the local hospital. No matter if it's glamorous or shabby, it's home while they're there.

BOBBY BERGE (GUITAR PLAYER):

I ventured out, took a long trip down that rock and roll highway and almost didn't make it back. The years 1975 and 1976 were years of great music and heavy partying. During the recording of Tommy Bolin's *Private Eyes* album, I had been drinking a lot and doing coke when it was around. One night, the toots weren't there, and I got so drunk I could hardly play. I fucked up the session for that night. I was doing an easy song, but I couldn't remember the simple changes in the arrangement. I wanted coke really badly, but there was none, or so I was told. Late into the night, we finally gave up and called it quits.

The next day, some time in mid-afternoon, I was at home and hungover as hell. The real hell was about to begin, though. I started experiencing the toxic effects of alcohol poisoning. I managed to contact a friend, who took me to the ER of a nearby Hollywood hospital. As I lay there cramping up and feeling pretty much like I was dying, all I could do was wait till the toxic effects wore off. Thank God, I made it back from that horrible experience. Later that evening, as I rested at home, I received a lot of encouragement and understanding from Tommy and my friends. Carmine Appice filled in for me on the next session. I went back to the studio in a couple of days and finished the album "straight." I'm willing to "tell it like it is," cuz I've been sober now for twelve years, and off powder and pills for eleven and a half years. I know I hurt my friends, and pissed a lot of people off due to my drinking and drugging. I am truly sorry. I can only offer my sincere apologies to all concerned!

GROUPIES: GOTTA LOVE 'EM

Two groupies revealing that they had slept with Rolling Stone Brian Jones claimed, "He was no Mick Jagger." After trying Keith Richards, they again claimed, "He was no Mick Jagger." Finally, after going to bed with Jagger himself they declared, guess what? "He was no Mick Jagger."

Life on the road is notorious for the easy sex that presents itself. The groupies (both male and female), of course, are ever-present and usually easy to spot. They come with a variety of attitudes: the overt fans who will do *anything* to get close to their heroes; the cool, "I'm oh-so-bored" types who are looking for a quick thrill; and the "professionals"—those who are always at the venue, ready for a good time regardless of who is performing. It is a given that most unmarried (and some married), healthy musicians are going to take advantage of the unencumbered sex tossed in their faces day after day. That's part of the gig, right? But there are times when maybe, just maybe, they should put their libidos on pause and think things through.

KARL KUENNING (ROADIE):

I got lucky every so often and a cakewalk gig would pop up. In the summer of 1976, I did a huge disco show in Washington, D.C., at the Capital Center. K. C. and the Sunshine Band, Rufus featuring Chaka Khan, Heatwave, The Robot Band, and The Trammps were on the bill. Showco was doing the sound and lights. The Capital Center was rigged for maximum capacity, and I was hired to truck in P.A. equipment and stack it on top of the existing gear. They didn't need mics and boards, just extra P.A. Only one roadie was needed so I was working solo that night. I drove to D.C., unloaded, hooked up to Showco, loaded, and drove home. It was pretty easy money. I had nothing to do during the show, so I actually got to go trolling in the audience for young ladies that wanted a lasting relationship (as long as it only lasted about two hours.)

Everything went according to plan It was a union house, with forklifts and all, so I didn't have to lift anything. My speakers stacked on top of theirs to create a monstrous tower of power. Once I confirmed that my system was on line and in sync with Showco, I took the rest of the day off. I met K. C., who was a very unassuming guy, during their sound check. I also got to sit at the main board during the Rufus sound check and put in my two cents to Chaka's soundman, a guy who had struck up a friendship with me. Chaka came to the soundboard and based on the conversation he wasn't just her soundman, if you catch my drift. All the other bands had their sound check and we all had a gourmet meal in the green room (I told you this was one of the best jobs I had ever been on, didn't I?). Then they opened the house.

K. C. was hot that night. It was the height of disco, and every female under the age of forty within a three-state area was at this show. I walked around the front edge of the crowd sporting my all-access backstage pass. It was during this time that *she* came up to me. Her name was Stacy or Leslie or something like that. She was probably sixteen, give or take a year, but she easily could have passed for twenty-one. She was decked out in the full groupie costume of the day: heavy makeup, a short tight dress, high heels. You get the picture. She wasted no time in asking me the two very important questions: "Are you with the band?" Then, "Can you get me back stage to meet K. C.?" My answer was, "Yes" then "Yes." I exaggerated a little bit and told her that K. C. was a personal friend of mine. (I *had* met him earlier in the day, after all). She said she'd do *anything* to get back stage.

128

I told myself to think fast. I'd need a pass for her, and I needed to think of a quiet place back stage where we wouldn't be disturbed. "Wait right here, don't move," I instructed as I headed for the backstage area to get my hands on a pass. In retrospect, this was a major tactical error. I should've already picked up a spare earlier in the day. I always carry a spare. But it slipped past me this night. Well, there was no sense in crying over spilt milk, so I approached K. C.'s road manager with "Hey, I just ran into an old college friend that wants to meet K. C. I need a pass, okay?" He looked at me and said, "She's not old enough to be in college." Damn! He'd seen me talking to her from where he stood on the stage. "No, really," I pleaded. "She's the sister of an old roommate of mine. She's like family to me." My desperation was obvious. "I'm going to do you a favor," he told me. Yes! The backstage pass! "I'm going to keep you from going to jail. She can't be a day over fifteen years old. They'll throw away the key." I was about to argue that she was at least sixteen, but I realized that it would be a losing battle.

I went back out to the audience, found Leslie/Stacy, whatever her name was, and told her they were all out of passes right now. Desperate now, I asked her if I could sit with her to watch the show. She just turned and walked away from me. As she left she told me, in her sweet little voice, "Too bad you couldn't get me back there. I'm *real* good."

For years after that night, I cursed that road manager. But with the hindsight of time I realize he was absolutely right. Karl's Roadie Rule #9 was born that night: "Everything happens for a reason." The show that night was fantastic, but for me it was a bitter consolation prize.

TAKE MY WIFE—PLEASE!

James Brown seems to have always had trouble with his many different wives. Once, he threw his significant other's furs out on the couple's front lawn and shot them full of holes with a shotgun.

It would be hard to imagine any red-blooded musician turning down all the interesting offers that are thrown in his or her way, but there are times when they do. Sometimes the company isn't quite what the rocker has in mind. Sometimes it's just plain trouble. In spite of their unbridled reputation, some rock and rollers actually do have ethics.

ZAK DANIELS (ZAK DANIELS AND THE ONE-EYED SNAKES):

On our first tour, the band was scheduled for a preshow interview to hype a concert. So, after checking into the hotel, we headed for a local radio station. Upon arriving at the station, we were greeted by a lovely young blonde whose duties, among others, included being the receptionist. From the second we rolled through the station's front door, I could feel the target she was painting on me. With hungry eyes, thirsty words, and no attempt to disguise her intentions, (I'll call her Blondie) Blondie continued to paint her target. By the time we left the station for sound check, I felt like a piece of meat with a freshly painted bull's-eye on my ass. As the station door closed behind me, I heard her say, "See ya tonight at the show Zak . . . and after the show, too!" she added with a giggle. (Okay, this was going to be a fun town!)

The interview had gone well, the sound check went smoothly, and the show not only rocked their socks, it rocked some undies too! Afterwards, we signed CDs and T-shirts for an hour or so, and then it was time for dealing with the money. Although the kids lined up around the block to see us, no matter how you do the math six hundred dollars was not the fifteen hundred dollars we had been promised. However, my deal was with the station owner, not the club owner, so I couldn't really bitch about it. I assumed the station would make up the difference. Okay, now where was the station owner?

I was informed that there was a party being thrown in our honor, and that the owner was going to meet us there. "Let's go have some fun at the party, and I'll work out the money later," I told my bandmates. While partying and waiting for the owner of the radio station to arrive, little Blondie was zeroing in on the target she had painted earlier that afternoon. There was at least one problem with this development. I found out that she was married, and her husband happened to be sitting across the room. I had met her husband earlier when he asked me to sign his CD. So, hubby is chatting with the other guests, just a few feet away from where his wife was coming on to me. Yeah, this was a little strange. Maybe too strange, even for me.

I expressed my discomfort with the situation, and as politely as possible, passed on Blondie's offer. However, I did let her know that treating her husband so coldly, right in front of his face, was, personally, a real turn off. She tried to convince me that he wouldn't mind, but I wasn't buying it. At this point, I just wanted to collect the balance of what was promised and grab a few hours of sleep before hitting the road again.

During the next hour, while waiting for the elusive station owner, the drinks flowed and magic dust flew. I was starting to feel pretty good and was also relieved that "Mrs. Horny-Blonde" (err, ugh, I mean Blondie) had gotten the message. I hadn't seen her for about twenty minutes, so hopefully she was busy painting a target on someone else's ass. Or so I thought. From out of nowhere, Blondie sailed across the room, slipped down next to me on the sofa, and with a whisper to my ear, suggested a threesome with her girlfriend. When I didn't chomp on the bait, a hot-tub orgy was enticingly offered. This girl was hungry! Seemingly unfazed by my polite rejection, she was determined to nail her prey. Blondie wasn't going to quit the hunt until she tried every weapon in her arsenal.

Now, you may think I'm crazy for turning down these wonderful offers, but something didn't feel right. I've had my share of "groupie therapy," and there were a few occasions where more than one really was merrier. But this town was stranger than fiction, and it just didn't feel like a story with a happy ending. This was not going to be a *Penthouse Forum* letter where everyone happily orgasms into the sunset. Seething beneath this veneer of sexual freedom, with its visions of hungry willing flesh and promise of lusty fun, was something else, and it wasn't pretty. I sensed some heavy baggage filled with fear, jealousy, and neurosis-driven anxiety. This was a small town with long and twisted relationship histories intertwined and tethered to most of the people at this party. It felt like a soap opera in progress, and I wanted out. But not without my money! The band headed back to the hotel, and I stayed to get paid. (Oh yes, being your own road manager is so much fun.)

Big Shot finally showed up, and we slipped into another room to discuss the money. He told me that he'd make up the difference in the morning. "Just stop by the station on the way out of town," he said, reassuringly. I finally left this Fellini cattle call of a party (Thank you, God!) and copped a few hours of sleep.

On the way out of town, we dropped by the radio station to collect the rest of our money, and yes, you guessed right: the station owner wasn't there. Nor was there a check waiting for us. The next show was three hundred miles away, so hanging out to haggle was not an option. It was time to roll. Fortunately, we sold a bundle of CDs and T-shirts, which more than made up the difference. Not to mention the fact that we made a ton of new fans.

A few weeks later, after we got back to L.A., I called the radio station to find out if I had left my "fave" stage jacket at the party. It was Blondie I spoke to, and she informed me that I had indeed left my jacket there. She said that she'd be happy to ship it to L.A. for me. I thanked her, and we said good-bye.

A month passed, but still no package from New Mexico. I phoned the station, and sounding quite the professional receptionist, Blondie chimed the familiar call letters, "This is KR_ _. Can I help you?" I said, "Hi, this is Zak Daniels. Just wondered if you've had a chance to ship that jacket yet?" I heard her start to cry, and then she said, "I'm so sorry." I asked, "Sorry about what?" Between her sobs Blondie replied, "Well, when someone found out that I was shipping your jacket to you, they took it out to the backyard and—sob, sob— shot it full of holes—sob, sob—I'm sooo sorry." As she continued to cry, I could only mutter, "Hey, it's no big deal, don't worry about it. I've got plenty of jackets. Take care of yourself, okay? Bye now."

I called one of the DJs later that evening, and he spit out all of the soap opera dirt. Turns out the guy who air-conditioned my jacket wasn't her husband, it was the station owner. It seems that Blondie was the station owner's mistress. To this day, I still don't know if he shot my jacket out of jealousy or because I wouldn't fuck her. Blondie was probably right about one thing: her husband didn't care. Strange fucking town! If Rod Serling was still alive he'd not only live there, he'd be Mayor.

Had I decided to take advantage of Blondie's orgy invitation, this story might have had a different ending, and most likely a different author. I can see the headline now: ROCK VOCALIST SHOT DEAD IN NEW MEXICO HOT TUB

Here's the moral of this story: enjoy being young and dumb and full of cum, but listen for the distant rumble of jealousy and fear before you jump into the tub. Rock and roll: it's not a job, it's an adventure. An adventure in the art of survival.

THE AFTER-GIG PARTY

At an after-party in Venice, Robert De Niro met Queen's Roger Taylor and Brian May. After expressing his respect for the band's music, De Niro decided to collaborate with the band members on a futuristic musical based on Queen's music that they would title We Will Rock You. *The play took six years to materialize, but finally, at a cost of 7.5 million dollars, the musical debuted on the London stage in 2003.*

Every gig must have an after-party of some sort—it's an unwritten law. Sometimes the label puts it together, sometimes the promoter does, and sometimes even the band takes care of it. The party can be back stage, in the venue's hospitality room, at a club, or in a hotel suite. The show's headliners are not required to attend. You'd think that maybe partying night after night would get old hat, and maybe it does. Yet the parties continue, whether the musicians are into them or not. Most of the time they show up, at least for a little while, but other times they have to leave right after the show to continue on their hectic tour. Whether the main attraction shows or not, the party *will* go on.

There's always the chance that there might be a big-star sighting at one of these parties, but one thing's for sure: liquid entertainment or something equally mind-altering will be available for the lucky few chosen to receive an invitation. There will also be an abundance of members of the opposite sex ready, willing, and able. Often, no one is happier to attend the after-party and take advantage of all this than the opening act.

ANDREW GOLD (SOLO ARTIST):

One of my favorite rock and roll moments was when I was touring with the Eagles. They used to have their roadies go through the crowd before the gigs and pick out gorgeous girls (always plentiful at Eagles concerts). They'd pass out these special buttons, which meant the girls were invited to an after-show party at the hotel the Eagles were staying in. I think they called this their "third encore" or something. Anyway, they would book a suite in the hotel especially for the party, and also book all the rooms above, below, and to the sides of this room so no one would complain about noise.

So, every night I'd go to these parties. Their road manager would stand guard at the door, and all these unbelievable women would knock and be let in with their buttons. The lads would order up everything on the menu, from room service with booze, drugs, and the usual rock and roll fare. They would just kind of graze, picking up women and taking them to their rooms. Some in the band would come back to the party an hour later and troll again!

Being the opening act, I had to settle for the ones not picked by the boys, who had first pick. The girls were certainly willing, so it wasn't as tacky as it sounds. Besides, these were beautiful women. Some of them smart, too!

The best moment was this: The knock comes at the door. The road manager opens it. There's a girl with a button standing there smiling, and with her is her boyfriend. The road manager says to the girl, without a trace of pity, "*You can

Andrew Gold
From the photo collection of Andrew Gold

come in; he can't." The boy turns, like, "Okay babe, let's go." She peers into the party for a second and then goes to the boyfriend, "Sorry!" She walks into the party without the suitably horrified boyfriend. The last thing I see is his incredulous look as the door is slammed in his face. Unbelievable. She went with Don Felder, I think, later.

DAZED AND CONFUSED

Guitarist Steve Rotherey of Marillion was once missing in action at a brewery launch party. After searching high and low for the musician as the band prepared to take the stage to perform, Rothery was found wedged into an empty barrel of brew surrounded by half-eaten, party-sized pork pies.

Drugs and booze, booze and drugs. As John Lennon sang, "Whatever gets you through the night." Touring is hard work, and when the time to kick back rolls around, a lot of musicians don't know how to work any less hard in their pursuit of relaxation. The elements of the party don't necessarily make their first appearance at the after-party, nor are they always left at the stage entrance. Booze and drugs, drugs and booze—they make for some strange tales . . .

LEE UNDERWOOD (GUITARIST WITH TIM BUCKLEY):

Late for the flight and stoned on reds (Seconal), Tim and I staggered as fast as we could toward the airport gate, laughing even as he lurched and fell. I got him back on his feet. We kept running down those shiny, endlessly long halls, barely making it to the plane. It was waiting for us, engines idling. The door was open. A stewardess reached out to close it just as we made it to the tarmac, yelling and waving at her. "Stop! Wait! Not yet! Don't go! Hey!"

Around noon the next day, sober and straight at Denver's Mile High Stadium, June 27, 1969, we admired Tim's name on the giant marquee beside those of Jimi Hendrix, Mothers of Invention, Iron Butterfly, Creedence Clearwater, Crosby, Stills & Nash, several others.

That afternoon, Tim and I stood on a stage in the middle of a baseball diamond, looking up at thousands of people, just the two of us playing our hearts out. Suddenly, after only four songs, a great roar erupted from the crowd on our left. Wire fences crashed down. Hundreds of fans that had been denied entrance to the sold-out festival rushed in. People screamed, ran, fell, tried to get away.

Cops in gas masks attacked the crowd with clubs. Other cops set off tear gas bombs. Smoke clouds billowed up into the stands and wafted out on the field. Tim and I heaved our guitars into cases and ran down the stairs at the side of the stage, out into right field.

People coughed, screamed, yelled, and cried while cops attacked them wherever they could. Tim and I got separated. Whenever a wave of smoke came my way, I lay down on the grass, covered my head, buried my face in soil, then got up clutching my guitar and kept running for the restrooms, coughing, crying, eyes stinging, lungs hurting. Inside, safe from the smoke, I watched a cop taking a leak. He propped his gas mask up on his forehead, chuckled, smiled a big grin, said to the guy standing next to him, "More fun than shootin' bunnies, ain't it?"

PLEASE STEP TO THE SIDE OF THE LINE

While on a train during a tour of Japan with Mötley Crüe, Tommy Lee and Nikki Sixx took handfuls of pills, drank dozens of shots of saki, and consumed a fifth of Jack Daniels. They threw food on the Japanese passengers and threw the empty bottle of Jack out a window. Sixx was arrested.

As with almost anything pertaining to the pursuit of fun, there are certain details of finding whatever form of entertainment you seek with which you'd rather not deal. If even Sir Paul McCartney can get busted for grass while on tour (okay, so he wasn't Sir Paul then, but still), just about anyone can. We've heard about members of the Rolling Stones and various other musicians being led away from their homes after a bust. Rockers, after all, are usually on-the-edge types of people. They can be risk takers and outlaws. They know what they want, and they are willing to risk the consequences. The fact remains that many musicians do like their recreational drugs, and sometimes thinking those drugs might be revealed to the wrong person isn't always paranoid.

DEREK BOSTROM (MEAT PUPPETS):

For even the most seasoned touring band, the long cross-country drives can get pretty monotonous. All you see is mile after mile of the same countryside, the same restaurant chains, and the same crappy coffee to keep you awake. (Not to mention the same smelly, crabby, hung-over companions.) But things pick up a bit when you have to cross an international border. Life takes on a heretofore-unfelt urgency. Lethargy gives way to desperate scurrying, futile cleaning, and furtive inserting. Suddenly, even waiting in long lines takes on a certain feverish intensity.

I recall one such crossing into Canada with my band the Meat Puppets. This incident took place almost twenty years ago, when I was much younger and much more foolish. Anyway, it was my turn to hold that night's worth of marijuana (which, back then, we refused to forgo for even a single show). Things went smoothly at first. We pulled up to the border, waited our turn, presented our identification, endured the standard snide comments about our band name, and submitted to the customary search of our vehicle. But something suspicious turned up in a suitcase: a sticky leaf, a green crumb, something. We were informed that we were to be strip-searched. The border guards said it would go much easier for us if we just gave up whatever we had, but I was damned if I was going to help them incriminate me. Besides, how much help did they really need? The weed was right there in my jacket pocket. They had no trouble finding it all by themselves.

I was quickly confined, for the first time in my life, in a room locked from the outside. As I sat there, deprived of my physical freedom, I suddenly found myself in the grip of primal urges. The door to my room had a window that looked out on to the hallway, and I began leering with uncharacteristic brazenness at any female officer or government employee who happened past. Finally, some guy came in and told me to sit down and get away from the window. Meanwhile, as we made ourselves comfortable in their various holding rooms, the authorities

Derek Bostrom
(Meat Puppets)
*Photograph by
Sonia Bovio*

conducted a thorough search of our vehicle and belongings. You see, they hadn't yet found enough contraband, actually, to make a proper arrest. But they had more than enough to allow them to terrorize me. They told me that I'd never again be allowed into their country; in fact, they were certain I'd have my passport revoked altogether. This, they reminded me, would make it difficult to earn my living. But that was okay, for by this time, I was thoroughly sick of touring.

But nothing like that actually happened. After their search turned up nothing else illegal, the guards were obliged to let us go. But there were consequences nonetheless. We arrived at the club far too late for a sound check; in fact we had barely enough time to set up our equipment before we were scheduled to go on. There, in front of a packed house at one of Toronto's most fashionable showcase lounges, we learned that the frustrated border guards had relieved our amplifiers of their tubes. After a long delay and much yelling and stumbling around, we used the opening band's equipment and played a decidedly inferior set.

We never got another shot at a club in Toronto of that size. Most of the people who'd shown up that night elected never to do so again, and henceforth we were relegated to smaller bars on the other side of town. Of course, it's always possible that audience might not have liked us even at our best, but I guess we'll never know.

Unfortunately, this was not our only run-in with international authorities. Since my passport was not revoked, my bandmates and I managed to get ourselves to another border: the gateway from Switzerland into Italy. I was no longer using controlled substances to enhance either my performances or any other aspect of my life. But on our little tour bus, I was definitely in the minority. We'd had no problems previously in any other part of the European community, so our border preparations had grown somewhat lax. The designated smugglers just kept their stashes in their hands, figuring they'd just fake-cough their way out of any trouble. But the Italians were onto our tricks, and they were quick about it. They had the cuffs on before anyone got their hands anywhere near their mouths.

The stash was discovered. And this time we were at a greater disadvantage than we were with the Canadians with whom, for the most part, we still share a common language. Here, on the edge of the Italian Alps, we could barely communicate with our captors. We were searched, of course, as was our vehicle, but no other drugs were found. However, when our merchandise woman was discovered in possession of several thousand dollars worth of T-shirt sales, she was suddenly separated from the rest of our party. Later, she told us she had been taken back on our tour bus where she was not only relieved of all the cash, but crudely propositioned as well.

Our entourage was herded into a small hallway off the main border kiosk, where we waited for the better part of an hour. Then three teenaged girls entered the room. They carried on a brief conversation in Italian with the highest-ranking guard, and then they left. We were released shortly thereafter without our T-shirt money and without the necessary stamps on our passports. (Because of this, we had to bribe our way out of the country a week later.)

Luckily, the guards had left our equipment intact, but just the same, we were way behind schedule. Or so we thought. We sped the rest of the way into town, arriving at the club in a panic but the promoter just shrugged. "You're early," he said. "They must have actually found something on you at the border." It turns out, the guards would routinely detain bands for as long is it took to shake them down. If they discovered something quick, you could be on your way in an hour or so. If not, you could be there for a lot longer. And if you were foolish enough to arrive with no contraband at all, it was so much the worse. You would then have no control over what they "found."

But I always wondered about those three girls. The best I can figure is that they were daughters of the highest-ranking guard. At first, I decided he had been making an example of us, an example of what can happen to those who choose the path of the illicit drug abuser. But later it occurred to me that those guards saw bands come through all the time. Maybe they had called the girls in to see if perhaps we were a group they'd heard of. Who knows? Maybe if we were cuter, or could play better, or could write hit songs, the girls would have taken pity on us, and we might have been allowed to keep some of our T-shirt money.

DON'T TRY THIS AT HOME

While on tour in England, Kurt Cobain was wheeled on stage in a hospital gown telling people that English people made him sick. It wasn't long after this that Cobain was being wheeled out of his hotel room on a very real stretcher.

So, a lot of rockers do drugs. Some get busted and some are lucky. Some—like the rock trinity of Jim Morrison, Jimi Hendrix, and Janis Joplin—die. The live-free, die-young-and-leave-a-good-looking-corpse mindset is in evidence nowhere if not in rock and roll. But most rockers age, as do all people. And with age comes a certain understanding that the party may not have been as much fun as it seemed to be at the time.

AL KOOPER (SOLO ARTIST):

Finding an apartment in New York City is a perilous task. It can take months. I was incredibly depressed, and emotionally weak; the perfect profile for a drug abuser. I had quit all drugs in 1967 while I was putting BS&T together, but now I suddenly crumbled and fell victim to the world of painkillers. I hesitate to document this part of my life (sound the serious alarm here for the next few paragraphs), but I feel it might help someone out there to see a foolishness of choices and light the way out of the tunnel for them. Back then, there were no rehab centers, and one had to take matters into one's own hands. At any rate, I'll be concise.

Percodan was the choice I made. Favored by doctors for migraines and dentists for post-op relief, in my eyes it was a chickenshit, Junior Miss heroin substitute. Not forlorn enough to punch a needle in my arm, I chose these convenient little escape tablets to cope with my problems. Completely unaware of the addictive features, I went hog wild. With the help of inspired tale-telling to various East and West Coast "Dr. Nick's," I built up a formidable stash. Behind my back, the members of my performing band would take bets on how many times I would walk into the microphone during each performance. My friends from Dr. Generosity's (an Upper East Side rock star hangout in Manhattan that had become my clubhouse) would literally carry me home on occasion, when I nodded out past closing time. Cute. And into this potentially lethal chemistry, I added the purchase of my first automobile: a brand new dark blue 1972 Corvette with two tops. Putting that car into the equation was the closest I had ever come to inadvertent suicide so far.

One night I was performing at a college in New Jersey. I had dated a woman twice before who was the sister of an actor who would become famous in two years on a television sitcom. I called her from the college and asked her if she wanted to spend the night together when I got back from New Jersey. The plan was that I would pick her up at her place on the way back home from the gig and we would "hang out" at my hotel for the rest of the night. I had driven the Corvette to

Al Kooper
*From the photo
collection of
Al Kooper*

Jersey since the gig was so close. As I headed back to the city with the top down, I realized I was starting to nod out. I drove faster toward her apartment and stumbled to the buzzer when I got there. Some Romeo.

This was a dangerous game I was playing. She came downstairs and got in the car. "Can we get something to eat?" she said. "I'm starving!" Just what I needed.

I answered, "Michelle, I'm seriously nodding out here. Let's just get something delivered to the hotel, OK?" She agreed, and I told her to call for food wherever she wanted and handed her a wad of bills.

"I have got to take a nap for two hours," I went on. "Order some food, make yourself comfortable, watch TV, and before you know it, I'll be up."

Another great date with Al. This was fine with her, however, so I headed off to the bedroom. It was one AM and I crashed instantly and awoke at four AM, refreshed and randy. I sashayed into the living room, and the little doll was attired in nothing but one of my shirts (quite oversized for her). She was out cold

141

with a drinking glass still in her hand. How cute, I thought. I kinda settled down next to her on the couch and made a few moves. I got zero response. I shook her gently to wake her up. No response. She began drooling.

Oh shit, am I in trouble, I was thinking. I tried the mirror trick, and to my relief she was still breathing.

I gave her one last tentative shake and said to her, "Okay, this is your last chance! If this is some method acting tour de force, now is the time to fess up 'cause I'm about to call an ambulance." No response.

I was really scared now. I called the hotel doctor and dressed her as best I could while waiting for him to arrive. He examined her and called for an ambulance. Suspected overdose. My world is just filled with irony, I was thinking. I'm nodding out a few hours ago, and now I'm taking her to the hospital!

She was rushed to an emergency room, where I paced around. The cops took her handbag and emptied it onto a gurney, looking for whatever had felled her. It was a moment out of a Woody Allen film. An incredible amount of stuff tumbled out: hairbrushes, makeup, cigarettes, magazines, address books, tampon holders, scraps of paper, and loose tobacco for starters. The cops looked incredulously at each other and began the task of weeding through all this feminine paraphernalia. I was actually able to grin for a moment until I started imagining the headlines in tomorrow's *New York Post*: DEAD NUDE GROUPIE FOUND IN ROCK STAR'S HOTEL ROOM

This sobered me up rather quickly. About an hour later, some doctor arrived with the news: "You got her here just in time. If you had slept through the night, you'd have awakened to a corpse in your room. She overdosed on something or other, and we were able to pump her stomach and save her. You're a lucky guy." Somehow, I didn't feel like a lucky guy.

Around lunchtime, she was discharged from the hospital, and I took her in a cab to her soon-to-be-famous brother's place. We walked into his soon-to-be-better-decorated apartment.

"She's all yours, big brother," I announced as I quickly took my leave. As I headed out the door, he looked at me with the look of a weary man who had done this before. Whew! Close call, kids . . .

CHAPTER 6

ARTIST ENCOUNTERS

P eople love celebrities. Television, film, and music personalities draw ridiculous amounts of attention not only from those in the United States but worldwide. Our entertainment icons are often surprised that they can be recognized even in some of the most remote places. Why there is such interest is a sociological complexity, but there is a basic underlying factor: we all find it interesting to come into contact with someone famous.

When those celebrities happen to also be people who are greatly admired, so much the better. Rock and rollers are no different than the rest of us. It's a kick for them to meet remarkable people and, just like us, always a thrill to remember.

SAM ANDREW (BIG BROTHER AND THE HOLDING COMPANY):

When I played with Janis Joplin in both Big Brother and the Holding Company and the Kozmic Blues Band, I met many remarkable people: Andy Warhol, Larry Rivers, Salvador Dalí, Tiny Tim, Debbie Harry, Larry Poons, Mick Jagger, George Harrison, Paul McCartney, Richard Chamberlain, and many other successful and interesting artists. There were three musicians, however, who meant a lot to me, and I always think of them with fondness and respect.

Jimi Hendrix was a quiet man who became Godzilla when he stepped on the stage. I met him at the Monterey Pop Festival after hearing his first album for a week and marveling at his incredible guitar work and song ideas. What could he be like in performance? Would he live up to his recording?

Jimi Hendrix was amazing at Monterey. He took the stage and ambushed the audience with a bombardment of the most unusual and advanced guitar playing that we had heard up to that point. He was dressed as a beautiful and exotic pirate from the eighteenth century, and there was a certain reptilian fascination about his movements. After he played, I talked with him back stage. I could hardly hear him in that environment because he spoke so softly. He was putting little white pills in his mouth. I thought they were breath mints—Tic Tacs—but no, they were LSD. He took a lot of them. I was amazed that he could talk at all, and yet he did so poetically and so aptly that his conversation sounded like a song.

Well, to put it mildly, we were all quite impressed with Mr. Hendrix. We all became friends because our band and his became successful at the same time and we played on the same bill a lot. Often, especially when we played the Midwest, we would be the only people around for hundreds of miles who spoke the same language, and so we played together and jammed together a lot. It is amazing to think of Jimi Hendrix in a place like Iowa where there are many cows and a lot of corn, but there he was and he was there often.

Jimi and I bought Super 8 movie cameras at about the same time, and we shot each other back stage. There is still a photograph around of him filming Janis, Ken Weaver from the Fugs, and me in the dressing room at the Fillmore. What that still photograph cannot show is that Jimi used his camera like a guitar. He gyrated around, zoomed in and out, took pictures from every possible angle, and generally behaved like a court jester. I filmed him filming us, but of course those films are lost now. I keep dreaming that they will appear one day, liberated from someone's basement.

When Big Brother played in Jimi's hometown of Seattle, we saw a man named Guitar Shorty play in a club called The Black and Tan. Guitar Shorty could do anything with the instrument. He played it with his teeth, with his tuchus (posterior or gluteus maximus), with his elbow, and during one breathtakingly beautiful guitar solo, Mr. Shorty did a flip off of the stage and did not miss a single note. It was clear that Jimi must have often seen this man play. Only recently I have learned that they were actually related. Guitar Shorty was married to Jimi's sister according to Caroline Newman in Portland, Oregon.

Jimi was new and revolutionary. B. B. King, on the other hand, carried on the tradition of the Memphis Blues. He was an established artist when we were all learning to play. I first saw him a long time ago in a scene that seemed old even then. It was a club somewhere in the Midwest, and I was the only white person there. There were a lot of people in their forties and fifties and it seemed like there were more women than men. They had all come in furs and their best jewelry. This was the first time I heard B. B. King do many of the songs that I have since heard many times, and we all laughed hard at the funny lyrics in "Sweet Sixteen" and all of those other great songs. It was a very organic scene, and it felt like being in an African-American church. Mr. King would sing or play a line, and the audience would respond immediately with encouragement, sympathy, and commentary. They were a part of the act as much as he was. I felt privileged to have witnessed this nightclub life in an intimate setting.

Big Brother played with B. B. King many times, but the most memorable was the weekend that Martin Luther King, Jr., was shot. There were riots in most major cities, the neighborhoods were in flames, and the situation was very critical for a while. It is hard to imagine today how close to disaster the country was. I sat back stage with B, as B. B. King is known to his friends, and he talked about the tragedy in such a beautiful and moving manner. Then he went out to play his set. His music, always moving, was especially sacred and religious that night. He seemed like a saint or a prophet to me, sanctified in his blues truth and ready to heal the wounds of a nation in pain. He is a hero to me and to many other musicians for his dignity, integrity, and blues invention.

Otis Redding was from Macon, Georgia, the same little town where James Brown, Little Richard, and the Allman Brothers started to play. Otis used to love Little Richard's style, and in fact, he would sing just like Richard Penniman. But when Otis started to sing his own tunes, he put a whole new meaning into the love ballad and into the funky tune, too. Like Jimi, he was a quiet man with a lot of feeling inside. He was so solidly built that he seemed like a bull, solid, powerful, and taciturn until he hit the stage. Then Otis would stomp his foot, yell "Shake!" and the band would be off and running. After he played at the Monterey Pop Festival, Otis stayed in San Francisco for a while to enjoy the city where he was now a famous and beloved figure. He went out to the nearby town of Sausalito, sat down on a pier, and wrote a song about the loneliness of being on the road that became his most well known song after he died.

Janis Joplin and the boys in Big Brother went to see Otis many times while he was here in San Francisco, and we both learned a lot from the incredible energy and yes, love that he put into his performances. The day that he died, she and I held a wake for him in her apartment. We drank some champagne, played all of his records, and then talked about how much he meant to us, what a gentleman he was, how his plain common sense meant so much in those insane times, and what an inspiration he was in the content and performance of his songs.

These three men—Mr. Hendrix, Mr. King, and Mr. Redding—were good friends to us. Otis and Jimi are dead. B. B. King is still very much alive, and we still see him play every now and then. He has become an elder statesman of the blues, and it is good to see such a talented man be honored and respected as he should be.

PETER NOONE (HERMAN AND THE HERMITS):

Our first concert as Pete Novac and the Heartbeats was at Urmston Football Club, and I can recall we also had a guitarist at the time called Al Chadwick. We stole the show. We were the only act. We were awful. We were paid four pounds, which was about six dollars. We all ate fish and chips and put petrol in the van. Our first success was behind us, and we were off on the road to our destiny.

Our first ever concert was watched by thirteen very bored looking girls whom we all knew by name, and their parents, whose names were Mr. and Mrs. Something or other or Beryl's mum and dad. My sister Denise and her friend refused to even come until she had auditioned us for coolness because they had been humiliated when I had played that one time in The Cyclones.

Then one day, the Beatles played on the field outside what was our sort of residence, Urmston Football Club. Can you imagine having the Beatles play on a field outside your little local teen club?

This was, of course, the thing that would change my life, and the truth is, I only went to see the openers, Brian Poole and the Tremeloes. I can never forget the strange feeling I felt as I watched Mel [Evans] and Neil [Aspinall] (both who would later become almost as famous as the Beatles would), push Ringo's drum kit forward. I knew that this was something special. What was this I asked myself? A drum riser? I had never seen anything so pompous in my life. Did they think their drummer was important like Sandy Nelson or Gene Krupa?

Then, they began to position three microphone stands. Three? What on earth was this? Wait. The drummer has a mic, too. These show-offs had so much money that they were even giving the drummer a mic? They must be rubbish and have to flash lots of expensive electronic equipment on stage to impress the audience I thought to myself. I always used to think to myself, especially when I was thinking about girls.

Peter Noone
(Herman's Hermits)
*From the photo
 collection of Peter
Noone*

I have to mention that the girls at this show were absolutely unmoved by all the bravado taking place on the stage. Only the local members of beat groups, as we were called, were paying any attention. The local girls were, of course, checking to see if any of the fair workers had managed to stay out of jail long enough to have one of his forty-five tattoos removed, but this was not the fair for them.

Then, the announcer said (as if he was annoyed that he had to stop eating his pork pie), "Here they are, from Liverpool: the Beatles." Being musicians ourselves, we pretended to applaud. At the same time, we hoped these blokes would trip over one of the cables of their four microphones or get struck by lightning and fall into one of the portable toilets right by the stage. Better still, we hoped they would be very spotty, and have the sort of zits which could possibly explode during a guitar solo.

With incredible casualness, I watched as these four lads nonchalantly plugged in their guitars and went about the "set-up" part of their show. Suddenly, I was absolutely transfixed. This was something completely different. I was witnessing the thing that would make these four lads the biggest musical event since Elvis Presley. Here it is necessary for me to say Elvis is, and was, my most favorite person and the greatest singer ever, and the Beatles would *agree,* so this moment was sort of important.

They began with a song called "Some Other Guy," and I will remember that moment forever. Then they did Ernie Maresca's "Fortune Teller." The rest is a blur. As you already know, I am wholly a man, and always was, but the music and the energy and charisma of these four young men was something indescribable. At the same time they were acting casually, they were also making eye contact with everyone in the small audience. Even Angela Denner (the coolest local girl that week), was smiling and forgetting how beautiful she was in order to try to catch the eye of the lead singer. In the early Beatles days, John Lennon was the clear leader and Paul was still a handsome second fiddle. George looked the coolest and the youngest, which drew all the pretty girls towards his edge of the stage because the other twenty-year-old Beatles were WAY too old for their tastes.

Ringo was a drummer, so no girls tried to catch his attention because he was so busy leading the band.

John was the one who captured all my attention because he epitomized everything that I liked about what was then called rock and roll music. He had the thing that all big stars need: charisma. Plus the thing that makes the charismatic ones useful: attitude. He was able to move quickly from casual nonchalance, to really aggressive and mean snarly stuff. He was also the funny one, and the other three clearly were his followers.

Paul was the best-looking man I had ever seen, which was not to his advantage. Even if he was the best bass player in the world that day, I hated him for being so totally cool, charming, cute, handsome, and talented, too. How could God have allowed these four people to meet and destroy all my hopes of ever being in the music business? Why me, Lord?

The guitarist, George, was young, handsome and thirty-five years ahead of the one in my band. Did that mean that my guitarist wasn't actually playing the guitar for hours on end in his bedroom? What was he doing all day up there anyway?

This bass player, Paul, had one of the greatest pretty voices I had ever heard, and could also do Little Richard. AAAaaaaaaaaaaaaaaaaargh. The bastard. He must have made a deal with the devil. Nobody can sing and play the bass that well.

Ringo had replaced Pete Best, and Pete had told me that Ringo was a great drummer but that he had no fans.

There was a rumor that they wrote songs, too, but I had heard that they were no good. Just as this thought settled in my tiny mind, they did "From Me to You."

That was when I decided to quit the music business and become a doctor. There was no way I would ever be able to compete with *that*. That was cheating. They were so much better than anything I had *ever seen* that I was speechless. That was when Alan Wrigley uttered these magic words. "F'ing 'ell." Actually, he said it maybe twenty-five times, as they began and finished a song that knocked our socks off and also shriveled the parts of our bodies that we desperately wanted not to become shriveled. Is it possible to be musically emasculated? Flaccid? "F'ing 'ell."

Then Alan said the words which were to change our lives: "No more f'ing around Pete!" Words to that effect. Alan always used the "f" word when he couldn't express his feelings properly, which was always. I was able to connect better words together, so I said, from this day hence no member of our musical enterprise would be allowed to have another job. No more part-timers. We had seen the truth. The Beatles were it. We had seen the real competition. This is not to say that The Hollies, Gerry and the Pacemakers, Freddie and the Dreamers, the Undertakers, or any of the other bands that we had seen recently were not great too, but these Beatles were fab.

That was the day we began to get serious. Alan and I had work to do. Luckily, we had Keith (Hopwood) and Karl (Green), who wanted to be great, too. We would, of course, need a name and a new style to go with our new idea. We couldn't do "Some Other Guy" anymore or "Fortune Teller." So? We would need to be different.

We were.

WE'RE ALL IN THIS TOGETHER

Emotions can run hot when a musician is up on stage. In 1973, during a concert at Knott's Berry Farm in Buena Park, California, the Everly Brothers terminated their partnership. It was common

knowledge that the brothers did not get along, but when an allegedly spaced-out Brother Don didn't perform up to Brother Phil's expectations, Phil threw his guitar down on the stage in fury and stalked off the stage.

As the Deserata tells us, many fears are borne out of loneliness and fatigue. Those emotions can also create massive opportunities for miscomunication. There's a lot of loneliness on the road and musicians experience more than their fair share of fatigue. When musicians are placed in anything-can-happen circumstances, well, anything can—and does—happen.

ROBIN BACHMAN (BACHMAN TURNER OVERDRIVE, B.T.O.):

It was May 17, 1973, which was B.T.O.'s first concert tour ever. We were in Nashville at an outdoor festival. Charlie Daniels was on the bill. We arrived at the concert early to check out the backstage area. We had a motor home as a dressing room, and it was full of goodies like Cokes, beer, fruit, sandwich meats, and desserts. I heard a band playing. They were jamming and burning up the stage. So, I went to see who it was.

I stood on the sidelines, shaking my leg to the beat. Charlie Daniels and his band were rockin' the crowd. It sounded great to me. I was really into it. I was smiling and laughing at the people having a good time dancing and grooving to Charlie's music. Charlie looked like he was really into it, too. He was shaking his head, stomping his feet, and singing up a storm. When he looked over at me, I gave him the thumbs up and a big smile and laugh. It sounded great to me by the side fill speakers. So I stood there, smiling and having a great time watching the crowd and anticipating B.T.O.'s turn on the stage.

I left the side of the stage to go get in sync with the other band members. I went into our motor home and sat down beside Lindsay, our stage manager. As I was drinking a Coke, Charlie came storming in the motor home and said, "Where is he?" Hearing this, I looked up and said, "There he is, man." I proceed to say, "Great job!" Charlie looked over at me, and before I could even think of a word or make a move, he stepped in front of me and grabbed me by the collar. He lifted me up off the couch, into the air and held me up by the collar, with my feet dangling.

Lindsay stood up and said, "Hey, what are you doing?" Charlie stared me in

B.T.O.: Robin Bachman, C. F. Turner, Randy Murray, Blair Thornton
Photo by Nick Seiflow, from the photo collection of Robin Bachman

the eyes and said, "Who in the fuck are you, and what were you doing on my stage?" So I was hanging there, staring back, wondering what the heck I'd done. I tell Charlie, "I'm Robbie Bachman, the drummer from B.T.O. I was watching you play. What the fuck's wrong?" Bruce Allen, our manager, walked in saying, "Show on. Let's go." Charlie puts me down, and I go to the stage to check out my drums.

We got done adjusting our equipment and C. F. Turner looked at me to count in the first song. The crowd cheered, and we were into it. In the middle of "Gimme Your Money, Please," I felt a tug on my left pant leg. Then another tug. I turned around and looked down and there was Charlie, on his hands and knees saying, "Hey man. I'm real sorry. I didn't know who you were or what you were doing." I told him, "It's okay, man!" Then he crawled behind the amps to the side of the stage.

We performed five more songs, and then I felt another tug. It was Charlie again. "Hey man. I'm really sorry, man. I'm sorry." So I tell him again, "Hey man. I'm cool. It's okay."

We finished our set, and then I found out what had happened and why Charlie was so upset. As it turned out, he was having a bad night. The monitors weren't working, the sound was bad, and he couldn't hear a thing. So he was real upset—very mad and frustrated. Charlie thought I was mocking him and having fun laughing at his expense. When I gave him thumbs up, a smile, and a laugh, he really was at his rope's end. So, it was all a misunderstanding. All was well, and a few years later, in 1976, Charlie was on tour with B.T.O.

STEVE ELLIS (SOLO ARTIST):

My life was confusing at one point, and I contacted Roger Daltrey. Roger was the closest to a big brother I had in those days. He said I should come and stay in his new house in Sussex. I packed a bag, grabbed the dog and left Zoot [Money] in charge of the flat. Off I went to see Roger and Heather. I got a taxi, and arrived about an hour later after getting totally lost in the winding lanes and farmland. The bill was £20—a lot of money in those days.

The house Roger had bought was, in fact, the sister house to Rudyard Kipling's and was bloody enormous. He got it from a guy named Perry, an estate agent who was very clued up about property. It was Perry who had found properties for George Harrison, Eric Clapton, and a host of other big names. Perry was the man to speak to regarding country houses, and I had spent a couple of days looking at cottages with him myself. I could have bought one in Berkshire for £2000. Times change.

Roger's house was actually a mansion in a state of neglect, but nothing that could not be fixed. Consequently, I spent most of the time helping Roger sort it out. This was both fun and very therapeutic after four years of complete pandemonium. It was a blessed relief to just do normal things and have no pressure put on me. The local country folk and farmers thought we were a bit of a novelty, and as we were of similar height and build, they named us "The Terrible Twins." Roger, who was, as I have said, as close as the brother I did not have, let me get on with things. I had my own room and the run of the place. He and Heather were very good to me indeed.

At the bottom of a rolling hillside behind the house were two massive lakes. We mucked about in an old boat we found. Roger loved fishing, and this turned out to be his passion. It probably kept his sanity all through the Who years. There were many board meetings at the house, and on those occasions, the Who entourage would all sit at a big long table in the dining room and discuss their agenda. I sat in on many of these and became a trusted member of the band family. This was the period when the band had released their greatest album *Who's Next*. I was lucky enough to see this glorious band in its prime. I used to go to gigs with Roger and lost count of the amount of times I saw them during this period. They were undoubtedly the best live band of the early '70s. Townshend was in supreme form, as both writer and guitarist. Keith Moon was a one-man army behind his enormous drum kit. John Entwistle stood stoically playing superb bass, and Roger turned in his very best performances, in my opinion.

En route to some concerts, Roger took his Corvette Stingray, an American classic. It was a left-hand drive. He took pleasure in accelerating out into the approaching oncoming lorries, as I sat on the right-hand side. At first I thought I was going to die, but it was a wind-up, and he would pull back into the lane effortlessly and laughing. On one occasion, he took Keith for a ride in the Corvette. Keith had bought a plastic steering wheel with a suction base and stuck it to the windscreen. Roger dropped back in his seat, and unsuspecting motorists thought they saw Keith Moon driving some futuristic car.

One day Roger and I went up to Sheffield for a Who gig. Love Affair and I had played with the Who, and the concert ended with me singing "Magic Bus" with Pete Townshend, Roger, the rest of the Love Affair, and Keith on drums and percussion. Roger invited me center stage, but Pete shot a look at Bob Pridden, their soundman, and the mic was turned off. I'll never know why. I asked Pridden afterwards, but he was evasive. Of all the road crew, he was the only one who, for reasons unknown, disliked me and apparently rubbishes me to this very day.

As Roger and I walked into the dressing room, the atmosphere was uncomfortable. We said hello to the crew—Cyragno, Wiggy, Keith, Dougall, and everyone else. They were all part of the well-oiled machine of the band and had been with the band from the beginning. They were far more than mere employees. From Shepherd's Bush to Woodstock, they had put their energies into furthering the Who legend, and they deserved much respect.

Apparently Pete was in a bad mood. As I walked to the toilet, Townshend snarled at me, "Why don't you stop moping around and get a band together?" As I rounded on him, Roger shouted, "Leave it, Steve." So I walked on. When I came back in, there was silence. Apparently Roger was fuming about what had happened, and had chinned Pete in my absence. I would not pretend that I knew Pete Townshend in all the years I had known Roger. I don't think I ever had a conversation with him that entailed much more than the usual exchange of pleasantries when we bumped into each other. I respected Townshend immensely, but frankly, I found him to be more than a little condescending towards me and I could not be bothered with his moods. I was not in awe of this man, but he was seriously talented. That is a fact of life.

HERO WORSHIP

John Lennon liked to recount that while the Beatles were visiting Elvis for the first time, the topic of "The King's" movies came up. Lennon said that when he asked if Elvis were preparing new ideas for his next movie, Elvis replied in his best Southern accent, "I sure am. I play a country boy with a guitar who meets a few gals along the way, and I sing a few songs." The Beatles looked at one another, and Presley and Colonel Parker started to laugh. Then they told Lennon that the only time they deviated from that formula, for the film Wild in the Country, *they lost money.*

Meeting your hero is an event you'll always remember. (I remember meeting Gene Pitney backstage at a taping of the *Mac Davis Show* when I was a kid. I had all of Pitney's records and just thought he was the greatest thing going. There was so much I wanted to tell him about how important his music was to me. I got the chance. I looked up into his eyes, shook his hand and said, "I think you're neat." He muttered something like, "Thanks," and I shuffled back to my seat, totally humiliated.)

Musicians are used to being fawned over by fans, so it's no big deal to them when someone comes off as a little awed by their presence. When musicians meet other musicians though, they are hopeful that they won't act like a doofus and when they remember the chance encounter down the road it will be without embarrassment. Sometimes something humiliating, at least to the person involved, will happen, but most often the encounters leave a positive lasting impression.

JANIS IAN (SOLO ARTIST):

At eleven years old, I fell in love with Joan Baez. Hungry for healthy, independent female artists to pattern myself after, I stumbled upon Joan—a woman who was also a leader, who could be articulate and funny, who marched bravely next to Martin Luther King. So what if she didn't seem gay? I didn't need her to be gay. I just needed her to be available for my beach parties.

I learned guitar by slowing down Joan's records. I set my curly hair (too unpredictable and free) in huge rollers, hoping it would fall languorously around my shoulders. I longed to be like her. I longed to be with her. In the life of the tragically un-hip, Baez was the epitome of cool.

Some years passed, and I attended the Newport Folk Festival as a sixteen-year-old "wunderkind." I was in the throes of teenage angst, dressed completely in black and terrified to speak with anyone. My early success with "Society's Child" had offended many of the performers there, who resented my youth and the apparent ease of my rise to fame. When I entered the dining room for the first time, everyone in it turned their backs on me, effectively freezing me out. For someone who had always dreamed of being "cool," I was being shunned publicly by those I admired most.

Then Joan spied me, and flew across the crowded room. She introduced herself and led me back to her family's table, where she rescued me from abject humiliation. And though she doesn't even remember it today, she gave me "The Queen's Stamp of Approval," making me loyal to her for life.

ERIC BARAO (THE CAUTIONS):

It's hard to think of myself as a Cars fan. The word "fan" seems to either belittle the enormous impact of the band's music on my life and musical career, or evokes the image of a creepy, obsessed loner trying to fill some emotional void by worshiping a celebrity. I don't consider myself even close to either end of that spectrum, and until my friends sit me down for an intervention, I'll continue to believe that.

My initiation into the music of The Cars came during recess in the sixth grade (regrettably, I was born too late to be able to have seen The Cars during the early or peak years of their career). I had walked past a large trash barrel and spotted a broken cassette tape at the top of the trash. The tape was all pulled-out like spaghetti and was unlabeled. Most likely, it had jammed in the tape deck of one of the many teens who used the playground as a drinking hangout at night. Curiosity and patience are qualities I had in spades back then, so I rescued the tape and spent at least a good hour winding the tape back into its case. It turned out to be a mix tape of '70s and '80s rock, and my hands-down favorite was "Let the Good Times Roll." Given that it was an unlabeled mix tape, I didn't know who this band was or where they were from. A year later, I would find out.

It was junior high, 1985, when I first found out who the Cars were. I was taking a class in metalworking, and someone had made a tintype caricature of Ric Ocasek. I didn't know who he was at that point, but I was intrigued by the spiky hair, skinny tie, and dark sunglasses. I questioned the student who made it, and

Eric Barao (The Cautions)
Photo by Eric Johnson

he told me it was Ric Ocasek of the Cars. He then proceeded to list out their hit songs, until he came to my beloved "Let the Good Times Roll."

As memory serves, it was that evening that I made my mom drive me to the record store so I could buy the Cars' first album. Song after song, each one seemed better than the one before it, and by the end of the record, I hadn't found one song not worthy of continuous listening. I bought every Cars record I could find after that, as quickly as I could get the cash.

A bit about why the Cars' music had such an immediate and lasting impact on me: As a lyricist, Ric's collage of beat poetry, fast-paced fragmented imagery, and sublime metaphors were far more meaningful to me than most other pop music pabulum and rock 'n' roll egotism of the period. I didn't want to be told how to "Walk This Way," I wanted to learn how to say "Bye Bye Love." As a teenager learning fast about love and heartbreak, I would slowly uncover new meanings and gain greater insight into the Cars' lyrics. They were puzzles that I could only work out through experience and empirical knowledge. No matter what romantic tragedies happened to me in those days, I would invariably find that there was an Ocasek lyric to help me through it, one that I had never known was there, waiting patiently for me to catch up.

Musically, I was transfixed by Greg Hawkes' synthesizer sounds, both melodic and space-age, and Ric's robotic, hypnotic, muted rhythm guitar mixed with Elliot's melodic lead guitar hooks, which when all mixed together, created a simultaneously cold and beautiful sound. The earlier albums were sparsely but masterfully arranged, and worked equally well as the soundtrack for a day at the beach or a night out in the city, anywhere a car could take you.

Sadly, I wasn't old enough to attend an arena concert until their "Door to Door" tour, which marked the end of their career together. My mom took me to the show at The Providence Civic Center, along with my junior-high-school sweetheart. After the show, I made them wait with me at the back of the arena for about an hour just to watch them get into their limos and drive off. I remember shouting things at them like, "Wooooo! We love you," and God knows what else.

The Cars' music was the beginning of my lifelong fascination and study of pop music. Soon after hearing their music, I knew I would devote the rest of my life to the craft of songwriting. The first impact they had on me in this direction was to influence me to *NOT* give up on my weekly piano lessons. I ended up taking twelve years of lessons before going on to Berklee College of Music to major in songwriting. I'm sure my parents would thank the Cars for that. While at Berklee,

I would use any opportunity I could find to bring the Cars into the classroom. If we had an analysis project for a songwriting class, I would invariably bring in a Cars song, every time. I tortured my instructors with them. In my spare time, I would transcribe entire Cars albums into musical notation, just for fun. Currently, I'm writing and playing with my band, the Cautions, a very Cars-inspired project, and we're hoping to get our next album to Ric Ocasek so he can hear the product of his years of inspiration.

The day I met Ric Ocasek was about 1996 or so. I was shopping in a computer store in Cambridge, Massachusetts, when I noticed the stitching on the pockets of the leather jacket on the tall guy in front of me. It was one of Ric Ocasek's trademark custom-tailored jackets. I recognized it immediately. I looked up and realized that it was more than just the jacket, it was Ric. I froze, too dazed to know what to do, so I patiently waited for him to finish his transaction with the store employee, and then engaged him in conversation. Of course, I didn't know what to say. I listened as he gave me updates on his upcoming solo album and his move to a new record label. I remember telling him that I thought "Time Bomb"(an obscure song from his first solo record *Beatitude*) was one of his finest works. I curiously left out the fact that I went to and graduated from Berklee College of Music because of him and his music, my own Cars-inspired band the Cautions, and everything else that mattered to me.

I eventually came to own Ric's living room furniture set. I was shopping in a now-defunct vintage shop in Boston. I found this great black suit with tiny white polka dots. I inquired about it, and learned that Ric Ocasek's ex-wife had put it on consignment there, along with Polaroids of his living room furniture, which was also up for sale. The store gave me her number, and I called her and arranged to buy the eccentric *Miami Vice*—era furniture: two custom-designed couches and an end table, made from fabric, mirrors, glass, black-lacquered wood, and internal lights. She was very polite and patient with me, answering a few Cars questions I had and such. She even said that she hoped the couch would bring me some inspiration. It did.

I've written many songs sitting there with my guitar.

SCREAMIN' SCOTT SIMON (SHA NA NA):

On the original 45 rpm releases on Sun Records, the name of the artist on such classic records as "Whole Lotta Shakin' Goin' On" and "Great Balls of Fire" is

"Jerry Lee Lewis and his Pumping Piano." The piano gets cobilling with the singer. The boogie-woogie, whorehouse piano style of Jerry Lee is a major character, too, in the Nick Tosches biography of Lewis that was made into the feature film—*Great Balls of Fire*—starring my next-door neighbor at the time, Dennis Quaid. With Wynona Rider playing his teenage bride, Quaid's characterization of the young Jerry Lee is as close as most people have gotten to a vision of this Louisiana wildman.

My own relationship with Jerry Lee began when I was first learning to play the piano in Kansas City. While avoiding practicing my little Haydn pieces, I listened instead to the sounds of Ray Charles playing "What'd I Say," Little Richard's "Slippin' and Slidin'," Fats Domino's "Blueberry Hill," and "Whole Lotta Shakin'" by Jerry Lee Lewis.

Fast-forward to joining Sha Na Na and casting for songs that I could perform as a piano player. The group's basic orientation was doo-wop songs recorded by one-hit wonders ("Book of Love" by the Monotones, "Blue Moon" by the Marcels). The visual recreation of these songs did not involve celebrity impersonations of these non-celebrities. Even when a well-known artist was represented, like Dion for "Teenager in Love," the key moment was for everyone to freeze with their eyes toward heaven to ask the eternal question, "Why must I be a teenager in love?" It was never a matter of Chico, who inherited the song from Bruno, who *inherited* the song from my piano-predecessor Joe Witkin, doing Dion. There were personality songs like Jocko's Big Bopper–inspired "Chantilly Lace," and Scott Powell's "Elvis in Gold Lamé," which we stopped doing after Elvis died. But Sha Na Na was fundamentally about fairly anonymous-looking greasers performing choreographed '50s and '60s classics, not Legends in Concert with look- and sound-alike renditions of Nat Cole or Bobby Darin material.

My strongest Sha Na Na audition song was "Whole Lotta Shakin," which I had been singing with the Royal Pythons. It showcases rock 'n' roll piano playing, has an exciting vocal, and in the opinion of John Lennon, was the greatest rock 'n' roll record of all time. I can't disagree. I've been performing this tune for virtually every show for the past thirty years, and have been wearing white patent leather shoes for that entire time as well. The white shit-kickin' piano player image is one that I present on stage, and the source for that look and sound is definitely Jerry Lee.

With the popularity of the television show, I knew in my *heart* that Jerry Lee himself would eventually get wind of this guy who was "doing" him in the Sha Na

Na group. Sometime during our second season on the air, the man himself was playing one of his infrequent shows at the Palomino Club in North Hollywood. I knew it was time to go and present myself to Jerry Lee, never having met him, and face whatever music there was to face about my using his look and sound with the "greasers" of Sha Na Na.

Between his early and late show at the "Pal," Lewis would retreat to a motor home in the back parking lot of the club. For a star of his magnitude and temperament, the dressing room area would not have adequately protected Jerry from his fans, and vice versa. During the first show, I had gotten word to his young wife, Garen (who one year later met an untimely demise), that I would like to get together with him, and when he came off stage after the early show, she found me and said to give him a couple of minutes, and then come back to the trailer. Jerry wanted to meet me.

I gave as little thought as possible to that last statement, waited a seemly amount of time, and went out past security (Garen had given them the word that I was okay) and knocked on the door. She welcomed me into the kitchen/dining area of the small motor home, where Jerry Lee was sitting in a subdued mood on one side of the bench seats that flanked a dining table. He wore a towel around his neck and had some serious bifocals on his face. He looked up after a moment, and said, "Do you want a beer, brother?" I said sure, and he had Garen get me one from the small fridge. He said he wasn't drinking hard, but that I should go ahead, and I toasted him with the neck of the beer bottle. Conserving his energy, he started in on why couldn't his agent get him onto our TV show as a guest, that it would be a good show for him to be on. I said we'd sure love to have him. He even joked about how I could play all those notes on my shirt and the sound kept coming out of the piano. Then he began talking about his new wife, how she'd been good for him, and then about his children in a somewhat disjointed way. I mostly sat drinking my beer and feeling that even though he seemed at low ebb, he was making an effort to be hospitable. Garen didn't have much to say although she was sitting right there, and I frankly didn't add much. There were times when it just got quiet, and that was okay, too. I finished my beer and thanked him for the time, and said that I hoped we would meet again down the road. He said, "Take it easy, killer," and returned to his silence. I came out of the trailer to find Link Wray sitting on a little bench, waiting for an audience with the Killer.

We did meet again down the road, about ten years later. He and Fats Domino were booked to do a co-bill at the North Shore Theater in the Round in Beverly, Massachusetts. Fats had long-term health problems, including a lack of desire to ever leave New Orleans. If he had a disinclination to travel, he had a ready-made letter from his doctor saying he had to cancel for medical reasons. A week before this particular show, he cancelled. We were in the general area and could fit the show into our routing without too much trouble, and for the first time were going to work co-billed with Mr. Jerry Lee Lewis.

The I.R.S. was spending much time and energy making an example out of Mr. Lewis around this period. The only way Jerry Lee would see *any* of the money he was making was if his manager would arrive earlier in the day and take a check made out to a third party and FedEx that off to a bank in Tennessee. Then when the I.R.S. came to attach Jerry's earnings, they would be too late to catch the cat that was already out of the bag. As we were setting up, we heard about this dodge that had clearly been played out.

MARTY JOURARD (THE MOTELS):

I've heard many stories about people who hope to someday meet one of their musical heroes and are disappointed when the big moment finally arrives. This story isn't one of them.

It was the summer of 1986 in Encino, California. The Motels were between albums. James Brown was in Los Angeles on a publicity tour, meeting people in the entertainment biz. Luckily, James' publicist thought it would be cool for Martha Davis and James to meet. When Martha excitedly called me one morning to say she was going to meet James Brown for lunch, I immediately offered to pick her up and drive her there. Just to be helpful, of course.

The rendezvous was a popular Ventura Boulevard cafe called, yep, Le Cafe. Back in the mid-'80s, "Le" was quite a popular prefix: Le Car, Le Freak, et al. Porsches, croissants, and big hair were the order of the day. Floating through the lunch-hour air were comments such as "Kiss! Kiss!" "Babe!" and "Call me!" (Q: How do you say, "Fuck you" in L.A.? A: "Call me!") After valet-parking my '66 Dodge station wagon, we entered the restaurant and were seated. I removed my Vuarnet sunglasses, hung them on the gold chain around my neck, ordered a Kir, leaned back in my chair, and tried to relax.

We were nervously chatting amongst ourselves at the table when suddenly the entire restaurant became silent and everyone's head turned toward the door.

Marty Jourard, James Brown, Dan Fritz, Martha Davis
From the photo collection of Marty Jourard

Enter James Brown, in full-length fur coat, aviator shades, dark green silk shirt, glossy hair, and a million-dollar smile. He had the whitest teeth I've ever seen. Accompanying him were a few management people and an L.A. publicist named Norm Winters.

James Brown was small, but stocky—built like a boxer. He was charismatic, extremely charming, very much "there," and he kept people laughing almost like a stand-up comic. When he smiled, you felt good. He knew how to lead a conversation, but it was almost impossible to understand what he said, and for three reasons: 1) He was very much from the South. 2) He spoke very quickly, in machine-gun-like bursts and with his trademark raspy voice. 3) He was James Brown and his thought processes were, well, unique. He would start on a subject, branch off into seemingly unrelated topics, and then veer back to the original thought at the last moment. It was strangely fascinating. We smiled and nodded. Publicist Norm Winters made two memorable comments: "James, I'm gonna

have your name on everyone's lips in this town if I have to print it on toothpicks!"
And (many times, to his assistant): "What did he say? What did he say?" Frankly,
it didn't matter what James Brown said. It was great just to be there.

We ordered lunch and I mentioned to "Mr. Dynamite" that my Emulator sampling keyboard came equipped with various James Brown grunts, screams, "Give
it up-ah!" and horn splats stolen directly from his classic recordings. He'd never
heard of this popular group of digital samples, but seemed more amused than
upset. I asked him what he did in his spare time. He told me he would sometimes
drive his van out into a field in his property in Macon, drink a little wine, and
then lay on the grass looking up at the sky.

A publicity photo was taken of Martha Davis and me with James, who looks
exactly like you figure he would look—smiling, self-contained, confident, very
showbiz.

At some point, he decided it was time to go. James made some comment to the
group that made everyone laugh, and at the EXACT moment we all began laughing, he smiled, stood up, put on his fur coat, made a little bow, turned, and
walked out, followed hastily by his entourage. The man's timing was flawless.

YOU SHOW ME YOURS AND I'LL SHOW YOU MINE

*In an episode titled "Cowboy George," Boy George appeared as a
character in the animated series* The A-Team. *Boy earned megabucks for uttering lines of encouragement to Mr. T and friends.*

In the movie *Rock Star,* the main character, played by Mark Wahlberg, gets the
opportunity to replace his hero as the singer in his all-time favorite band.
Though that actually has happened—think metal—it's not something that often
just pops up. But just getting the opportunity to play with a musical legend in his
or her band is something not only unique, but also immensely rewarding. The
fame by association that takes place is tremendously cool, and can often be the
start of a career—think of Duane Allman playing with Eric Clapton as one of
Clapton's Dominos on "Layla," or Poco's Timothy B. Schmidt playing with the
Eagles. Does Tom Petty as one of the Traveling Wilburys, along with George
Harrison, Bob Dylan, and Roy Orbison, count? Maybe not, but what a thrill for
Petty. Just spending time with a musical legend is a memorable moment in and

of itself, but when musicians can walk away with something more, it's a tremendous boon to their careers.

Sometimes, though, when musicians get together socially it's about the fun. But even then, there are sometimes bonuses. It probably never crosses the minds of lesser-known musicians that the person they might be trying to impress might actually be impressed by something *they* do or say.

DAN PEAK (AMERICA):

Hollywood never looked better. The success of *Holiday,* hailed as our comeback (hard to imagine we'd been gone), lent a rosy glow to everything. "Tin Man," the first single, climbed sure-footedly to the top of the charts, topping even the soul chart, interestingly. George Martin's contributions did not go unnoticed by the press, and though our intent was to avail ourselves solely of his musical abilities, it certainly paid off handsomely in the PR department to have hitched our wagon to his ever-burgeoning star.

Concurrently with *Holiday,* George had also been producing guitar virtuoso Jeff Beck. This pairing produced two award-winning albums and made for interesting chat in the studio during breaks.

Jeff stretched George musically, and vice versa. A lifelong fan of Beck, I loved trying to get a personal analysis of him from George, but ever the gentleman, George kept the details to a minimum. He did give high praise to Jann Hammer, Beck's keyboardist. Hammer, of course, went on to write and produce the groundbreaking soundtrack to *Miami Vice.*

It seemed like half of London's musical luminaries had taken refuge in L.A. "Brain drain" resulted in not only more "brain," but more "partayin'" with the likes of Harry Nilsson, Ringo, John, Paul, George, and Derek Taylor. Harry, an American, became an Edwardian caricature of himself. Oh, the wild exploits! Being married put a certain braking effect on all this partying for me, but just barely.

Paul would come to town and throw a party for his closest five hundred friends. Paul had style, panache, elegance, good taste, and lovely Linda always at his side. One year the venue was the Queen Mary, the next, the Harold Lloyd Estate. The Harold Lloyd Estate, saved from the wrecking ball at the eleventh hour, was a seventeen-acre estate nestled into the hills of Beverly. Built by one of the earliest superstars, an eerie reflection of the past was conjured up by the complete refurbishment of the building, complete with Grecian-style gardens and architectural adornments. All the dollying up was underwritten by Paul McCartney for the party. We guests were asked to wear white—and only white— formal wear. Like a scene from the lodge in *The Shining*, time warped, we were transported to a long-gone era of gentility and civility. A perfect Riviera clime set the scene for five hundred of Hollywood's heavy hitters to hang out on the lawn and rub white dinner jacket sleeves together.

Jack Nicholson and Warren Beatty kept a rapid-fire convo going near the pool, stopping only long enough to flirt with my astonishingly beautiful wife (who won rave reviews from Linda and Paul for her kind housewarming gift).

Frank Zappa stood to the side, and I introduced myself as a fan of his music. The seminal Zappa album with "Peaches in Regalia" is a particular fave of mine, and we chatted amiably. Mr. Zappa was probably one of the most individualistic, avant-garde, musically savvy, culturally challenging players to ever walk the streets of that city.

There was an intensity to these gatherings that overshadowed everything else. Paul brought together the A-list of celebrities and people who most often liked and celebrated the work of their fellow partygoers.

The evening ended with Catherine and I hosting Rod Stewart and Britt Ekland back to our house in the hills. Rod is as gentlemanly and charming a person as one would ever hope to meet in this life. His joie de vivre is contagious. That evening, and late into the next morning, he and I sat and played in my studio. I played "Today's the Day," the song I had been working on. Rod said he liked it, and that it gave him an idea for a song. Of course, after his recording of "Tonight's the Night" came out, I laughed when I remembered what he'd said. I'm sure I probably smacked my forehead and said, "Why didn't I think of that!"

THE KING

On one single day, Elvis bought thirty-two Cadillacs. By afternoon, he had given them all away.

This collection of stories wouldn't be complete without a story or two about rock and roll's king: Elvis Presley. Tales of Elvis sightings aren't as popular among musicians as they might be among those on the periphery of public life, but Elvis stories remain an interesting diversion to those who seek to realize their own rock and roll dream. Elvis was, and always will be, bigger than life. Even to other icons.

DICK DALE ("KING OF THE SURF GUITAR"):

In Hollywood, California, back in the late '60s or so, Elvis was preparing for his big show in Vegas. He was so excited to take me for a ride in his new Stutz Bearcat sport car, but he couldn't get it unlocked. So he put his fist though the passenger window. The glass splattered into a million pieces, all over the passenger seat.

El jumped in and said "D! Let's go!" I jumped in and had to sit on all the millions of pieces of glass, freezing my butt off 'cause there was no more window to roll 'cause El busted it.

Dick Dale
From the photo collection
of Dick Dale

He burned the tires as he drove to the gates, with the Memphis Mafia follow-ing behind us in the Rolls Royce. Every time he hit the gas pedal, I thought my butt was going to look like red, tenderized mincemeat. El kept laughing away, say-ing, "Ohhh, you'll be all right, you'll be all right." I said "Yeah, bullshit. I feel like my hemorrhoids just got cut out."

It was late at night, and El was wearing shades because he was having trouble with his eye. A girl fan had poked him in the eye a while back with her pen because she was so excited to see him. El drove down to Hollywood Boulevard and was doing sixty miles per hour coming up to the stoplight. He screeched on the brakes saying, "Don't this baby just scream? I just love her, man."

I said, "Well someone just loves you, too. Look over here." There was a police squad car pulled up right next to us, and the cop driver looked over and said, "Oh, it's you. You want a manager?" El looked over, nodded at him, and said, "Thank yuh very much," and sped off, leaving them behind.

We went back to his estate with the Memphis Mafia following behind. And of course, I kept feeling for my behind. Great night.

NEAL CASAL (SOLO ARTIST):

I was in a diner in Spartanburg, South Carolina, called the Piedmont Café one late night during the tour behind my first solo record back in '95. After my show at a club across the street, me and the band were the only people in the place. Of course, we noticed the Elvis chair on the wall right away and asked our waitress about it. She had worked at the diner for over thirty years and was happy to give us the story.

In 1955, on one of Elvis' first tours, he passed through Spartanburg and played a couple of shows. This was before he was really well known and was still quite shocking to most people. Well, I guess the audiences didn't like Elvis and his band very much, and let him know it—loudly. They booed and threw things, and completely ruined his shows there.

Elvis stopped into the Piedmont after the second show (just like we were doing forty years later) for a quick meal before getting out of town. He politely told the waitress that he had a terrible time in Spartanburg and that, no offense ma'am, he would never come back. And, as our waitress told us, "He never did."

Well, it wouldn't be too long before Elvis became the "King," and the folks at the Piedmont proudly hoisted the famous chair into its present lofty position,

Piedmont Café, Spartanburg, South
Carolina, Elvis' chair
Photo by Neal Casal

complete with its very own sign. We looked closely, and couldn't help but notice that his name had been misspelled. We thought about it, but didn't have the heart to tell the waitress. In fact, it made the story a little bit funnier and a whole lot sweeter. I couldn't leave without snapping a picture.

GRIEVOUS ANGEL

Gram Parsons liked to tell the story about the night that two girls drove their convertible into a wall of The Prelude, a club on Lankershim Boulevard in North Hollywood. As people screamed and the car fumed, the two chicks remained in the car and smoked a cigarette. Not willing to risk having the public think there might be an interruption in his money making endeavor, the club owner looked at the damage to his building and loudly announced, "Business as usual tomorrow night!"

Gram Parson was one of a kind. He is generally acknowledged as being the musician who melded together two distinct forms of music and created the rock and roll subgenre known as "country rock." Parsons left behind a legacy of unique and sometimes thrilling performances, but is probably better known for his trendsetting style and hedonistic life. Perhaps he enjoyed the excesses of the rock musician's world a little too much, but Gram Parsons would exit the world recognized as unique an individual as rock has ever known.

RUSTY YOUNG (POCO):

This happened in the fall of 1967. Richie Furay had been roommates with Gram Parsons in New York during the folk era of the '60s. Gram came to rehearsals when we were putting Poco together. We thought maybe he would fit into what we were doing—a new thing called country rock. But after a few rehearsals, Gram pulled me and Richie aside and said that he couldn't be in the band with Jim Messina. He thought Jimmy would never make it in the biz. Hmmmm. So Gram didn't work out in the band, but we stayed friends.

So, it was a warm summer Sunday afternoon when Richie and I were going to meet Gram at Disneyland to see Buck Owens playing there. Richie didn't know much about Buck, and since we were putting the band sound together, I thought he'd get some ideas from Buck's edgy country sound. We were supposed to meet Gram at the entrance to the park. Well, we waited for a while and then heard a big commotion at the gates. We went over to see what was going on.

Well, there was Gram being held by security. He was raising a fuss! You have to remember this was Disneyland in 1968. They were a little more uptight than they might be today. They weren't going to let him into the park wearing a dog collar, sandals, and a full-length white dress. Mickey didn't approve! Gram was shouting that he was friends with Buck, but they didn't believe him. It was a *Three Stooges* scene. It ended when Buck's manager came down and rescued Gram.

When Gram finally went through the gates, Richie and I walked with him down Main Street. People stopped dead in their tracks to look at him. I remember him turning to me and saying, "Just wait. Pretty soon everyone will be dressing like this!"

Many years later, I got a chance to talk to Buck about that afternoon. He remembered, and told me that it was one of Johnny Cash's favorite stories. Funny, I don't remember Cash there. But that's how stories live on.

YOU HAD TO BE THERE

In 2001, an *NSYNC fan threatened suit against Justin Timberlake for "intentional infliction of emotional distress." According to the fan, when the band passed by her in a hotel lobby, all the band members acknowledged her except Timberlake. The fan blurted that she liked J. C. Chasez better, proclaiming, "He's cuter." The rejected lady was summoned up to the band's suite later by a security guard. She alleged that Timberlake backed her against a wall and gave her a piece of his mind.

Encounters with superstars can be much different than what one might expect, for fans and other musicians alike. Usually, when rockers cross paths with someone who might like to get to know them better, they will either acknowledge the person or completely ignore them. It's the encounters that fall in between those two extremes that can be noteworthy.

GOLDY MCJOHN (STEPPENWOLF):

I was at a party at some actor's house in the Hollywood Hills in 1974. It was a huge place, and there were a lot of celebrities there. You name them and they were there, from basketball players to everyone else. Al Kooper was sitting about ten feet away from me.

I kept making a move to sit beside Mick [Jagger] and strike up a conversation with him because it's Mick! What do you say to Mick? First of all, you have to get his attention. I finally got in the position by sitting beside him. I tried to introduce myself to him. I was like, "Do you want my green card number? We're Steppenwolf. Have you ever heard of us?" He used to come in to hear us in 1966 in Greenwich Village. He told us how great he thought we were then.

Mick kept sort of moving over and giving me that look like, "What kind of shit are you again?" I'm sitting there just starting to froth. I was starting to get biker attitude. I finally said to the guy in his ear, "When are you going to give J. K. [John Kay] some swimming lessons?" No response. Not a fucking thing. I said, "It's a real drag what you and Keith did to Brian." He got up and goes to throw his plate of food at me.

Al Kooper says to me, "I don't know what you said to him, but you got his

Goldy McJohn in the '60s (Steppenwolf)
From the photo collection of Goldy McJohn

goat. Right on." I said, "Yeah, I guess. Let's blow this pop stand because he is acting like a fag. Fuck him." So Al Kooper and his girlfriend jump in the car with me and my girlfriend, and we go to Al's hotel room. I don't think another thing of it.

I heard later that I made a really nasty remark to Mick Jagger. I spent a month in my own limo and nobody would talk to me. All of a sudden there was the article in *Rolling Stone* magazine where it said, "Even if they had been friends, it still wouldn't have been funny." How did that get there, unless Mick told someone else, unless he told somebody what an asshole he had met? They took the word of Mick Jagger over the word of some asshole with an Afro and a biker attitude.

CHAPTER 7

BEGINNINGS, INSPIRATIONS, AND REFLECTIONS

Every story has a beginning, and the various stories of how bands and musicians begin their careers are numerous and varied. Establishing a career is not always as simple as starting up a band in your mom and dad's garage and practicing until you have a recording contract, although that has been known to happen. There are dues to be paid, and most of those who succeed in the music business have paid them—big time.

After they have enjoyed some success, a time comes when musicians reflect on the beginning of their careers, and on who was there along the way to encourage and inspire them, or maybe on a particular event that laid the groundwork for a band's philosophy or direction. The early years in a musician's career aren't just for practicing. They're also for observing, listening, and learning.

DONNA FROST (SOLO ARTIST):

I first met Carl Perkins back in 1978. My uncle, Felton Jarvis, was producing an album on Carl entitled *Ol' Blue Suede's Back,* which did end up out on Jet Records, I believe. Uncle Felton was Elvis' record producer from the mid-'60s until Elvis died. Carl and Uncle Felton had so much fun doing that album! They even said they sensed the spirit of Elvis in the studio on more than one occasion.

Carl stayed with my Uncle Felton and Aunt Mary while he was recording. I would go over to hang out and hear Carl's stories (especially about when he met the Beatles) and get him to play for me. I wanted to know how he wrote all those

Donna Frost
From the photo collection of Donna Frost

great songs and how to play them! I was twenty-one and eager to learn from the master. Imagine my reaction when he then asked ME to play for HIM! I about fainted. I played and sang some songs for him, and he looked at my uncle and said, "She's going to be a star someday."

I was floating for weeks after that. It meant so much to me. And all these years later, I'm not a big star yet, but I am a touring indie artist and have never given up my dream.

As the years went by, I'd go see Carl at shows in Nashville. My uncle had passed away a couple of years after they did the album. He always played "Blue Suede Shoes" for me. The last time I saw Carl was the year before he died. He and his lovely and sweet wife Val were in town for the Beatle Fest.

My brother Tony, his wife Dawn, and I went to visit Carl and Val and hang out for a while up at their hotel room. It was a very special day! We were talking about so many things, and remembering my Aunt Mary and Uncle Felton (Mary had passed away the previous year). I took Carl a tape of some new songs I had written and recorded. He invited me to come down to Jackson and go fishing with him and do some writing. I said that would be great! We never got to do that. Not long after, he went out on tour to promote his new album and I was touring around. Then he became ill, and passed away. I regret we never got to have that fishing trip and writing session. But I will never forget the kindness and encouragement he showed me.

BOBBY WHITLOCK (LEGENDARY KEYBOARD PLAYER)[1]:

I guess it's a natural thing to say that when you've had a life like mine, especially my early childhood, "I was born to play the blues." It's the way that I was raised. Hard physical work was expected to be done by a child to help make money to help support our family. If that meant bending over in the fields, doing backbreaking work like the other adults, then it was understood that this was my way of contributing. I'm talking about *real* little, like a little bitty boy. Not even eight years old; much smaller. I chopped and picked cotton until my fingers were stiff and sore. Cotton's nasty stuff. It can make your skin dry up and bleed if you handle too much of it. I rode the back of bean planters in the countryside out there in Arkansas. The sun would be beating down, the air would be hot and dusty and our throats were parched, but we had to work. There wasn't much else to do and we had to pitch in and help. I hauled all kinds of produce.

Did you ever hear the phrase "a shotgun house?" Well, we lived in one, down there in Marmaduke, Arkansas. That meant you could fire a shotgun from one side and there wasn't anything like a wall or any other rooms to stop the pellets or buckshot from going anywhere but straight out the door. It was kinda like a three-room, one-house deal. It was also known as a high-water house because it was sort of built on stilts to keep it dry when the high water rose. You could literally read last year's news through the cracks in the walls, because that was the insulation in this house. Sometimes, it was necessary to scare off—or worse—anything or anyone on two or four legs that might be trying to break into the place. Yes, we knew we were poor. I could tell that by having to sleep head-to-toe in a bed with my grandfather, "Peapaw" Whitlock. For heat, all we had was a pot-

---

[1] This story comes from an interview of Bobby Whitlock by journalist Mitch Lopate (first published in this book with the permission of both parties).

bellied stove, and food . . . well, I remember one time when a rat ate through a loaf of bread that we had saved. It looked like a train had gone through a tunnel from one end to another.

My daddy was a preacher and what you'd call a "professional student." He felt that this would take the mischief out of me, as well as teach me discipline that was necessary to be a son of a man of the gospel. I took my share of beatings, too—tied up by the wrists and whipped because I wasn't acting serious-like during church services. I'm talking about this happening to me as a young fella of eleven years—not a child any more, either! He took me out back to the barn and trussed me up and used the leader-line of a mule team on me. I'm talking about a seriously thick piece of leather! He kind of had what they call a "Napoleon complex." I didn't know he wasn't six feet tall until I grew bigger than he did. My daddy would drag my mother and me and my sister and brother—they were too young to work—all over, looking for some place to work while he did his preaching. I can still see pictures in my mind of her in a homemade dress and high heels, standing over a hot wood stove and cooking on a Sunday. My mother and I had to go work in the fields to feed ourselves because my father would come home for two days and be gone again.

On Sundays and Wednesdays, folks would take the preacher's family into their house and show their hospitality that way. I remember one family—the Turberville's—whom I thought was rich because Mr. Ross Turberville had two mules and a tractor.

You would have to meet my kind of kinfolk to understand them. They just did things their own way and nobody had better interfere—what we called "rounders." They would as soon as fight, steal, make moonshine or just get into plain mischief. Just imagine how a raccoon would act if they were part human. It just had to rub off on me, growing up with people like this. I can remember Peapaw Whitlock living with us, whittling and then *spitting* on that stove, and drinking boiling coffee. I never would have believed it in my life, but it was that hot. He also did something that I learned about when I was on the road as a musician: Peapaw would smoke regular tobacco—Bull Durham was his brand—during the day, but at night, then he'd take something else from another pocket and light up that. When I first smoked marijuana, I knew what it was! I said to myself, "That old sonovabitch, he was smoking pot!" Of course, it was during the '30s and '40s, and people's attitudes were different, and so was the practice of indulging in those kinds of things. Especially for us folks who lived back in the hills and hollows. It was more understood as a way of combining medicine with driving out the pain of making ends meet and getting through the harshness of living.

For example, there was Aunt Berthie and Uncle Elvin—they were my kin from Marked Tree, Arkansas. Aunt Berthie was a great big woman, with hair down to the ground, and Uncle Elvin was my Peapaw (grandfather) King's brother. Well, you sure can say they were a little bit odd: in their home, they had pigs in the bedroom and chickens roosting on the head of the bed. They ran a store there, a kind of general store where you could buy all kinds of goods. I can see those wooden sidewalks in my mind. But the point is, the government wouldn't let them sell anything out of that store unless it had a lid on it or a wrapper. I would have been hard pressed and double-dealt to buy *anything* from them, but they were kinfolk.

Well, it wasn't too long before Aunt Berthie went into an institution for the mentally handicapped. One day, Uncle Elvin called Peapaw King and said, "Hey, one of Berthie's relatives has died. We gotta take her to the funeral." They had a pickup truck with a chair in the back of it—it was something straight out of *The Beverly Hillbillies.* So, they took her out of the side door, which was quite a feat for a woman of her size, and put her up in that chair. Then they took off, doing about forty-five miles an hour down a bumpy gravel road with Berthie perched up there, and rocks zinging from under the tires and smoke flying in the air. Peapaw said, "I felt the truck hit a bump and looked up and everything got real springy under the wheels, as though we had just shucked ourselves of some extra weight." Both men looked in the rearview mirror, and saw Berthie tumbling end-over-end in the gravel behind them. Uncle Elvin said, "Doggone, she's gone and dove out of the back of the truck!" So, both men went and picked her up, dusted her off and put her back in the chair, turned around and drove all the way back to the institution. They hauled her out of the chair, dusted her off, and backed the truck up to the side door. Then they went to the front desk and declared, "She ain't quite ready yet!"

Like I said, growing up with these folk can leave a lasting imprint on a young boy's mind—and I was an impressionable child. Being poor was a way of life that was just something that we accepted, so the petty criminal activities in which the family participated was just considered another way to make ends meet. It was a way to survive! Let me give you another example of how they survived: they were "miners." Oh, no, there was no prospecting for gold or other precious minerals—

that was too much hard work for nothing. Their theory was simple: what was once yours is now *mine.*

One time, Peapaw and Uncle Elvin—this must go back about fifty-five years or so—were out on an "excavating" mission in Mississippi, riding around in an old beat-up car. They were gonna dig up *something* somewhere, but they just weren't sure what it would be. Then they came upon a farmhouse and went out and stole this farmer's chickens—chicken coop and all! They opened up the back of this old car and put the whole thing in there—chickens and coop and all—and drove away in the dead of night.

Well, sure enough, just like Aunt Berthie and the truck, the chicken coop *and* the chickens fell out of the back of the car, and there were chickens running around loose all over the place. My grandpa, Peapaw King, went back to the farmer's house—the guy from whom they'd just stolen the chickens and the chicken coop! And knocked on the door. "Could you give us a hand out here?" he asked, "we got ourselves a problem with all these chickens!" The farmer followed him back to the car, helped them round up all those loose birds and tie up the chicken coop, and put it in the back of the car again!

They started up the car and began to drive away—but that's not the King family way of doing things, so they stopped and thought a minute. As a token of their appreciation, they backed the car up alongside the farmer, who was still standing on the side of the road. Uncle Elvin stepped out and handed the farmer a chicken, which the startled man placed under his arm like a loaf of bread. Sure enough, my grandfather and Uncle Elvin drove off and left the poor farmer standing on the side of the road, scratching his head with one hand, holding a hen in the other, and wondering why two men were out in the dead of night with a trunk full of squawking chickens and a coop that looked a lot like his. To tell the truth, a Pentecostal preacher was holding a revival in Lepanto, Arkansas, and he, Peapaw, and Uncle Elvin were in cahoots with this chicken stealing. After he stole the chickens, Peapaw left a note on the chicken house, "We steal from the rich and give to the poor. We left you six, to raise us some more."

Peapaw King also got himself thrown into the Polk County Farm in Arkansas for stealing a loaf of bread and a quart of milk—don't forget that I'm talking about the times of the Great Depression—and my grandmother, "Big Momma" King, got a job working there in the kitchen. It was like a complete scenario from the Paul Newman movie *Cool Hand Luke:* they bull-whipped him with a cat-o'-nine-tails, and "Big Momma" slipped him some red pepper powder to put in his shoes and helped him break out of there. They had the hounds on his trail real quick-like, but that pepper stuffed them up. I saw those scars on his back from when they whipped him.

On the other side, it was the Whitlock's that were trouble. My Peapaw Whitlock was a moonshiner, and he died because of it. I remember him literally lighting that stuff up—if it had a blue flame, it meant it was real, real good! He was going out on a delivery, but of course, he had to sample it a bit to make sure it was of the proper quality and strength. And he got himself drunk. So, there he was, taking a case of freshly made brew across a newly cut cornfield during the night on what must have been the coldest Thanksgiving Day on record. I mean, it was *nasty* bitter cold, down near New Albany, Mississippi. He was carrying a pint jug with him on the way back—that was to be expected—but he didn't see or *couldn't* see— depending on his condition—where he was going, and he tripped over a corn stalk. The fall didn't kill him; it just knocked the wind out of him for a minute. He turned over on his back in the middle of the rows and just froze to death. The boy who was running the fence on that farm came out the next day to work, and found my grandfather lying there with his arms outstretched to the heavens and a pint of moonshine behind him. Lord knows if he was trying to ask for help to raise himself up or he was trying to reach out first for that lost jug!

The only joy I had was when I would have a few spare moments to hear music at the church, or when I sat with my grandmother, "Big Momma" King, who would play her dobro for me.

Thank heaven for those moments. They were the shining light in my life as a three-year-old boy! It was a beautiful National dobro, made in the late 1880s, and there were hula dancers on the front and back. Big Momma would sit me down and play gospel-style to me, "Turn your radio on, get in touch with Jesus." I can still hear her now! I have that dobro with me. I've gone and had it painted. At one time, a lady named Genya Ravan, who played with 10-Wheel Drive, had it and kept it safe for me. See, it was always with me—the music—it was in my soul and in my spirit. So when I look back at those hard times, I can say I was a singer, and I sang *all* the time! I'd be working out in the fields with the migrant workers and the poor black folk who were sharecroppers, and they'd sing all the way to the fields in the back of rickety, bouncing trucks, and then they'd be singing while they were working, and then on the way back home. I'd be singing right along with them. So, yes, I'd say my roots were always there in gospel, blues, and soul music. I was born living the blues, and I learned to sing them to get through those harsh times!

RANDALL HALL (LYNYRD SKYNYRD/WORLD CLASSIC ROCKERS):

In many interviews and bios, I have said that I started playing guitar after seeing the Jimi Hendrix Experience open for The Monkees two weeks after the infamous Monterey Pop Festival in June 1967 at the Jacksonville Coliseum, Florida. In fact, my first paying gig was the day Jimi died in 1970. I was fortunate to see him headline at the same venue in 1968, when only a year before he was booed and moms covered their kid's eyes.

I performed with the folk singer Melanie in 1979, and she told me about flying with Jimi between New York and the U.K. and what a gentleman he was.

Thanks to my first show performing with Lynyrd Skynyrd in '87, I met Bill Graham, who later managed us. I immediately asked him of his encounters with Jimi, and he told me about the Band of Gypsies at the Fillmore East, where Jimi got in his face.

Jimi Hendrix Experience poster
From the collection of Randall Hall

Again, thanks to being on the road with Lynyrd Skynyrd, I was exposed to many others who had worked with or had personal encounters with Jimi Hendrix. I was fortunate enough to play one of Jimi's guitars, thanks to Al Kooper. I asked Dave Mason how it was recording with Jimi. "Was it good, bad, or indifferent?" He said, "Oh it was definitely different." That was on the *Electric Ladyland* album. Mackenzie Phillips told me that in Memphis as a little girl her father introduced her to Jimi. She said she just remembered a black man, dressed in all purple, and she was a little taken back by all that color. My good friends Nick St. Nicholas and Michael Monarch, formerly of Steppenwolf, had their own encounters with Jimi in the old days.

Although I haven't elaborated on everyone's experience, I am just happy to have rubbed elbows with these people. Especially Bill Graham, who was a great man himself. That brought me that much closer to the MAIN MAN, who inspired me to be the guitarist I am today.

Bill Graham and Randall Hall,
Lynyrd Sknyrd Tribute Tour, 1987
From the photo collection of
Randall Hall

THE ART OF SURVIVAL

While recording in a studio at Montreux, Switzerland, Deep Purple watched the Montreux Casino burn and the smoke from the fire drift across Lake Geneva. This experience inspired the lyrics to "Smoke On the Water." Coincidentally, Frank Zappa and the Mothers of Invention were playing at the Casino at the time of the fire and had to run out without their equipment, which ended up being destroyed.

We have all had life experiences that have been out of the ordinary and that stick in our minds. We sometimes recount some of our more outrageous adventures to our friends, but other events can remain buried in our subconscious minds until they're triggered by something. Often, what's held within the nooks and crannies of a songwriter's memory becomes the basis for a song. Sometimes, things happen in musicians' lives that make them realize they aren't exactly like other people. Perhaps this realization is the nucleus of the idea that leads them to express their eccentricity in music. Musicians—because of their unique creative and artistic abilities—are not like the majority of the population. Because of this, many of their life experiences are unlike most people's, too.

PRAIRIE PRINCE (THE TUBES):

It all started when the only thing to do was watch TV while eating frozen softballs made of wonder bread in a darkly smiling room. It was refrigerated to heavenly degrees, and located next to the newly dug fallout shelter stuffed to the brim with more canned food than the PX at Paris Island and even more Wonder Bread that one could use as insulation in case the air conditioning malfunctioned. I was approaching draft age and watching a lot of war news on TV. I was getting cold sweats thinking about the reality of getting plucked out of art school, locks jarred, dreams of being a hippie or rock star or both shattered by a spray of shrapnel and no helmet to protect my nuts. Jimi Hendrix ruled my world. The year was 1969, and all my friends were in the same boat. We all said, "Hell no, we won't go!" but they wanted us anyway, at least that's what everyone said. The Tubes all originated from Phoenix, Arizona, which was where the local draft board had all of our names registered from high school. And they were not accepting a student deferment, especially if it was signed by an art school official.

Prairie Prince
From the photo collection of Prairie Prince

Some of our group had moved to San Francisco, California, by the fall of 1969, and the rest were still stuck in Phoenix ("Refrigerator Hell" as Alice Cooper coined the phrase.) We had all just gone to the maniacal Altamont scene and were hanging tough with the Peace and Love Theory that the mid-'60s were raging. I was going to the Art Institute on Chestnut Street, one of the oldest and most respected schools in the country, painting images of my musical heroes and glorifying visions of youth and anarchy in smelly oil and turpentine. The birth of The Tubes was bubbling under our TV-saturated brains, and with the threat of going to Vietnam tugging at our earlobes, we all vowed to make it impossible for these military-clad warmongers to take away our right to make art and music. A lot of our friends, who maybe were a little more straight minded than we were and were drafted, had already been killed. Bill Spooner penned a song about a friend whose legs were blown off in a minefield. This song was named "Empty Shoes" and became the Tubes' first protest song. It stands today as one of the most poignant songs about war ever. My best friend Rognald Johnson was killed in a helicopter crash in 1970, and I have found his name on the wall in Washington, D.C. I did a rubbing of his name in the rain.

The call came. I was in the middle of a painting of Jimi Hendrix writhing on a stormy beach, turning into a merman as the world explodes behind him and the saucers come down to take him away. The letter was from the draft board in Phoenix, advising me to report the following week for a physical and induction into the military, as well as immediate transferal overseas to Vietnam. I knew what I had to do. Take a lot of mescaline and get prepared for war. First, drop two tabs of pure mescaline, given to me by one of my teachers. Next, continue working on my painting, avoiding the canvas and applying most of the paint to my clothes and body. Besides oil paints, I was using glitter, which was all over me as well. Stay awake until the said appointment, which was three or four days away. Find many items to distract me from reality during the inquisition, such as irritating toys, a collection of odd photos, burned and tattered, that I eventually ended up folding and unfolding as if possessed. I was.

I flew to Phoenix the night before my call and spent time with the two craziest friends I knew. They prepped me to no end (more on that later). Next: a quick nap on the lawn at dawn, then rudely awakened by a gardener with the power mower covering me with grass clippings. I was ready for inspection. Uh oh, two hours late—shouldn't have taken that nap.

I drug myself into the room for preinduction. Everyone had completed filling out their questionnaires and was listening to some sergeant speaking on the pros of war. I was escorted to the opposite side of the room, away from the thirty or forty gung-ho pig-farmer types, straight backed and glaring in their perfectly aligned desks.

I was a pathetic sight in my Snoopy and the Red Baron bomber helmet, red silk pj's with ballet-type slippers, and a tank top. Completely radiating mescaline-induced acrid sonic waves. Covered with green and orange glitter, purple oil paint, and long stringy hair, matted and greasy. Not to mention the layer of grass cuttings that had dried nicely, giving me a grand patina for supporting the anti-war statement. After failing to fill out the war statement correctly (I marked all the boxes), and maintaining the plea for assistance at all times, I marched into the room for my physical exam. Now as I mentioned, the night before, my dear friends (names withheld to protect the innocents) doctored my lower regions with several appropriate substances that seemed to extremely offend my chief examiner. As I bent over to spread my cheeks as instructed, a gasp and harsh

"What the hell is that?" exclaimed the astonished military physician. I reached between my legs displayed two fingers full of peanut butter, popped them into my mouth, and proudly announced, "Tastes like peanut butter!" Needless to say, I was on report. Next, I fucked up the hearing test, the eye test, the reflex test, the breath test, and then on to the psychiatric test. This guy had heard it all, but to me he looked like he believed the shit I was trying to convince him of. Murdering my mother, fucking my friend's mother while trying to drown myself in my own urine, all of course, untrue. But, I even convinced myself for a moment, I was so wrapped up in the psycho character.

The mescaline come-down definitely helped in the tragic and apathetic bull I was slinging in that induction center that day. I was ushered to the door with not so much as a good-bye. They practically pushed me out. With only a piece of paper that claimed I was now a 4F (unsuitable for military life). Yahoo! I kicked up my heels (I had no heels, I was in ballet shoes), and ran all the way to the airport and back to my beloved San Francisco.

The ironic conclusion to this story is that The Tubes as a rock group, whose members were all transported to San Francisco from Phoenix, gained status in popularity and shortly became local heroes, held in high esteem back in our hometown. By 1976, we had quite a reputation in the U.S.A. and elsewhere as a theatrical band of musicians and artists, who would do just about anything for good or bad publicity. We jumped at an offer by a promoter to return to that same induction center as a special "no war time" promotion for the selective service center as it was now named. The draft had long since been banished. We arrived by helicopters, decked out in glam rock fatigues and mirrored sunglasses with our dancers dressed as military nurses. Our choreographer and head wardrobe/dancer, acting as FBI agents, escorted us into the venue singing and dancing "The Funky Revolution" by James Brown. Fee Waybill, our lead singer, was his FEEdel Castro character and Re Styles portrayed Patty Hearst for the lunchtime crowd of over a thousand fans. The induction center officials posed and smiled for photos with the band, all of who received official 4F notices from military service six years prior. A good time was had by all, and not a word was mentioned about Vietnam or the next war on the horizon.

I would like to bless those who felt in their hearts as we did, but were not so lucky as to escape the war. All those who made it through and those who didn't, we admire you for trying and dying for an unknown cause. Make music, not war. Speak not with guns, say it on the drums.

PAUL GRAY (THE DAMNED):

In February 1980, I got a call from Chiswick Records' Roger Armstrong. The Damned were booked into Wessex Studios to demo new songs, and they wanted me to play bass. It was the first time I'd seen them in eighteen months, and it was a breath of fresh air. The ideas were flowing, the atmosphere was buzzing, and the studio was well stocked with goodies. As well as being grossly underrated as musicians, there was an element with this band that anything could happen. I soon learned that the first rule was: there *were* no rules. They knew they'd got me and dropped a small bombshell: "By the way, Paul. We've got a twenty-date British tour. Starts next week." Two days rehearsal was booked, but singer Dave Vanian never showed, so we spent the time wisely in the pub next door.

The very first gig was recorded for the *Live at Shepperton* album, for Damned fans only. Talk about baptism by fire! When I pointed out that we'd never actually got round to rehearsing, they dismissed it with an airy, "Don't worry, we can tart it up afterwards. Anyway, you can learn the songs on tour!" For the record, we didn't tart it up, and the next night we hit the stage at a sold-out Newcastle Polytechnic. Nothing could have prepared me for the adrenaline rush and sheer mayhem of playing live with these guys. There was absolutely no boundary between on and off stage. I'd also never seen so much gob in my life, and took a leaf out of Captains' book, prancing about the stage in a vain attempt to avoid it.

They lived being The Damned twenty-four hours a day. The audience was wild, the band was wilder, and there was constant competition to outdo each other. A club was quickly formed called "The 24 Hour Club." Criteria for joining—well, use your imagination! It was a marvelous tour, and I had been well and truly baptized.

Almost immediately after recording, we embarked upon the infamous Barge Trip on the Oxford Canal. Somehow, Rat and Cap had managed to persuade Chiswick to hire a narrow boat and a few amps on which we could routine songs for the new album. "Nice and relaxing," they said. "And away from pubs!" Roger phoned. "Meet them at Didcot station. Just bring your bass," he told me. Great idea, I thought, but when I arrived the next day they had other plans. "Whaddaya got that for!" they screamed, pointing at my bass. "Red Star it back to Cardiff immediately!" They were shrieking with laughter and had no intention of working at all.

There was no food on board, just beer and an air rifle. The next morning, I awoke to see my boots floating by the porthole, on fire. They'd doused them with lighter fuel and chucked them overboard. The boat had been booked for a week, but on the fifth day we had to dump it. By the second day, there was no crockery left, it was all used as target practice. Locks were filled with washing up liquid, engines revved, and we'd laugh helplessly as the bubbles flowed over the gates onto the puzzled boaters below. We visited every pub within reach, and then practiced the waterways equivalent of handbrake turns. We'd navigate by torchlight and use the barge as a bumper car. When the river police came after us, we'd quickly pull in and pretend to be asleep. If anyone shouted at us, Rat would turn round and shoot them in the arse. It was *that* sort of a trip.

At this time we were managed by Doug Smith (he also looked after Hawkwind and Motorhead) and had a jovial Scottish tour manager, Tommy Crosson. We'd asked for a coach for the next tour in April of Holland and Italy, as the drives were horrendously long. But Doug was having none of it, and booked us a minibus. Over to Tommy: "There was silence in the van for the first half mile, then all hell let loose. Within half an hour it was devastated. All the seats were on fire. The roof was ripped off. They made me stop at a post office, took a piece of roof, put a stamp on it, wrote a message: 'So you don't want us to have a coach, eh?' and sent it to Doug. He got it as well. When we got back, the van was gaffa-taped all over."

We duly arrived at the Palais Sports in Turin for the first Italian date. The stage was bare. Our crew had had a run-in with the local mayor in a restaurant, become unduly paranoid due to certain substances sampled in Amsterdam, panicked, and buggered off towards the border, leaving the truck driver locked in his cab. The promoter arrived with the local heavy mob, and they had guns in their pockets. Politely, but firmly, he intimated it would be a jolly good idea if they escorted us to the hotel. They then confiscated our passports and put us all on separate floors. Dire retributions were threatened. He obviously had contacts in high places, and was phoning border customs to make sure the crew didn't get through, but it was too late. It was now our turn to panic. I even called my girlfriend back home and made a will!

By this time, punters had got to the gig, found out it had been pulled and were amassing outside the hotel baying for blood. I was starting to wonder if I'd made the right move joining The Damned. But the rest of the tour went ahead—a press gang was dispatched around the pubs and clubs of London that night to bribe a new road crew to fly out to Italy the next day. But that's another story.

RAY DORSET (MUNGO JERRY):

The Mungo Jerry early success came from my playing of the Leadbelley/Woody Guthrie—type songs. When I could find no more material, I began to write songs in a similar style. I had also become interested in the jug band music of the Memphis Jug Band and the Picanini Jug Band.

By November/December 1968, my rock band, The Good Earth, had split up because we had no bass player or drummer. But we had a gig booked at Oxford University—a Christmas ball. So, Colin Earl, Joe Rush, and myself did the job as a kind of skiffle/jug band and we were a resounding success. On the same bill were the Keef Hartley band and Mick Farren and The Deviants. We were asked to play again after all of the other bands had finished. We stopped at about 3:45 in the morning.

Barry Murray, an old friend, had got a job as a house producer at Pye

Ray Dorset (Mungo Jerry)
From the photo collection of Ray Dorset

Records. He had also started a management agency with Eliot Cohen. He called me one day to see what I was up to, and he had a listen to the band, which by now included Paul King. Joe had left and was replaced by Mike Cole on double bass.

In February 1970, we got signed to do an album and recorded seventeen titles including "In the Summertime," which Barry was convinced was a hit! The title was written by me, probably in late 1968. It was released as the very first maxi-single on the Friday before the Whitsun bank holiday. That day we played our first gig as Mungo Jerry at the Hollywood Music Festival in England, together with such artists as Free, Black Sabbath, Traffic, the Grateful Dead, Jose Feliciano, Ginger Bakers' Airforce, and others.

The record company and management wanted a change of name, and Mungo Jerry from T. S. Eliot's *Old Possum's Book of Practical Cats* ("Mungojerrie" was a cat in the book) was picked out of a hat. By June, "In the Summertime" went straight into the U.K. charts at number thirteen and went to number one the following week.

After a seven-week tour of the Far East, Australia, and New Zealand in February 1972, Colin and Paul fired me and took over the name of Mungo Jerry, with Dave Lambert on vocals and guitar. The record company did not like the idea and decided that, as I was the front man and main writer of the band, I should become Mungo Jerry, the performing artist, and Ray Dorset the songwriter.

"In the Summertime" goes on and on all around the world. Now, more than thirty years after its first release, it is still going strong. I never tire of singing and playing it.

INSPIRATION IS WHERE YOU FIND IT

Eric Clapton wore his heart on his sleeve singing about "Layla." The lady about whom Clapton sang was actually his best friend George Harrison's wife, Patti Boyd. Evidently, the song played a role in Patti's decision to leave George and marry Eric. The song remains a classic, but their marriage was doomed to fail.

Many hit songs have been inspired by a particular woman who was important to the songwriter: Toto's "Roseanna" is about actress Roseanna Arquette;

the Stones' "Angie" is about Angela Bowie; "Oh Donna" is about Ritchie Valens' girlfriend. And the list goes on. (We'll probably never know for sure who "You're So Vain" is *really* about . . .) Many songwriters work from scratch on their creations, but more often than not, a real person or a real-life event has inspired at least a part of the song.

Some songwriters are inspired by a specific event or by a need to voice their beliefs: "Woodstock" by Joni Mitchell, "Dust in the Wind" by Kansas, "My Sweet Lord" by George Harrison, and almost any Bruce Springsteen song come to mind.

Most songwriters don't reveal the story behind the song—it's up to us to either use our imaginations or to connect the dots. Sometimes, the inspiration is so important to them that they share it with us.

GARY WRIGHT (SOLO ARTIST):

In 1972, my friend George Harrison invited me to accompany him on a trip to India. A few days before we left, he gave me a copy of the book *Autobiography of a Yogi* by Paramahansa Yogananda. Needless to say, the book inspired me deeply, and I became totally fascinated with Indian culture and philosophy. My trip was an experience I will never forget.

During the early '70s, while reading more of the writings of Paramahansa Yogananda, I came across a poem called "God! God! God!" One of the lines in the poem referred to the idea of the mind weaving dreams, and the thought immediately occurred to me: weaver of dreams, dream weaver. I wrote it down in my journal of song titles and forgot about it.

Several months passed, and one weekend while in the English countryside, I picked up my journal and came across the title "Dream Weaver." Feeling inspired, I picked up my acoustic guitar and began writing. The song was finished in an hour. The lyrics and music seemed to have flown out of me as if written by an unseen source.

After the record was released and became successful, many people asked me what the song meant. I really wasn't sure myself, and would answer, "It is about a kind of fantasy experience: a Dream Weaver train taking you through the cosmos." But I was never satisfied with that explanation, and as the years went by, I began to reflect on what the song actually meant. And then it came to me: "Dream Weaver, I believe that you can get me through the night" was a song about someone with infinite compassion and love, carrying us through the night of our trials and suffering. None other than God Himself.

REACHING OUT

Bill Berry of R.E.M. experienced a severe headache while performing in Lausanne, Switzerland, and was forced to leave in the middle of a show. Feeling worse off stage, he was taken to the hospital where he eventually underwent brain surgery to repair two ruptured blood vessels. This was only the latest event in Berry's run of bad luck. Earlier in the band's career, he developed Rocky Mountain spotted fever while in Munich, Germany.

Life is sometimes too short. When musicians are out on the road doing what they need to do to establish themselves and their music, it becomes easy for them to focus only on themselves and their careers. Those who extend themselves into their communities often find inspiration, a sense of personal accomplishment, and a belief that what they are doing is somehow, in some way, having a positive effect on society. Music is a gift, and it can be a means for great emotional healing. Music is a wonderful conduit of communication; it transcends all barriers and sometimes allows the songbearer—the one who created the music—to enjoy the special gift of giving.

LARRY HOPPEN (ORLEANS):

In the mid-'80s, I was in a band with some good friends—my brother Lance, of course, and some other friends from Woodstock, one of whom was Robby Dupree (who had that big hit with "Steal Away"). We got bored in Woodstock one winter, and we said, "Well, let's just put a band together for the winter." The band ended up being together for like five years and doing some great gigs in the Caribbean, Hawaii, wherever. We called it Mood Ring. We did all our hits and a bunch of covers. Mood Ring was pretty funny. We had a lot of props. We used to give out mood rings and dress up on Halloween.

One thing that we did each year around Christmastime, we'd go down to New York City to Sloan-Kettering to the children's ward and visit the kids who were really sick, most of whom had some form of cancer. It just felt great. We'd go there and sing songs, Christmas carols, and hang out.

I'll never forget this. One year we went down there and were going to do what we always did. It was fifteen to twenty kids and the staff in seats. And they wheeled this twelve-year-old kid in on a gurney. He was hooked up to all kinds of meds. He was bald from the cancer treatment. We started singing "Dance With Me." He was laying there in the gurney, and he was singing the words. I'll never forget that. It's hard to put things like that into words, what it meant to me. It's a graphic illustration of the power and universality of music. It was happy, but it was extremely emotional. I remember feeling at the moment that I was basically trying to keep it together. It was heart wrenching. A joyous universality.

When Orleans went to Japan for the first time in 1991, we played in Tokyo, Nagoya, and Osaka. The crowds there knew all the lyrics. We couldn't speak any Japanese. Most of them could barely speak English, if at all. But they knew all the lyrics, not just to our hits, but also to our ballads. They cried during the music. The experience was so transcendent of language.

DOUG ANDERSON (FAN):

I had seen Harry Chapin perform a few times live. Once in Bridgeport, Connecticut, where I was a disc jockey on the campus radio station, and later in Portland, Maine. But the first time I actually met him was at a place called the Club Casino in Hampton Beach, New Hampshire, in 1980.

During that time, Harry was often flying in from Washington, D.C., where he was actively lobbying Congress on the issue of world hunger. He would lobby during the day and then catch a flight to wherever he was playing that night, which often made him late. This particular night was no exception.

Harry was about forty-five minutes late, but came onto the stage and apologized, saying he was going to "sing his ass off" for us. He then proceeded to sing for about two hours, taking time out to tell us about his work with World Hunger Year (WHY), a group that he started with Reverend Bill Ayers in 1975 and that is still going strong today.

After the concert, Harry, as was his custom, came out to the lobby to sign autographs and solicit donations for WHY. (Profits from the sale of programs and the like also went to WHY). I waited for my turn, and as I gave my donation, Harry signed my program and thanked me for coming out and waiting for him to get there. We shook hands, and there was a bit more small talk. Finally, Harry's attention turned to the next person in line.

Harry always seemed to make each audience member feel as though he was singing to only them, and the fact that he took the time to thank me for coming to one of his shows never left me. Sadly, Harry was killed in 1981, just days before he was to return to the Club Casino, so I never got to talk with him again. But the program that he signed for me twenty-two years ago is framed and on the wall in my living room, and he still speaks with me through his music. I often hear his song "Cat's in the Cradle" on days when I get home from work tired-out and my sons want to play, and it somehow gives me a bit more energy.

Aside from my parents, Harry was, and is, one of the most influential people in my life. As I try to do some small part to be a positive influence in my part of the world, some of the things Harry used to say and sing still hold true. Harry was often known to say on the subject of helping those in need, "When in doubt, do something."

Perhaps one of the best ways to sum up Harry's philosophy (if there truly is a way) would be to quote his epitaph, which is also a lyric from one of his songs: "If a man tried to take his time on earth and show before he died what one man's life would be worth, I wonder what would happen to this world."

LIFE'S OPPORTUNITIES

Steven Tyler once trashed a backstage buffet because turkey loaf was served instead of the roasted turkey demanded in Aerosmith's contract rider.

Being a rock star isn't all about the perks. It's first and foremost a career. There are many phases to a performing career. First of all, there's the point in time at which musicians decide they want to make music their life's work. Then comes the hard part: paying dues. If fortune shines upon a musician, he or she realizes a career in music unlike anything he or she could possibly imagine.

As the years roll by, the career either grows or quickly becomes just a fond memory. It helps to be reflective in this business. Not everyone can be the

Rolling Stones, performing at the median age of 60, but if a musician sees his career for what it is or was—a unique opportunity—there can be plenty to be thankful for when it's all said and done.

NICK GILDER (SOLO ARTIST):

I have been working on the new CD, and every once in a while I wander back to the '70s and those tour days. Funny how the years have a way of softening the edges. One thing that is still very clear is that the band rocked! Then and now, I have always found myself with great rockin' players. Not that much has changed from those days. Actually, that's not entirely true. I wish we still had the budgets we had then!

We had our share of excesses, but not to the extent of some, who have suggested it remarkable they are still alive to reflect on their outrageous glory days, let alone remember them. Somehow, it seemed we were always tryin' to keep the road crew out of trouble, as much as any other activity. I remember one night

Nick Gilder
Photo by L. Mastromonaco-Gilder

hearing a thud in the aisle of the bus as one of the guys fell out of his bunk. This was thanks, I am sure, to the bus driver forgetting it was a new gig and not his old truck route.

We had the almost cliché tour experiences with the ladies wanting to express their appreciation with as much affection as possible. It wasn't unusual to see one of God's beauties in her birthday suit, walking down the hallway of a hotel to an after-gig party room. Oh, yeah.

Outrageous is not something new. The kids liked to show their fashion sense in kaleidoscopic extravagance then, and they do now. The touring, though, is the same. You wait for the stage time that night. It's somehow the focus of your day, whatever comes your way.

It's still dreamlike in some way, as I think of a fateful day in a piano refinishing shop in Vancouver when a young guitar hopeful named Randy Shepard asked if I would like to sing in their band, after my exhortations of music experience in England. From there, a chance meeting with Jim McCulloch, who claimed to have connections with a real booking agent, and did!

Our first gig was opening for Heart at The Cave in Vancouver. We played every nook and cranny after that. And suddenly I saw "Roxy" [Gilder's hit song "Roxy Roller"] all around me. Then I saw her at the top of the charts! It gets way too confusing after that. Next thing I know, Jim and I and the guys of the Nick Gilder Band are shaking hands with Dick Clark, and I'm accepting awards and propositions of every artistic nature.

I have truly enjoyed, and continue to enjoy, my life as a recording and performing artist.

TOMMY MANDEL (KEYBOARD PLAYER):

Here I sit, PowerBook on my lap, in this cold basement. The prunes I ate this morning in front of the iMac checking for eBay e-mail are finally doing their job. Or maybe it's the cappuccino, quaffed at the diner around three-thirty PM while sitting with my eleven-year-old-daughter and her boyfriends during our court-allowed time together between school and Hebrew school. Has it really come to this?

Once I slept in the finest hotel in South Africa. Zebra skins adorned my floor. Strange pagan woodcarvings the size of baby elephants stood watch outside my door. Bryan Adams' room even had a baby grand piano in it. He'd invited me up, and as I played Journey, Duke Ellington, Beatles, and Stones, I believe I realized that it didn't get much better than that . . .

Or the time Little Steven, Jackson Browne, Darryl Hannah, my ex-wife, and I were invited to a special sushi place in Tokyo after we played Tokyo's Giants Stadium. It was the inauguration of Japan Amnesty International, organized by Peter Gabriel, with whom I shared the dressing room's one electric razor before our shows. (Nona Hendryx had a KILLER band and set that night, as did Lou Reed.) Jackson B. had the fish that if not properly slaughtered could kill ya. He lived.

Now if I wake at three thirty AM, it's not due to jet lag, or three crazed Djakartan fans pounding on my door. It's not because a scorpion has mysteriously joined me in bed in Canberra, or due to the nearly killing heartache I felt being so far from my baby daughters. It's just the fourth cup of coffee I drank at nine PM to get me through her geometry homework. I'm a used Volvo owner, with the self-satisfaction that comes with having serenaded Lady Di and conversed with the future King of England. I play "Santa Claus is Coming to Town," with the wrong chords, at my kids' school assemblies with a group of dads. I brave the wilds of Astoria to rock out on a tiny keyboard with Stevie Blue, the garment center rockabilly, who interrupts his recording sessions to haggle with a fabric supplier from Hong Kong.

My ex-wife has followed her trajectory from Rock Chick studio love, to serious f*ck, to confidant, Merchandise Lady on my Dire Straits tour, wife, mother of my children, Faithful Heart, to the Road Warrior, harridan, Divorce Aggressor, visitation fiend, and now is sinking into the Indian Ocean of farther away tolerance. The kids continue to grow and out-pass me in every area except piano practice. My girlfriend is amazing, and she ain't twenty-two.

I don't call Mutt Lange anymore, but Bob Clearmountain still invites me to his birthday parties. The last time I saw Bruce Springsteen close up was at a wake. I haven't seen Madonna in years, and that's okay with me, too. I do miss Kurt Cobain, though I only dined with him once, and he probably never knew my name. I was instrumental in Bob Dylan's choice of a piano for his latest tour, but the last time he saw me, he was probably wondering where I'd gotten the food.

My gut empty, my heart full, and my calves and feet asleep with pins and needles, I close the PowerBook and head back upstairs, to the Volvo, to pick up my youngest kid from Hebrew school.

CHAPTER 8

INTERNATIONAL TOURING

A
s we've seen, strange things happen along the road. As if traipsing all over the United States isn't hard enough, some of the real money and adventure that can be experienced by performing live is found internationally. At first glance, traveling abroad seems as though it could be very interesting—and it is—but there are also things to be dealt with that are problematic, at best.

In addition to the differences in culture, the way of life in another country is not always what we have experienced or been led to believe and expect. Different lifestyles, language barriers, accommodations, and the customs of basic pleasantries provide unique challenges. It can be difficult for musicians to deal with people whom they don't know or with whom they have little or nothing in common, especially when they're in a different country. Sometimes running into someone "from home" is a welcome relief from new cities and different cultures. Being on your own to explore and experience these things isn't always what it's cracked up to be.

JOHN NOVELLO (A TASTE OF HONEY):

In 1978, I was the musical director for the R&B disco group A Taste of Honey. They had a huge record in 1978 on Capital Records called "Boogie Oogie Oogie." Just being with them is an interesting story, as R&B disco is not my type of music. I am an instrumental, progressive rock, fusion keyboardist; currently

John Novello at keyboards
From the photo collection of John Novello

cofounder of the project Niacin featuring Billy Sheehan on bass and Dennis Chambers on drums and me, of course, on Hammond B3.

But anyway, in 1978 I had just moved out West to L.A. from Boston, where I had been studying at Berklee College of Music. I was pretty broke in those days, especially since I had literally just arrived in L.A. from a cross-country trip with my stripper girlfriend at the time.

I was jamming away at the famed Guitar Center on Sunset Blvd when Perry Kibble (God rest his soul as he passed away since that time), the keyboardist of A Taste of Honey, heard me playing and asked me if I needed a job. I said, "Sure, what ya have, mate?" He told me about the band and that they had a record due out in a few weeks on Capitol. They needed an MD keyboardist and a percussionist to augment the group. I took his number down and gave him mine, but really didn't think it would amount to anything because in those days everybody said they had "deal and management" as a lure to get you to play for free.

About five weeks later, my girlfriend at the time was getting up for work. She had this god-awful disco station on that I hated (she got up early as she was a

197

computer programmer). I was half asleep, and was telling her to turn the damn thing off. She didn't and left for work. Next thing I know, the DJ said "That was a new song called 'Boogie Oogie Oogie' by A Taste of Honey." He said that it was number forty-one with a bullet, and fast climbing up the charts. Being broke, I just about fell out of bed. Holy shit! I thought to myself. Where is this cat's number? I looked all over the house and finally found it in one of my shirts. I called him up, and he said he'd been looking for my number because their record was a big hit and they were going out with the Commodores. They needed a keyboardist and a percussionist and someone who could do arrangements, etc. I went and played with the band, got the job, and we went out on tour. By the end of the tour, we had the world's number one record, and the single alone had sold nine million records. I was making lots of money, but playing music that was not really my cup of tea.

But here's the weird part of the story. We were in Japan playing at the Buda Kahn for the Tokyo Music Festival in 1978/79. One day I went out by myself, exploring the old wharfs of Tokyo. I ate at some neighborhood restaurant that was incredible, real local cuisine, but by the time I was ready to leave it was dark. I was dead lost, far from the hotel, and far from any taxis.

Earlier in the day I had seen Donna Summer rehearsing, as she was the headliner. She had a great band, and she really had pipes in those days—a class act, actually! I remember saying to myself that I should be in that band, as it was a better musical situation (still not my exact cup of tea but much better players). Anyway, just when I was starting to freak out, as I was lost in an old part of Tokyo in the dark and didn't know how the hell I was going to find my way back to civilization, I heard a voice say, "Hey, white boy. What ya doing down here all by yourself?" I turned around and saw a big black stretch limo. I began walking towards the car, and when the window came down more I saw it was Donna Summer!

Apparently she went exploring too, and ended up synchronistically in the same neighborhood. (What're the odds of this?) She spotted me in the dark as I was, of course, the only foreigner, and she recognized me. We had a great ride home and hit it off very well. The next year she asked me to tour with her, which I did. I found this interesting, as it shows the power of destiny and positive thinking in one stroke, in my humble opinion.

Of course, I eventually began playing the music that I was destined for, but those good old days were loaded with invaluable experience.

ROBIN BROCK (SOLO ARTIST):

I waited for my suitcases at the airport in Brisbane. I waited and waited and waited. They had failed to show up. My custom-made stage clothes were in there, as well as my makeup and everything I needed for my performance at the South Pacific International Song Contest. Up until this point, I had always had good luck with my baggage whenever I traveled. So I checked my garment bag at this time. Bad idea. As my manager gave the department all the details, I walked around looking at other people's bags, hoping someone had at least maybe picked up the bag with the huge Canadian flags and fluorescent pink ribbons on them. A lady with an adorable little beagle was walking around, and never seeing a sniffer beagle in an airport before, I knelt down to pet it. The handler held up her hand to stop me, as the little dog went crazy sniffing my packsack. I don't do drugs, so I had no idea what was going on. My dirty laundry couldn't smell that bad. She asked if I had any fruit. No, I didn't. The dog kept going. I had to upend my bag in the middle of the floor. Nothing. I kept trying to convince her that I didn't have any fruit on me and wasn't hiding it anywhere on my body either, when I remembered the banana I had had in my bag fifteen hours or so earlier, in Hawaii, which I ate in the Honolulu Airport. Now that's a nose.

We arrived sans luggage to our apartment in Surfer's Paradise. It was ten thirty AM and we were hungry so we walked a few blocks to find at least a cup of coffee. Every thing was closed pretty much, it being Sunday. We hadn't brought Australian currency because part of the festival deal was that they gave us spending money, but we wouldn't get it until we met our hosts later that afternoon. We came across a bank and my manager slipped her card in the machine. Her brand new, not ever used before Visa Gold. The machine started making strange noises and promptly swallowed the card, refusing to give it back. In our jet-lagged stupor, we stared at each other. This had never happened to either of us before. Did this mean if we left, it would get itself together and spit the card out onto the sidewalk? Louise went to see if there was anyone in the bank by chance and I stood guard, chasing people away from the machine.

I often wonder what people thought, watching this freaked out Canadian babbling on about who knows what at that point. There was someone in the bank, but they couldn't help us, although they explained that the card would be okay, and they would hold it until the bank reopened.

It was a long weekend, and it was Sunday now. Of course, in our rush to get to the airport, we had left all our credit card information at home, and the only way to get it in order to cancel the card was to fax the bank at home to let them know what was going on, seeing that they had all the data. We walked through the closed-up village, until we came across a real estate kiosk whose owners took pity on us and gave us a coffee and let us use their fax. This was before e-mail was so popular. The stores started to open up at noon, and we found another ATM. We were wary of putting another card in, so with mine the closest to its credit limit, I really didn't have a lot to lose, and of course the card worked.

We woke up the next day, and what a relief it was that our bags had been delivered and our new adventure with our hosts and the new people we met had begun. The next day, my manager (who never ever gets sick) couldn't get out of bed. I was really worried because she has the immune system of a bull. Of course, she rested for a little while and insisted it was just a little cold. I finally convinced her to go to the clinic I found around the block first thing the next morning. The finalists for this contest were people from all over the world, so it was a surprise when I saw Monica, a singer I had met in Romania the year before. I had only met her momentarily, and was convinced she wouldn't remember who I was until I heard my name being yelled from across the room and the next minute I was being hugged into a large pair of breasts. Monica had remembered me. Then, moments later, I felt a tap on my shoulder. It was one of the judges from Romania who lived in the U.K. I somehow didn't feel so lonely anymore.

The rehearsal the day of that evening's performance, we all got our own dressing rooms and were treated extremely well. It was fun doing a radio interview in my curlers and bathrobe. Finally show time. I went and performed my song "Rockin' On the Airwaves," and won for the rock category. The cool thing about the festival was that there were many different genres being performed, everything from rock to opera—literally. After my performance, I went out at intermission. Not having seen the Arts Center at its finest, I was amazed to see people of every age and many older women dripping with diamonds. This was a big deal. It really gave me a kick to be congratulated for my performance first by some young kids and then some little old ladies with bright red and pink lipstick who came over and hugged me and told me how much they loved my song. Very bizarre, but it goes to show how music has no age.

I returned with my trophy to my dressing room, and went to get my stuff. My makeup bag was gone along with five hundred dollars of makeup, a very inexpensive but very valuable watch, my crystal necklace, and a makeup bag and mirror my Nana had given me. We looked everywhere, and our hosts apologized profusely for the rest of the trip. (Hmmm, was that because they were sorry or because they had to look at me without makeup?) Every stitch of makeup was gone. The next day I went to the drugstore to buy the basics because I had nothing. Being the cheap/broke musician I am, I found a kit that was on sale. I checked it over and decided it would do for the next remaining days of the festival. When I got the kit home, I realized why it was on sale. What a deal. The makeup was like wax and would barely go on, and when it hit my skin, it did something strange and I looked like a clown. Oh well, at least they would remember me.

The last day, we went into the Hinterlands with two of the other performers and actually got to see some of the beauty that is Australia. Credit card loss, sickness, and clown faces suddenly faded away as I found a little rock shop where I bought some opals and tiger's-eye in their raw form. After tea and biscuits, I was in heaven. As the skies opened up to rain on us, I really didn't care. There I was in Australia; I had been there to perform, and I had seen so many great things and met so many wonderful people. That is what I remember most.

THIS IS FROM THE NEW ALBUM . . .

The always outrageous Led Zeppelin held a press conference in an art gallery while in Copenhagen. When asked if he liked the paintings, John Bonham selected one and smashed it over the man's head, asking if there were "other paintings you'd like me to criticize tonight?"

What's considered art—in any form—is truly in the eye or ear of the beholder. When they are performing in another country, some musicians figure that if they stick to the music or persona for which they are known, they should be home free. Most of the time that works, but not always. On the other side of the stage lights, returning fans sometimes expect to hear new material or see at least some sort of change in a show they have seen before. The tricky part is figuring out what any one particular audience might prefer. Most performers try to include a variety of their past successes while they introduce the audience to their

201

new material. Everyone likes to hear the songs they know and have grown fond of, and in the end, exposing the audience to the development of the artist's music and sharing new songs is a crapshoot.

IAN COOKE (RICK NELSON'S COLLEAGUE):

A favorite story for me is about Rick Nelson playing the Royal Albert Hall in February 1972. Rick and the Stone Canyon Band played in England after much persuading by George Harrison (Rick's L.A. neighbor) and Elton John. His opening act during this British tour was Seals and Croft, who were much larger in the U.S. than Rick was at the time. During this tour, Rick went to visit George Harrison at his estate. On his way to see Rick perform at the Royal Albert Hall, George had his much publicized car accident.

Anyway, Rick had been feeling very confused about his place in music after the October 1971 Richard Nader Rock and Roll Spectacular fiasco. [Nelson was seeking to get away from the "Ricky" persona and refused to do the oldies he was famous for. He was soundly booed off the stage.] Attending the Royal Albert Hall performance were Paul McCartney, Olivia Newton-John, Cliff Richard, and Elton John. Rick was mobbed on stage and had to do four encores. Girls ripped his shirt off (ticking off his wife, Kris), and Rick used this concert as the impetus to come back to the states and write "Garden Party."

In 1985, Rick toured Britain again, this time with a basic rock-and-roll-band format. On the tour were Bobby Vee, Bo Diddley, The Marvellettes, Frankie Ford, and Del Shannon. Rick just blew every act off the stage and received some of his best notices of all time. He was to come back and tour Europe in 1986 with Fats Domino. Richard Nader was the promoter of the '85 British Tour. [This time Rick was well received.]

ANOTHER DAY, ANOTHER WAR ZONE

In 1960, on his way to Gatwick Airport after a successful tour of Britain, popular rock and roll pioneer Eddie Cochran was killed in a London taxicab. His girlfriend Sharon Sheeley and fellow rocker Gene Vincent were also injured.

With all the intricate preparations that are part of the rock and roll tour, you'd think that international travel would be easier for musicians than for "regular" people. But because of their love of adventure and need to share their music with as many types of audiences as possible, musicians sometimes place themselves in precarious situations where anything can and does happen to them. When you factor in foreign customs that are little known or understood by the musicians and their crews, the traveling circus becomes prime for whirlwind confusion and lots of stories to take back to the folks at home.

FROM THE DIARY OF BRUCE WATSON (BIG COUNTRY):

KOSOVO
DAY 1
After a two-hour flight from Munich to Skopje, our charismatic yet unlucky singer Stuart got pulled by Macedonian customs officers and was given a full body search. This included the dreaded "digit up bum" procedure that scares the hell out of rock bands the world over. Cries of "didn't they buy you a drink first?" and "you lucky bastard" echoed around the tour bus.

On the road from the airport to the hotel, we passed cornfields growing on either side. The farmhouses in the fields were basic shacks, and there was a strong military presence here, with two Apache helicopters hovering above the bus. A convoy of KFOR and aid vehicles drove by, and in the distance we saw the high mountain ranges that lead to Kosovo. Our base for the weekend was the Hotel Continental in Skopje, which, according to the brochure, had "state of the art service, provided by highly competent staff." This is, of course, a complete lie, since two days after I accidentally broke the flusher in my bathroom it still hadn't been repaired. In fact, the sanitation was so bad that when guests asked directions for the toilets, they were simply told, "Just down the corridor mate; follow your nose."

Music journalist Billy Sloan and photographer Ronnie Anderson from the *London Sunday Mail* are out to do a story about the band over the next few days. Also, here is the West End theatre impresario Bill Kenwright, who, along with Vanessa Redgrave, has organized the event. In the hotel bar, I was introduced to the "Men of the Deeps' Canadian Miners Choir," who coincidentally worked in the same pit that my dad worked in back in 1962. Small world. These guys take a ten-week break from mining every year and go out on tour singing about life down the mines. Their songs are quite heartrending, and their cheeriest song, "Dust in the Air," contains the chorus: "Dust in the air, all through the mine. It's concrete on your lungs and you're old before your time."

In the foyer, we were presented with a plaque from Vanessa on behalf of the *Sunday Mail* for performing at the "Scotland for Kosovo" gig in Glasgow. Vanessa has the energy and enthusiasm of a small child and talks nonstop. She invited us to a modern jazz concert in the evening where Philip Glass was performing. Modern jazz is not my bag, and Stuart [Adamson] said it just made him chuckle, but we decided to go along and show face anyway. After a twenty-minute speech from Vanessa, which then had to be translated for the locals, Philip took to the stage. Things were going along just fine until he introduced an avant-garde clarinet player to accompany him. The second he put his "bugle" to his lips and "farted" out the first note, Stuart and I just creased up laughing hysterically. We immediately covered our mouths with our hands to stifle our guffaws, but this made it even worse as we couldn't breathe properly. Every time the clarinet player "tromboned" another jazz lick, it just cracked us up. Tears poured from our eyes, snot bubbled out our noses, and both of us started sweating profusely. At one point, I had to pull my jersey over my head. I immediately tried to think about mundane things like hoovering or watching a Dunfermline Athletic football game to take my mind off him, but that didn't help. All of a sudden, for some insane reason, I thought about starting a Mexican wave and that was it. My underpants were now damp, as I was losing control of my bladder. When Philip and "bugle boy" brought the music to a climax, the crowd rose to its foot and applauded. Stuart, who was now under his seat crying, got up and ran out with me right behind him. He would never listen to the clarinet again.

Back at the bar, we banged into Lulu, whose bandleader, Alan Derby, comes from Dunfermline. Also in attendance is Angus McFadyen, who appeared in *Braveheart* as Robert the Bruce, whose body was buried in Dunfermline. Is that a link? Lulu is over here to sing her big hit "Shout," and Angus is going to do a poem about death. Angus may be a great actor, but his pool playing and sportsmanship leave a lot to be desired. He was severely thrashed by Shorty (our guitar tech) and didn't take it too well. Lulu looked great, and had a fantastic, bubbly personality. Angus, on the other hand, had a face like a flitting after Shorty again thrashed him on the green baize. In fact, Angus was so dour he made Victor Meldrew seem positively happy. For some strange reason I imagined that if Mother Teresa were alive today, she would have shot him.

INTERNATIONAL TOURING

DAY 2

We boarded the buses at eight and prepared ourselves for the long drive to Pristina. The Italian carabinieri were escorting us. They are the scariest looking guys I have ever met, and if it came down to having the Terminator or the carabinieri chasing me, I would rather face the Terminator. These guys are not to be fucked with. On the way, aid trucks were held up trying to get through the border, as the queue was around five miles long. We passed a lot of burnt-out farm buildings and abandoned cars. Our convoy arrived in Pristina around midday, and we were ushered to the gig, which was right next door to the police headquarters that were bombed during the war. As usual, we got our priorities right and set off to find a football. Once procured, we got a game going with Angus and some of the local children. Not only did they hammer us but they also stole the ball.

Billy organized a meeting with some of the guys from the Royal Marine commandos. Their headquarters were opposite the derelict building, and they welcomed us with open arms. They were mostly from Scotland, and had a visit from Vanessa Redgrave the previous day and were expecting Prince Charles the next day. As you can imagine, they were extremely pleased it was a bunch of fellow jocks that were visiting them today, which meant they didn't have to dress up, hide their scud books, or mind their language in front of more "luvvie darlings." Suddenly, a heavy Glaswegian voice from the back of the room bellowed forth. "Vanessa Redgrave, ye say? I thought it was fuckin' Vanessa Feltz who wis comin." Big Mick was as wide as he was tall, and like all the lads in the squad, had a great sense of humor. I suppose you would need a large one if you had to deal with the problems these guys have to face. On the wall of one office were Polaroids of children. It didn't dawn on me at first, but these were pictures of missing children. Like myself, most people I know who have young children worry like mad if their bairns are a few hours late, or if one goes missing in a busy supermarket. Most of these kids have been missing for months. A few more horror stories were intertwined with some of the funniest jokes I have ever heard. I must salute Mick, his squad leader Frank, and all the rest of the guys out there as they are extraordinary people and do an excellent job keeping the peace. Through the office window we could plainly see the bombed-out police building. A young lad around the age of ten popped up from a hole in the ground and threw out a spent shell casing. Up on the top of the dangerously crumbling building were two teenagers collecting scrap metal.

After sound check, we decided to go and check out the local market, which was so big it made the Barras look like a car boot sale on a wet Saturday morning. The market specialized in fruit, fags, and dodgy Levis. Ronnie the Smudger bought a pair, only to discover that the pockets hadn't been stitched up, unlike his good self. Further into the city center, the pavements were choc-a-bloc with young entrepreneurs selling everything from bootleg cassettes to flick knives and laser pens. We must have walked about a quarter of a mile, when suddenly in front of us stood the remains of the post office. It was quite a high building, and I was amazed it was still standing. There was a huge gaping hole in the middle of it. This was the main telephone exchange, so it was one of the prime targets. Just as we were about to take a closer look, a young man came out of the building and started speaking to us in pretty good English. It turns out he used to work in the post office, but was on vacation in Dusseldorf when the shelling started. He was now employed as a security guard, and invited us in to the building to have a look round. It was still very unstable, but he knew the safer areas. We carefully climbed the stairs to the top of the building. Most of the time the banisters were missing, so it was a sheer drop. At the top, we could see most of the surrounding damage. The air conditioning unit that was once housed on the roof of the post office had been blown off and was now residing on the hotel roof across the road. Further to our left was a washing machine embedded in a wall. The middle of the building had a huge hole that ran from the top to the bottom where the missile had struck it. False ceiling tiles hung by their wires, and burnt out circuit boards littered the floor. Ronnie shot some film off, and we made our way back downstairs. We invited the security man over to the Pink Panther bar for a drink with us. He told us his house had sustained some damage after the bombing of the post office. When he returned from Dusseldorf to find his family in a partially destroyed home, he decided that he should make some plans to take refuge. He asked his neighbor, who was a policeman, to help him get his family out of there. His neighbor took him to the police HQ and was told by his superiors that he should take him back home and shoot him. Luckily, he decided to let him go, and he and his family escaped to a refugee camp and spent months living in a tent. He is now rebuilding his life slowly but surely, and I wish him all the happiness in the world.

Back at the gig, Lulu was posing for photos with squaddies, while Angus was alone in a tent rehearsing his death poem. Vanessa took the stage, and started reciting another speech that was so dull and monotonous that I was forced to give her a damn good listening to. Various clog dancers and jazzers got up and strutted their stuff, which really warmed the audience up—not! Angus was up next with "The Poem of Death," which incidentally goes down like a cruise liner hitting something large and frozen in the middle of the Atlantic. He wasn't impressed, but then again, neither was the audience. It was only when Lulu got up and sang "Shout" that the place went nuts. Big Country was up next, and when Bill Kenwright introduced us as "The best rock 'n' roll band in the building" you just knew he wasn't wrong.

On the return drive back to the Macedonian border, everyone, with the exception of Vanessa and Lulu, decided to get off the bus to do what comes naturally. Five minutes later, everyone got back on the bus, totally relieved. That is, everybody except Angus, who had the entire bus in stitches when he slipped in the biggest puddle of raw sewage I have ever seen.

And they said tragedy is dead.

ANDY POWELL (WISHBONE ASH):

Over the last thirty-plus years, Wishbone Ash has been a much-traveled band. Even these days, we play around a hundred shows each year. We've toured all the usual places like Europe and the U.S.A., together with some of the more unusual and exotic rock destinations. These situations often require a great deal of adaptability and flexibility from the band and crew alike. But in terms of life experience, they are just invaluable, even though at the time you were wondering just how you were going to get through the tour, or show, and in some cases, how you would even survive.

We've had guns pulled on us in Italy by angry promoters when our gear didn't arrive for a show deep in mafia country. We privately fought apartheid in South Africa during a show that ran counter to the U.N. ban on entertainers working there. Our entire crew was deported from the U.S.A. back in the '70s during one of several drug busts our organization endured in our travels. There was the time in the former Soviet Union where my brother was nearly arrested and detained, thanks to our tour guides and interpreters, who turned out to be junior KGB officers. He'd gotten involved with a Muscovite beauty, and I was told that if he didn't leave town quickly "passports could disappear."

Steve Upton, our original drummer, was arrested during a 1970s world tour and spent the night in a New Zealand jail for using bad language on stage in

Auckland during an open-air festival. Today, this wouldn't even raise an eyebrow. The list of incidents goes on. Keith Moon broke into my hotel room during the Tommy tour when Wishbone opened for the Who. He was brandishing a submachine gun, shouting, "Your money or your wife!"

However, for the truly exotic location where every day produced a crazy incident of some kind or another, one need look no further than India, a continent we've toured not one, not two, but three times! There's only a handful of intrepid Western rock/pop acts who have taken this one on, including The Police, Jethro Tull, Osibisa, Bony M, and Uriah Heep . . . and that's about it as far as I know!

A couple of years ago, I received a letter from Ian Anderson of Jethro Tull, who actually went out there as a result of seeing that we'd ventured forth. Unless you've done it, it's very difficult to describe. In his letter he thanked me for being the reason that Tull had taken the plunge. It seemed that he took our visit as some sort of endorsement! He shared some moments, and I felt a bonding there, a kindred spirit, as if he wanted to somehow share the experience with someone who'd also been through this very unique event.

From the moment you deplane in Bombay, your senses are assaulted with the sights, sounds, and smells of this mysterious continent. You are immediately aware of the sheer numbers of people and, of course, the attendant poverty on your way into the city. There are whole families living in what look like makeshift houses often made of little more than cardboard boxes. They live right by the roadside. There are beggars and lepers, exotic street weddings, cripples, people giving birth, people dying, in fact every kind of thing to make your eyes pop out of your head. Life is lived right out in the open—truly medieval. Your jaw gets ever lower, and then you are transported into a hotel of extreme opulence, unlike anything you've ever experienced. That's just for starters.

On our first tour, we were greeted by our promoter, who I believe had worked in the Indian film business and was connected to an upper caste family. Vikhram was an honorable man who, against overwhelming odds, did a splendid job on the arrangements, with the aid of an exotic assistant by the name of Nareesh. I never saw this man travel with any luggage, but each day he would arrive in the hotel lobby in clothes of exquisite hue and design. He wore only skirts and tunic tops, and could have walked off the canvas of a Mogul painting.

On our first day, he greeted us at the airport and, as was his custom, clapped his hands together, whereupon half a dozen helpers appeared hanging off a strange, three-wheeled, open flatbed truck with some gaily colored red-and-white plaid mattresses draped in the back for our guitars, drums, etc. This was how the equipment was to travel! Sometimes we'd travel by plane, and at the airport it was the same. Nareesh would clap his hands together, and people /servants would appear out of nowhere to do his bidding.

There were so many episodes in India, we had to give them all names. There was "Baby on a Stick," "The Ox Cart Incident," "Lights Out," "The Streets of Shame," "Fishing in Madras," "The Children of God," etc. "Baby on a Stick" started when we checked into our Bombay Hotel, which had a garden/pool area overlooking the beach. Like no other, this beach was an entire movie epic from dawn to dusk with entertainers, magicians, jugglers, snake charmers, fire-eaters, high wire acts, and musicians, all fighting for the tourist rupee. We were looking down over a high wall at all of this, when all of a sudden, a tiny baby appeared next to us, and in it's hand was a bowl for money. This child was tied to a twenty-foot long pole, which the child's father was balancing on his chin below us at beach level! That was our first experience. It only got weirder.

We were touring with Richie Havens, who must have been one of the few black men in India at the time. Being a native New Yorker, he was reacting to all of this as we were. Our hosts, believing that as rock and rollers we would need to see some real Indian "ladies of the night," took us down to an area of Bombay where the brothels are. I forget the name of the district, but its translation came to us as "The Streets of Shame." We walked, or rather cowered, down the middle of this one street, which was lined with garishly colored buildings of every hue with literally hundreds of women and girls of all ages leaning out of windows or lounging in groups. When they caught sight of our group, there started a slow murmuring that gradually rose into a caterwauling, whistling and whooping—truly scary! There were the most amazing makeup jobs, and piercings, and nose chains—enough to make even the most hardened punk sit up and pay attention. At one point an old hag of about seventy years of age ventured out into the street to confront us, and made a grab for Laurie Wisefield. The place really erupted. Even our hosts were getting scared now, fearing a riot or something. We were quickly hustled into a couple of cars, and sped out of there. We did later get a song out of this one, titled—you guessed it—"The Streets of Shame."

Driving in Calcutta was very interesting, and not a little nerve-wracking. Indian taxis are tiny. After a show in an outdoor arena where we'd witnessed vultures encircling the stage during sound check while also watching stagehands erect the flimsiest of bamboo security barriers to protect us from an overenthusiastic crowd, we took a couple of taxis across town to our hotel. It turned out that large parts of this city of almost twenty million inhabitants have no electricity. When we encountered one of these sections, we were alarmed to see that our driver turned the lights off on his taxi. "What's going on? Why are you turning the headlights off?" we screamed, as he narrowly missed oncoming traffic. "Oh," he replied, while shaking his head from side to side and grinning broadly. "It's to save electricity."

When we got to Madras, deep in the south, we were by now intrigued by how each city was entirely different from the last. Unlike Bombay, this place was full of low buildings and very rural in feel. There were all the usual street vendors and a good number of oxen pulling carts loaded with every kind of merchandise. Another wild taxi ride had us literally screaming at our driver to slow down when, sure enough, the inevitable happened. We collided in a great broadside with one of the beautiful beasts that had been pulling the obligatory cart loaded with vegetables like some thing out of an Indiana Jones movie. Wild stuff! Luckily, the ox lived to see another day. The amazing thing was that people never seemed fazed by these kinds of events. It was seen as God's will, or some kind of divine intervention, as to whether you lived or died. We would often see trucks broken down in very rural situations by the side of the road, and the driver would be camped next to the vehicle for days and weeks even, we were told, until something happened to change his situation. Naturally, there was no such thing as AAA roadside assistance.

Steve Upton and I went walkabout on this huge beach, and came upon a community of tiny loinclothed and turbaned fishermen. Though they didn't speak English, two of them offered, through sign language, to take us out in their canoe for some fishing. It was something like a journey back in time to be able to see how these people functioned, relying on their skill and instincts. Later we hung out with them on the beach, smoking and sharing some of our belongings with them. They were as fascinated by us as we were by them. Way off in the distance, one of their younger sisters could be seen running towards us, obviously inquisitive as to who her brothers were talking to. As she got closer and saw our white faces, she burst into a fearful kind of crying and ran off shrieking. We couldn't understand it until one of the fishermen pointed to our faces and skin, explaining that this young girl had never seen white people before. She was suddenly very scared.

Years earlier in Los Angeles, we followed Fleetwood Mac into town and, like everyone else, heard the rumors of drug overdoses and religious cults making their impact on the band. We subsequently lost our guitarist, Ted Turner, for three days in the desert to a bunch of well-intentioned hippies. He returned fifteen minutes before our showcase for the label chiefs at MCA/Universal. Unfortunately, he was tripping! As our bass player Martin Turner later commented, his body was there on stage, but his mind was still somewhere out there in the desert.

Anyway, back to Fleetwood Mac. That particular week, the L.A. rock and roll community was abuzz with the fact that Jeremy Spencer, their diminutive slide guitarist, had been kidnapped and brainwashed by a religious cult called The Children of God. He was never to be heard from again as far as we were concerned, until that is, many years later we played in Banglore, India. We had finished playing in front of about 5,000 people at this open-air concert, and two Americans introduced themselves to us. They said that they had been on a radio ship in the Indian Ocean with Jeremy. He was apparently currently engaged in doing a fine job of broadcasting the word of God to anyone who would listen. Incidentally, he was still playing and making music, and I was given a cassette of his music to prove it. It was too strange for words, but nonetheless good to know that he was still alive. Leaving New Delhi right around Christmas, we got to the airport only to be told that our flight was overbooked. We could see there was a problem since people were camped out all over the terminal and looked like they'd been there for a couple of days at least. We were turned away, only to return the next day, determined to get on a plane to be home for Christmas. Eventually, we were assigned a plane. That, too, had been overbooked. In the end, it became a first-come, first-served, free-for-all with peace-loving Indians and us, too, literally fighting to get into the plane.

A while after the thing finally became airborne, we passed over a desert area. We could see that there was smoke coming from underneath one of the 747's wings. The captain came over the intercom to say that a part of one of the engines had "fallen off." We were to land in Kuwait City and wait for a new part to be sent out.

Needless to say, the Kuwaitis were none too pleased about us landing at their pristine airport, and we were immediately put under armed guard and we had our passports forcibly taken off us. A couple of American oil workers protested loudly as some of the ladies were rudely pushed around. These guys were promptly kneecapped and beaten to the ground. We realized these Arab folks were seriously pissed off. We were taken to another opulent hotel and kept under house arrest for a couple of days while the necessary repairs were made to the plane. Eventually we did make it out of there in time for Christmas in New York, which seemed just as surreal. The culture shock was palpable as we were thrown into the feeding frenzy that now passes for Christmas in the West.

JIGA AND JINNO (ANALOG PUSSY):

Our connection flight to Mexico from Germany landed in Houston, U.S.A. We were stopped by an agriculture officer cause we "smuggled" two apples and a tomato in our bag. He checked our tomato carefully. "Normally, you should pay 250 bucks penalty for entering the U.S. with this. But I will let you go." He continued in a Clint Eastwood style: "Because today is your lucky day."

Jiga and Jinno (Analog Pussy)
From the photo collection of Jiga and Jinno/Analog Pussy

I'm not sure what he meant, but from that moment on, everything went weird. When we arrived in Mexico City, we lost one piece of luggage with our "Soundscape" studio hardware inside, the one we use for the live show. It was found the next day, and we had to pay a huge tax on it. Then we got sick. High fever, shivering, vomiting. We assumed it was some kind of a nasty flu.

The night of the rave in Mexico City, DJ Vazik was playing his last track. We were next. We were both still sick, and very weak. We were almost about to faint. I don't believe in God normally, but this time I closed my eyes and prayed: "Dear, dear God, please make me well for one hour and twenty minutes."

My wish came true. For one hour and twenty minutes I got an adrenaline rush. I can't tell you what went on during the show. I don't remember much. It's all quite blurry. One picture is stuck in my head—when I took my spacey bass guitar out, everybody screamed. They were waiting for that.

We didn't play an encore 'cause God interpreted my wish literally and gave me exactly one hour and twenty minutes, not more. I just went off stage. Somebody held my arm and helped me to walk. Apologies to our lovely crowd. They were so disappointed!

The following week, Jinno and I were still sick in the hotel. Plans to visit the pyramids were cancelled. Thursday, we were at Mexico City airport just about to catch a flight to Monterey for our next gig. Jinno collapsed on the floor at the airport, weak and feverish. I immediately called a security guard. They took him to the airport clinic, and the doctor told us we had a bad stomach infection. A few days later we felt fine, thanks to megadoses of antibiotics.

The gig in Monterey was a blast. I spotted this gorgeous girl in our crowd. She was really into the music. I invited her to come up. We sat on stage and hugged, a synth on my knees. She played it, and I turned the cutoff knob. Suddenly I realized that the guys in the audience are freaking out. Then I got it. Two hugging girls playing a synth to a psy-trance beat. They saw this as a lesbo show!

A day later, we returned to Germany. At Cologne airport, I was stopped by a giant German customs officer. I had nothing to hide, but he scared the hell out of me. He ordered me to open my bass case. I did, and then he goes, in an admiring voice, "Wawwo, a five-string bass. Where did you find it? I'm a bassist myself. I got a Fender Jazz." On and on he talked about his instrument, waving his giant hands in the air. Everything seemed surreal, trippy, hallucinated. Inside my head I can still hear the American agriculture officer: "Today is your lucky day."

JOHN "MARMADUKE" DAWSON (NEW RIDERS OF THE PURPLE SAGE):

Here's some of what I think I remember about The Festival Express [in Canada]. The first and maybe the best part about the train was that it was only hauling us musicians, our crews, and the train's staff. It had a bunch of sleeper cars with seats that converted into upper and lower closeable berths (they were wide enough for two people). Once you were inside, it was kinda like your own super-small motel room, but with a spectacular view out the window.

The front two cars were quickly made the official jamming cars. One had a twenty-four-hour-a-day blues, rock, weird stuff, and jazz jam going, and the other was more country and folkie oriented. I'll tell you the names of the acts that I can remember. There were the Grateful Dead, New Riders, Janis Joplin and her new band, Leslie West (a grossly overweight guitar player who made a Les Paul look like a ukulele balancing on his huge belly), Ian and Sylvia and their band, Eric Anderson (all by himself), Delaney and Bonnie and their band, and I can't remember who-all else. Oh, and Rick Danko of the Band (the others flew up for the actual gigs).

One night we were (a lot of us were, at least) jamming away in the C&W car, trading songs and chops. I think Janis liked the way I sang "Tonight the Bottle Let Me Down," because later that night I had the pleasure (she was my favorite girl singer) of getting dragged off by her. It was fabulous, and the next morning John Cooke, who was her road manager, came by Janis's little place to wake her up with a generous screwdriver. Good man.

We were about two hours out of Saskatoon when somebody noticed that the train was about to run out of liquor. We wouldn't make it through the night if somebody didn't go into Saskatoon when we got there and restock. A few good souls went through the train soliciting money for a booze run in Saskatoon. We were routed onto a sidetrack, but the train stopped at a station that was only a couple of miles out of town. The good souls jumped into a taxi and told the driver to take them to the nearest good liquor store. When they got there, they went in, plopped over four hundred dollars on the counter and said, "Tell us when we've reached that much." Then they started pulling bottles off the shelves.

They came back to the train with a great collection of all sorts of this and that, including a three-foot tall bottle of C. C., around the bottom of which Buddy Cage was found passed out the next morning. (Apologies to Mr. Cage, who's been in A.A. for at least fifteen years now.) That night I heard the most amazing version of "No More Cane on the Brazos," performed by Janis and Rick Danko. They were trading verses, trying to outdo each other for at least an hour. They were amazing. That's also the only night I ever saw Garcia drunk. (Cuervo Gold, as I remember.)

Well, the train got to Calgary. We did a good gig there and then came home, as the organizers were running out of money, so we didn't continue on to Vancouver, which had been planned. I loved the constant clickety-clack of the train's wheels.

ROCKERS AS ACTIVISTS

In 1968, the Byrds were scheduled to play several dates in South Africa. Gram Parsons, who was a member of the band at the time, felt uncomfortable playing that country because of the apartheid issue. When Keith Richards told Parsons that the Stones would never play South Africa, Parsons quit the the Byrds . . . on the night they were scheduled to leave.

As interesting as it is for musicians to travel the world and encounter cultures far different from their own, politics sometimes come into play. Since rock and roll lyrics can be a direct reflection of our life and times, certain acts are frequently requested to play at politically tinged events such as campaigns, voter-registration drives, protests over such issues as nuclear energy, and ecological and pro-animal-rights rallies and the like. In this day and age, musicians have to decide if they want to take that step beyond entertainment to raise their voices either for or against an issue currently being debated or that is close to their hearts. Doing so is a career risk, at best.

Some musicians, such as Jackson Browne, have chosen to endanger their commercial careers by taking strong political and ethical stands and not only appearing at protest events but by releasing politically themed albums. Others, such as Bonnie Raitt, Bruce Springsteen, and Neil Young, have been able to use their celebrity to speak out, but at the same time successfully deliver their contemporary music to the masses. Sometimes the combination works for the musician, other times it doesn't. One thing is for certain: rock and roll and the politics of our lives and times will continue to be intertwined.

ARLO JENNINGS (MANAGER OF SHAWN PHILLIPS):

From my travel diary:
SOUTH AFRICA (APRIL 26, 1994)
"As you know, South Africa is about to be liberated," said festival promoter David Marks in his last faxed memo to me regarding Shawn Phillips' proposed South African music tour.

MEMO: Our first free and democratic elections take place on April 27, 1994—so naturally we are very excited and want to celebrate the occasion with those who supported the struggle against apartheid. The music festival gates will open at ten AM on April 28, 1994, regardless of politics. Either way, you will be the first, since the '70s cultural embargo, to enjoy the first major music and cultural happening in the new South Africa. What better way to celebrate the birth of a new nation and the death of apartheid?

I accepted Marks' invitation and booked Shawn Phillips' first tour of South Africa. Because it was illegal to exchange South African rand for U.S. dollars in 1994, payment for the tour would come later. An oversight I made in the planning for the tour was the cost to ship Phillips' music equipment. The fees to ship a quarter-ton from Minneapolis to Johannesburg was more than I had. In exchange for lowering his excess baggage fees, I offered the person behind the airline check-in counter free CDs. "A portion of the concert fee is going to charity," I added, persuasively. After a round of push back, and holding up a long line, the check-in person accepted his four-anvil guitar cases without the extra $150 each excess weight and baggage charges.

"Seriously, he's a rock star"—I told airport security that the man with hair down to his ass, dressed in a full, dark military blue uniform, which uncannily resembled a police uniform, was not a terrorist, (proud to be a volunteer firefighter, Phillips liked to travel in public in his full dress fireman uniform) but actually, and none other, a famous music cult legend. As I copied the last word of Marks' fax over to my travel diary, the captain of South African Airways flight #202 announced, "At five AM you will see the sunrise over Africa."

Following the announcement, I picked up a Johannesburg newspaper stuck in the seat in front of me. HEADLINE: "April 25, 1994. Eight bombs exploded around South Africa, including one at a crowded taxi stand in Germiston, killing ten and injuring thirty-six. Yesterday, 150 pounds of TNT took the lives of nine innocent people in the largest bomb to date outside the Monte Carlo Hotel on Bree Street in Central Johannesburg." I was safe flying over the Atlantic at thirty thousand feet. During the twenty-hour flight however, the international arrival section of Johannesburg's airport had been blown up. Back home, my wife had no idea if I had been killed.

After reading the paper, I was having second thoughts. "A rock 'n' roll tour in South Africa?" I showed the paper to Phillips. "I don't care about the money. I think a lot of my music really relates to what's going on over there right now. Compassion for the human condition has always interested me. I want to share that with the people. It's for that reason that I want to perform in South Africa no matter what the risks," he said with great conviction. I must have look scared because he added, "Don't worry so much." But it was my job to worry about everything.

I was glad he had organized his thoughts about this unusual tour. Upon our arrival, journalists from all the major South Africa newspapers, television, and radio were scheduled to meet us at the airport. Our trip to South Africa was the fulfillment of two great personal journeys. For Phillips, it was a reconnection to thousands of lost fans, a self-confidence booster, and an aid to his recovery from depression. For me, because I had struggled my entire life (and probably my past lives too) to pursue my calling in the arts, going to South Africa as Phillips' manager, and to experience the birth of a new nation, felt like a dream come true. It was a moment of divine inspiration. My soul and destiny had finally met.

The tour had come together in less than a week. That was all the time I had to learn about the complexities of South African politics and Phillips' multi-million-selling seventeen-album repertoire. For over twenty-five years, Phillips heard rumors that he might be popular in South Africa. Not until the sanctions were lifted, did I learn that Phillips was a triple platinum (150,000 records) selling artist in that country—a lot of records considering that it was a market of only nine million people.

Finally, after trying to canvass South Africa by phone for a promoter, I received an answer from my queries: "Want to celebrate the birth of a new nation?" Marks asked. His message continued to tell me about a five-year-old South African music festival called Splashy Fen. Its purpose was to bring together all peoples through music. The steward brought me a glass of the formerly banned Cape Town wine. I took a guilty sip of the wonderful tasting Merlot and wondered if the winery had used slaves to pick the grapes. The jet engines hummed a luring lullaby. Unable to sleep sitting up, I remained awake and reflected on whether I was out of my mind for accepting this tour.

SOUTH AFRICA (APRIL 27, 1994)
I awoke in Theo Coetzee's home in a suburb of Johannesburg called Randburg. Like all suburbs in Johannesburg, it was exclusively white and guarded by private security and electrical razor wire. Theo was our retired Afrikaner, former management consultant, and Zen mystic tour promoter. While South Africa prepared for the mother of elections, on April 27, 1994 we packed for our five-hundred-mile journey to an outdoor music festival located in the heart of Zulu county, Kwa-Zulu Natal, despite reports that travel to the area was not recommended. On our way out of Johannesburg, we passed a voting hall where thousands of Afrikaner, British, Zulu, Nedebele, Venda, Xhosa, and Indian people, speaking more than eleven different languages, stood together for the first time in history. Mendela supporters ran up and down the street, waving yellow, green, and black flags into the air, shouting, "Tata" (father). Watchful of the crowd, the police rested nearby against a footlocker filled with machine guns.

"The reason apartheid is ending is because the South African rugby team was beaten to a pulp by the worst team in the league (British)," Theo said humorously. "Therefore, unable to sign new players because of international sanctions, the government had no choice other than to abolish apartheid in order to save their rugby team from further humiliation."

Breaking all bets of an impending civil war, Johannesburg was strangely peaceful on the first day of the elections. The highway to Natal Province, however, was cluttered with armored convoys.

SOUTH AFRICA (APRIL 28, 1994)
"Look out," Phillips yelled at Theo to drive carefully. Along the highveld roadside a sign read, "Beware—Rhino Crossing." Theo assured us that there had not been a rhino anywhere near the highveld toll route for decades. "Like the American buffalo," he explained, "once they were everywhere, now they can only be found in game reserves."

By dusk, the road climbed into the fog-clasped Drakensburg Mountains. Darkness, weaving roads, rain, and cattle slowed our journey further. Hours behind schedule, Phillips and I reached a hand-painted sign, Splashy Fen—15k.

We arrived at the entrance to the Zulu wilderness area campground and were pounded by a raging storm off the Indian Ocean. Between bursts of lightning, thousands of cars stretched bumper to bumper across the mountainside. Our joy had to wait—our van got stuck in a foot of mud. Word of our arrival made its way to Bart Fokkens, a professional hang glider and the festival manager.

"Sawubona," a tall person said with his face darkened by the hood of a raincoat as he approached the kombie (van) in the darkness. We breathed a sigh of relief. It was Bart. "To roll over the mud you need to deflate the tires and to avoid the bad ruts. Stick to the right, and whatever you do, don't stop," he told us. The next hour passed like a log chute ride at an amusement park. Up and down a grade that would put any four-wheeler to the test, we slid our way past the music tent and on to the musician's cottage, which we were pleased to discover was a warm, three-bedroom, thatched-roof cottage. The cottage had more room than was needed, so I invited about a dozen musicians out of the rain to stay with us. Our first night at Splashy Fen was remarkable. Grounds owner Peter Ferraz, a retired journalist, and his wife and lovely three daughters, put my fears of being caught in some kind of Zulu uprising to rest. They built a fire, passed guitars, wine, and smiles. For hours, many Splashy Fen musicians like Saranti from the band Keep the Change entertained us with her original songs about growing up with a family of black servants that lived in her parents' backyard shed.

SOUTH AFRICA (APRIL 29, 1994)
"Splashy Fen, the Woodstock of South Africa, am I really here?" I said the next morning, looking out the cottage door and at the Dragons Head, the highest peak in the Southern Drakensburg Mountains of Kwa Zulu, Natal, at 10,000 feet above sea level. The mountain air outside the cottage was wet and cold. It had been raining for days. The clouds rolled over the peak like steam rising from a lake of fire. Below Dragons Head, five thousand mixed-race barefoot, soaked-to-the-bone, graying '60s flower children, new age ethnics, professionals, teenagers, and toddlers danced about smoldering campfires. As strange rhythms echoed across the valley floor, their tent doors flapped like Mandela's green flags in the freezing drizzle. Exploring the campgrounds, I discovered the food gardens (a group of tents with outdoor grills), which included some South African delights like Bunny Chow, Zulu Porridge, and beer. After I choose a Bunny Chow, Phillips met mud-clad, smiling fans. "Far out," a young person

said, stumbling into Phillips. His companion just stared, stoned. Recognizing the American artist, they offered him a toke of their Durban poison stick (marijuana), which Phillips declined saying, "Besides water, I never put anything into my body before I perform." (Marijuana, called dagga by the locals, is an unofficial export of the Natal province, which accounts for its popularity and its abundance. Earlier that morning the police had set up a roadblock in front of the festival entrance and arrested dozens of people who had dagga. Phillips and I were puzzled by the busts: despite all the heavily publicized rumor of civil war, how is it the police could afford to spare so many officers over a few harmless joints?)

SOUTH AFRICA (APRIL 30, 1994)

I went to the information tent to check out the local South African music scene. Guitars For Africa—*3rd Ear Music,* a compilation cassette featuring twenty-four of South Africa's finest guitarists, was as good as any I heard in the states. One outstanding performance on the tape was by Sipho Mchunu, who demonstrated a unique guitar technique called Zulu guitar: a special tuning/strumming system. There was also a festival program guide that told about the beneficiaries of the festival: the Wildlife Society, Ladysmith Black Mambazo Trust, the Underburg Himeville Education Foundation, and DASH, the Drakensburg African Schools Organization. Following the melody of Joni Mitchell's song "Woodstock," we discovered the first of thirty performing groups—Saranti's band Keep the Change. They sang, "By the time I get to Splashy Fen." Keep the Change also created an original sound by combining elements of jazz, folk, and rock with their own Euro/American pop style. The group reminded me of the Roaches meets Crosby, Stills, & Nash. Another highlight of Splashy Fen was Ladysmith Black Mambazo. The legendary ten-man a cappella group that sang on Paul Simon's Grammy-winning album *Graceland* filled the music tent with their authentic, chain-gang gospel with voices deeper than a South African diamond mine. In approval, the crowd saluted the group as heroes, exploding in applause. The University of Natal African Music Ensemble was another group that caught our ear. Using handmade, otherworldly looking instruments, the group created a rich, Afro-tapestry of plucked, strummed, and shaken traditional folk songs from Uganda, Zimbabwe, and Mozambique. The Hairy Legged Lentil Eaters put on an unforgettable show. They combined banjo, violin, and electric guitar to create new mixtures of folk and political satire.

SOUTH AFRICA (APRIL 31, 1994)

Later that night, it was Phillips' turn to perform. At 6,000 feet, combined with heavy fog, Phillips found it hard to sing and keep his guitars tuned. Regardless of the elements, he performed a couple of his favorite songs from each of his seventeen albums. Songs like "Steel Eyes," "Ballad of Casey Deiss," and "Woman" brought cheers from the crowd. Phillips finished his last show at Splashy Fen with the "Peace Song." Taking a final bow he raised his arms as if he were about to fly and said in Zulu, "Hambe Kahle" (Go well, go with God).

After the show, Marks, who was a soundman at Woodstock, spoke about the days not too long ago when audiences of mixed race in South Africa were prohibited by law. "So, when bands had black and white musicians like the Flames and Freedom's Children, there had to be one show for black people and another show for white people. White and black musicians in the same band were not permitted to play on the same stage together. The way around that one was for the black musicians to play behind a curtain when they were entertaining a white audience, and the other way around when the audience was black."

I began to realize what a cultural embargo meant. South Africa had one of the largest and most vibrant music scenes in the world, but no one knew it. Because there was no South African export, record companies and businesses worldwide took advantage of the cultural embargo by paying the artists less or not paying them at all. Marks was never paid by American publishers for his apartheid protest hit song "Master Jack." "When I called to ask for my royalties in the States the publisher called me a racist and hung up."

During the music festival, Shawn and I hung out backstage and spoke with many South African musicians. Zakes Myataza, a Zulu musician who had not stopped playing his guitar since we arrived, said, "My grandmother taught me to throw harmonies like bones: both tell the future." Enoch Lengoasa, a Xhosa percussionist remarked, "Every tribe has its own record of dreams: ours is the praise song."

The first cultural event of the new South Africa was leeker cracker (super good). Hundreds of musicians performed nearly every type of music imaginable. Over 5,000 people gladly listened. There was no violence. Blacks danced with whites and celebrated their new democracy.

JANIS IAN (SOLO ARTIST):

When *At Seventeen,* which I recorded in 1976, received five Grammy nominations—incidentally the most any solo female had received to that date—I was accused of selling out to the commercial interests. People said I was "mainstreaming my message" by using strings on the record and "disguising my message with pretty words and music." Still later, I was attacked for going to South Africa during the apartheid years, though I took an integrated band and played to integrated audiences and avoided Sun City, which was played by artists ranging from Linda Ronstadt to various black Americans who couldn't even order dinner there. The same English committee that prevented Johnny Clegg—probably the best-known white South African artist in the world—from performing at a tribute to Nelson Mandela because he'd performed in his residence country of South Africa, also banned me from playing in England.

CHAPTER 9

FAN ENCOUNTERS

Rock musicians, like any other performers, would be nothing without their fans. From the moment that audiences started dancing to live performances of Bill Haley & His Comets and Buddy Holly, and shrieking at Elvis and the Beatles, rock fans have been an integral part of the show. Yes, rockers are sometimes held in awe by fans, and the term "Rock God" has been applied all too frequently, but the fans' interactions with those on stage has always been part of the concert experience.

To be a fan of a particular artist is to accept that artist's songs. The lyrical content of those songs defines the rocker's opinions. Some lyrics pay homage to excessive drug or alcohol use, promoting the party-hardy lifestyle. Other songwriters employ music as a conduit for their political beliefs and convictions. Because of the renegade nature of the genre, there are few, if any, topics or perspectives that are off limits.

Lyrics, and the artist's intent, are always open to interpretation. That said, sometimes lyrics are misinterpreted by fans. In the end, the listener takes away what he or she chooses. It goes without saying that what they think they are hearing isn't necessarily always what is being said.

ALICE NUTTER (CHUMBAWAMBA):

For a bunch of serious politicos, we were never that serious. Like any gang, we had front—our front was skinny, angry, and extreme—but when we were with each other, we were more likely to talk about records and food and Deirdre from Coronation Street than we were about "issues." We demonstrated, played benefits, produced pamphlets, broke the law, and read stuff, but didn't need to talk about it to prove we had. When [Johnny] Lydon sneered, "We mean it, maaan!" he really did, and so did we, but we never really cared whether or not anybody believed it. Our job was to be arrogant little bastards who didn't look up to anybody and who were secretly nicer than we seemed. Since the first rule of punk was Kill Your Idols and we were Beatles fans, our first single—1986's "Revolution"—started with the sound of us scratching Lennon's "Imagine." Couldn't get any bigger or better than Lennon, so we aimed high and went straight for the jugular.

The first dead bird arrived a couple of weeks later. Wayne the postman had to knock because he couldn't get the package through the letterbox. Knowing nothing about nature, it was just a bird with black feathers to me. A large bird nestled

Alice Nutter (Chumbawamba)
From the photo collection of Alice Nutter

in cotton wool inside a shoebox wrapped in old-fashioned brown paper and finished off with string. No scrawled "I'm a Madman Me!" handwriting to give it away. Addressed in a neat hand, it seemed impressively formal and normal until we opened it. A dead bird. A scrap of paper bearing a written date: February 14, Valentine's Day. We sat on the bottom of the stairs across from the front door gawking at the bird.

"Maybe it's because we're into animal rights!"

"Has it been shot?"

"It'll have maggots."

We gave it a newspaper shroud and put it in the bin. The cats were always killing birds, and that's where they ended up. We weren't sensitive enough to be properly spooked by a dead bird.

We knew what the next package was before we opened it. Same as the last one, except one of its feet was twisted sideways, toes curled where it had been wrenched away from life. Death always inserts individual details—an upturned palm or a last chesty rattle. Even a bird gets a final signature. And the date was there: February 14.

"How Stephen King!"

"He's crap, Stephen King."

"No, he's great. Totally underrated."

"Stephen King's not the point! Someone is sending us dead birds!"

The birds kept coming, and we got used to them, wondered whether we should just bin them unopened. But we always unwrapped. Over the next few weeks, our fingers got slower, and the anticipation and shock turned into the fatigue of routine. Always a bird and a date. They were weird and momentarily worrying, but we were too preoccupied with ourselves, sex, the revolution, our hormones, gossip, and whatever cause we were being arrested for that week to give the birds the consideration their untimely deaths deserved.

We weren't just a rock 'n' roll band; we were a gang you couldn't join, and that riled a lot of people. Politicos tried to sleep with us, and when sex wasn't enough to get them into the inner circle, they tried to force Maoist self-criticism on us. We were too insensitive for that, too. The year 1986 turned into '87, and in the new year we played in Aberdeen. Dan [Nobacon] started the set by putting Lennon's "Imagine" on an old Dancette we'd mic'd up, and then pointedly wrenching the needle off. Lennon was a scratched record singing "living for today" over and over until, from the blur of dark bodies on the dance floor, someone jumped on stage, sprayed Dan with lighter fuel and halfheartedly tried to light and throw a match at him. As assassination attempts go, it was a bit lame. [Fred] Dunst and Boff manhandled the arsonist out of the building. It made the evening. We were young, it was rock 'n' roll, and setting fire to Dan was the difference between a memorable gig and just another venue.

Valentine's Day came and went and there was no bird to mark it. February 15 we got a rabbit. It was the same size box, and the rabbit was awkwardly squashed in with "February 14" pinned to its fur. The pinning seemed cruel, but having a pin stuck in its dead carcass was the least of the rabbit's problems. A few days later, days uncommonly free of gift-wrapped carcasses, a friend who lived in a Vauxhall Viva in Kettering rang and told us that some kid he knew had jumped off the old glue factory on Valentine's Day, and that his death was somehow linked to us. The glue factory is a proper *kill yourself* building. If jumping off its roof is a cry for help, it's a cry that ends abruptly 150 feet below.

Next time we played in London, a curly-headed student wearing his Dad's jumper came up and asked if he could come to Leeds and talk to us. That wasn't particularly abnormal. People were always ringing up and speaking in code before visiting us with conspiratorial proposals. It was part and string-wrapped parcel of being a political band. Then as now, there were always cases coming to appeal, disputes, community groups, international struggles, and an alternative media that needed funding. It wasn't unusual for people to knock on our door asking for donation; but this time it was different.

Instead of asking us to play a benefit gig for something highly illegal, the man in his dad's clothes turned up with an apology. He'd posted the rabbit. The whole sorry story came out. The guy who'd committed suicide was his best mate, the same boy who'd tried to set fire to Dan. They'd moved from Scotland to London together, listened to the same music, and obsessed over the same minute details of which band did what and why. Which is what we all did. Sometimes you were so busy monitoring pop culture that you didn't know if you were a cop or a punk.

He'd posted the rabbit at his friend's behest: "It has to go on the 14th, and I won't be here to mail it." Dragged into a suicide that didn't seem real until it happened, he was obviously guilty, sad, and sorry, because he hadn't stopped his friend from killing himself, and worse, he felt like he'd aided and abetted him.

We wanted to know what it had to do with us. You could tell the explanation sounded as stupid to his ears as it did to ours. *We'd released records.* His friend had killed himself because we'd betrayed our DIY principles by moving from mailing out cassette tapes on to selling vinyl in shops. There it was. It supposedly mattered so much that this kid had to die to prove a point. Peace punk, or anarcho-pop, or whatever you wanted to call it, was in danger of being submerged by the mainstream way of doing things because bands like Chumbawamba were being sold in record shops.

A boy's life was too important for us to pretend he'd died because of us. Disappointment at a pop group isn't the launch pad off the glue factory; it's all the details that come before, the stuff that lurks behind the cheap color snapshots of kids smiling on the beach. We were sorry, but not for anything we'd done. We couldn't take the blame for mental illness, or for whatever hurts had pushed him to climb onto the roof, pushed him to fall, wingless, another dead bird wrapped up and buried. But still, we were strangely, numbly sorry. There wasn't anything else to be.

MEET AND GREET

While on stage one day, the Grateful Dead's Mickey Hart was greeted by a fan who proceeded to give Hart his brother's skull. The fan explained that his brother had been a huge fan and would have liked Hart to have it. Looking at the skull, Hart proclaimed it a true "dead-head."

Not all fan encounters are as disturbing as those experienced by Chumbawama and the Grateful Dead. Most are fairly lighthearted, chance meetings between people who like a band's music and the band members. Frequently, though, there are little twists in fan-encounter stories that make them something a little more than just "how ya doin'" and an autograph.

MEL CARTER (SOLO ARTIST):

I remember a time in Atlanta, Georgia, early on in my career when I was with the Dick Clark Caravan of Stars. I did several of them, as many of us did in those days. The year was 1963, when my first hit record, "When a Boy Falls In Love," was high and hot on the charts. We had played the Coliseum in Atlanta, and upon leaving the auditorium and getting on the bus, the fans broke the police line and

Mel Carter in the '60s
From the photo collection of Mel Carter

ran up to us. One of them had a stick in her hand, and got so excited when she saw me, she hit me in the eye and then fainted.

I must say, that was the first black eye I ever had, and it wasn't even a fight. Need I say that for a while on the remaining tour dates, I had to use heavy makeup to cover the black eye. This is a road story that sticks firmly in my head and eye (smile).

GEORGE MCCORKLE (MARSHALL TUCKER BAND):

In Norfolk, Virginia, Marshall Tucker Band was playing The Scope. It was a sold-out house and a great audience. When the stage went black after the show, all of us went behind the amp line to dry off. With the roar of the crowd, we knew we would do an encore. When we went back on stage, Toy Caldwell's guitar tech noticed Toy's white Les Paul Custom was missing! He asked all the other roadies and stagehands, but no one knew what had happened to it.

Our road manager told a Norfolk police officer there would be a "hundred dollar bill" for the man that found the Les Paul. Now that was when a hundred dollars meant something.

After the show was over and we were in the dressing room, a police officer walked in with it! He told us a fan just couldn't help himself and jumped on the stage when it went black, grabbed the beautiful Les Paul Custom, and ran back into the crowd. Somehow he got out the door and into his van where police found him playing it. He offered no resistance and gave it up. I guess he and the police officer were happy. The cop got a C note, and the fan got to play one of Toy Caldwell's Guitars!

GEORGE "SOUTHERN GEORGE" PIESCH (FAN):

It was in 1975 when I met this pretty girl on a street in Vienna. We got together and had a great relationship for a few years. She moved from Alabama to Vienna to study to be a doctor at our university. She had a lot of great music with her, old vinyl and tapes.

One tape had really great music on it, but it was unlabeled and nobody could tell me who the band was. So I listened to it and kept asking everybody what their name was, but nobody could give me an answer.

In summer 1976, I heard about a big one-day open-air concert in Knebworth, England, with a few bands like Todd Rundgen, 10cc, a few others I don't remember, and the Rolling Stones as headliner. I was a big Stones fan then (I still love

George McCorkle (Marshall Tucker Band)
From the photo collection of George McCorkle

them), and I hit the road and hitchhiked to Great Britain. It took me two days to get there. I was impressed with the huge audience. Later on I found out that about a hundred thousand rock and roll fans were there.

I had a great day there. The weather was beautiful (remember, it is England), and I spent the day drinkin' and partyin'. Before the Stones hit the stage, there was a band that I had never heard of before. This band was a bunch of long-haired, wild-looking guys with guitars. They started playing, and the music went straight to my heart, brain, and soul. It made me get up and jump and go closer to the stage. "Workin' for MCA!" LYNYRD SKYNYRD! The band from the unlabeled tape I had listened to for so long. MY BAND! MY MUSIC!

I got hooked on Skynyrd from that moment on. I didn't care about the Stones that day, because Skynyrd blew them off and away. It was not just me, a lot of people left the area after Skynyrd. On my way home, I stopped in London and bought myself all the albums I could get. Back in Vienna, I just played Skynyrd and told everybody about that band, that music.

TERRY MORRIS (AUTHOR):

As I was deciding if I wanted to choose a "Nathan's Famous Hot Dog" or a slice of "New York Pizza," I was standing at the crosswalk on the corner of Fifth Avenue and West Fifty-Seventh Street and was watching for the street lights to change colors. They did. Typically, there would be what seemed like a zillion people dashing in front of me at a street crossing like this, but today as I looked up to get ready to step into the crosswalk, I noticed that there were only a few people moving. I was shocked to realize and recognize, along with the other stalled pedestrians, that the two people directly approaching me were John Lennon and Yoko Ono. They were crossing the street right at me! As you can imagine, I was stunned. Everyone was. We couldn't budge. But we all stared.

Yoko Ono was decked out in a full length mink fur coat and was dripping in jewelry as if on her way to receive a prestigious award, while John Lennon had on faded jeans and a worn, almost shredded in places, green army jacket and was looking at the ground and his feet as if he were lost in thought or perhaps humming a tune. She strided along with purpose while he sluffed and shuffled next to and slightly behind her. Personally, I always thought they looked odd together. I thought this even more so now that I was viewing them in person. She looked very "New York" and he looked surprisingly down-to-earth and "normal." I probably could have said "hello" to him as he passed by me, but I didn't want to mess up his silent tune humming. He might have been creating an important new piece of music. You just never know what exactly a genius might be thinking. Yoko stopped for a minute to let John catch up with her.

I watched in awe as John and Yoko walked right by me. And right by everyone else who was standing there with their mouths gaping to the sidewalk. If I had put my hand out, I could have touched them as they glided by me. But, out of respect, I didn't attempt such an invasion of privacy. I think I held my breath for a minute. No one said a word. No one moved. We just watched them walk by as if time were standing still.

There are a few times in your life when something will happen and right after, you say to yourself, "I'm never going to forget that." Unfortunately, we also will always remember what happened on December 8, 1980. For those of us who were on that corner in New York City that day, frozen in the moment, we seemed to feel that it was necessary to stand quietly and observe. It was important, in our minds, that we record every single detail of this one fleeting moment to tell about later to anyone who would listen.

ALLEN METZ (AUTHOR):

This wasn't my first meeting with Blondie. I had spoken to Deborah Harry in 1999, following a concert in Concord, California. I broached the still-forming concept of a book I was planning on the band, which would document their musical/pop culture legacy. Ms. Harry expressed an interest in the project.

Fast forward to August 16, 2002. Just the previous evening I had the first opportunity to see advance copies of my book, which I was hoping to present to the band following a concert at the Mountain Winery in Saratoga, California. All I knew in advance was that one of the webmasters of the official Blondie Web site, and also owner of the very popular Deborah Harry and Blondie Information Service Yahoo group, Louis A. Bustamante, was also planning on being at this concert. He was driving up from Southern California with fellow Blondie fan and journalist Luther Orrick-Guzman. The afternoon of the concert, I called the other Blondie webmaster and de facto Blondie archivist, Barry L. Kramer. The long distance connection back East was rather poor, but the main point I gleaned was that I should wait around the stage after the show.

I left early and arrived shortly after the gates opened. I drove up a long, winding, and narrow road into the hills, hoping to meet up with Louis, who arranged in advance for the distribution of backstage passes to members of his Yahoo group. Not finding him, I bided my time among the "beautiful people." I crammed as many books into my trusty, weathered briefcase as I could. This 500-plus page monster of a book weighs some three pounds. You do the math! Finally, just a half hour before Blondie was scheduled to go on stage, I ambled back to my car, retrieved said briefcase, and gingerly approached the entrance gate (again), but this time with books in tow. As you can imagine, there was no way I was going to be allowed to take a briefcase into the venue. So I was asked to step aside and open up the case. I explained "the plan" and that I was waiting for Louis to arrive. The personnel at the box office were expecting him, but he hadn't shown up yet. Following some discussion, I was instructed to leave the briefcase at the box office and retrieve it after the show.

I enjoyed the concert, but was wondering if I would be permitted to return to the box office to retrieve my precious cargo. As suggested, at the end of the performance, I approached the stage looking around, but there was no sign of my contact, the holder of the backstage passes. A few minutes passed, and I was having doubts about whether I could pull this thing off after all. While in the midst of that reverie, I heard someone behind me call out my first name. I turned around, and there was Louis and his driving companion, Luther, who had arrived at the show just as Blondie took to the stage. What timing!

Louis gathered up the other DHBIS members. We waited a short time, and then received our backstage entrée, the passes. One of the venue staff overheard me express concerns about needing to get back to the box office to claim my newly minted books. "If you go there now, you won't be able to go back stage," I was informed. Hmmm. So I waited until they led us down a short ramp, where there was another venue staff member, a big burly guy. I explained the situation and how I was hoping to present advance copies of my book to the band. My words fell upon sympathetic ears, and he said, "Go ahead." The box office was right nearby, up the hill. The staff at the box office communicated via cell phone with the big guy and, following a brief exchange, I heard the box office staff member answer slowly in reply to a question regarding the nature of the briefcase's contents, "It's all books, just books," as he carefully examined the contents. Then I was allowed to secure the case, and was on my way back down the hill where the big guy waved me into a large room, which had the appearance of a wine cellar (appropriate enough décor for a winery).

Having triumphantly secured the books (actually relieved might be a more accurate description), I headed over to one of the round tables where about a dozen Blondie fans were seated, eagerly awaiting the opportunity to meet and greet their heroes. A copy of the book was passed around the table, but I eventually retrieved it, as that and all the other copies were for the band. The band slowly trickled in. Louis assisted me by carrying several copies of the book and introducing me first to Debbie. After Louis explained who I was, she asked, "Will I like this book?" And, as if in reply to her own question, she signed and inscribed my copy, "You will make me very happy!" Then Louis introduced me to Chris (who knew about the project). With Debbie still in earshot, Chris greeted me with his typical animated welcome—something to the effect of, "Here's that editor guy," in response to which Debbie's eyebrows and expressive face perked up. (Chris had received an early book galley so that he could get a feel for the nature of this book). Chris was very gracious, thanking me a couple times for my "devotion/dedication" to the band. After signing my copy, Clem, the drummer, asked me to sign and inscribe his, which I happily obliged, addressing it to the world's "premier" drummer. Leigh Fox and Paul Carbonara also were also very gracious. I approached Paul, asking him to excuse me for interrupting him as he was reading and browsing through the book. Having dispatched with all the books I had brought with me (mission accomplished!), save my autographed copy, I spoke with fans and others from the Blondie entourage. By the time I knew it, the gathering gradually melted away until I was the last person to exit the room.

JENETTE WALDVOGEL (FAN):

I was at a Bob Dylan show in Terre Haute, Indiana, in 2002, and I started talking with a security guard outside of the venue a few hours before show time. We chatted, and he gave me one of Bob's cigarette butts and told me Bob was going to do two encores.

During the last one, I went out by where the buses were parked. When Bob came out, I told him how his music has changed my life. He waited for me to come talk to him. I hugged him and kissed him, and before I could stop myself, I blurted out, "You smell really good." He laughed and asked me what he smelled like. I told him he smelled like strawberries and that I thought it was maybe his shampoo. He leaned into me and sniffed my neck, then grabbed my long hair and buried his nose in it. "You smell good, too," he told me.

MARK E. JOHNSON (FAN):

On Sunday, July 28, 2002, me and my friend Joe made the two-hour drive to Atlantic City, New Jersey, to attend a concert called "A Walk Down Abbey Road." This was a concert consisting of an all-star lineup of musicians performing Beatles' songs, as well as songs from each person's past. The show consisted of performances by Jack Bruce (Cream), Todd Rundgren, Mark Farner (Grand Funk Railroad), Christopher Cross, and Alan Parsons.

The plan was to get to Atlantic City in the early afternoon to hang out on the boardwalk, in the casino, and by the concert hall in hopes of meeting any of the musicians in the lineup. It was such a nice day, I figured they would probably be hanging out somewhere close.

After arriving in Atlantic City, we parked the car and I took my camera and a few items to get signed with me. In less than ten minutes of parking the car and walking through the Hilton casino to get to the boardwalk, I see Todd Rundgren walking quickly through the crowded corridor. I stopped Todd and shook his hand. I talked to him briefly, and then he was off. I was so surprised and awestruck that I forgot to ask for an autograph or to take a photo with him.

We decided to walk the boardwalk to see if we could find any of the other musicians. About an hour later, I see a long-haired guy leisurely strolling the boardwalk holding hands with a beautiful woman. "That's him," I told my friend Joe. "Who? Where?" he said. The one and only Mark Farner of Grand Funk

Mark Johnson with
Todd Rundgren
*From the photo
collection of Mark
Johnson*

Railroad. We politely introduced ourselves to him. He introduced the woman as his wife and we all talked. Mark was very nice and cordial, posing with us for pictures. No one else on the busy boardwalk that day seemed to know or recognize him. We thanked Mark for everything, then continued on.

Soon after, I see a gentleman taking his time walking towards us. He looked like a typical middle-aged man, who blended into the crowd of people on the boardwalk. After he passed by us, I told my friend, "I think that was Jack Bruce of Cream." We cautiously approached him and verified that it was Jack Bruce. He was gracious enough to have his photo taken with us. We shook his hand and thanked him, then parted ways.

We walked back to the Hilton casino and patiently waited outside on the boardwalk, hoping for another possible encounter. After some time had passed, coming out the casino doors we again see Todd Rundgren. Todd took the time to talk to us and was very cool. We got our photos taken with him, shook his hand, and then he was on his way. About twenty minutes later as he was walking back, I stopped him one more time for an autograph. He kindly obliged.

We still had the concert to look forward to, but I was already completely satisfied. Meeting three of my rock and roll heroes in one day in such a completely relaxed setting was very fulfilling. Although I've met all of these musicians before, I never cease to be a little starstruck in such encounters. The impact some of these musicians have had on my life has been monumental. My personality, career choices, choice of friends, and image has been significantly influenced by many of these musical icons. I always feel honored, privileged, and grateful when I get the opportunity to meet one of my musical heroes.

TONY HALL (FAN):

In 1997, during Glen Campbell's concert tour of the U.K., I contacted his management to ask if he would be interested in seeing a guitar, a banjo, and other exceptional 1930s string instruments—all made entirely with used wooden matchsticks by my dad. To my great delight, I received a response from his road manager Bill Maclay, saying that Glen was interested in seeing the instruments, and he invited me to meet him at Fairfields Hall Theatre, in London, prior to his concert.

I arrived at the theatre at six-thirty PM, and received a welcome from Bill, who helped me carry the instruments into a backstage room. It was a wonderful moment, and a big surprise, when Glen entered the room. He had his band and management team with him, too! I showed him the matchstick guitar and matchboxes carrying case, explaining the detail and the outstanding story behind their construction. He then played the guitar and banjo, prior to seeing the mandolin and the violin and bow. I took some photos of Glen with each instrument, and then Bill took some photos of us together. He then autographed some photos of the guitar for me and for my mum, Grace, who has an "amazing" connection with Glen's performance on the *Ripley's Believe It or Not!* show.

Glen was absolutely fantastic throughout our twenty-minute meeting. We had an in-depth conversation about the instruments, and he told me that neither he nor the rest of his team realized they were full-size, playable instruments. They were expecting to see only little tiny models! I felt extremely privileged that Glen afforded me so much time, and was overwhelmed with his interest and the wonderful comments he made about my dad's work. I had no idea he would actually play the guitar and banjo. I was thrilled that he did. It brought back memories of a time in the '70s when my dad and I sat in awe watching Glen perform "Dueling Banjos" on BBC television. At the end of the tune, my dad said, "I wonder what Glen would think of my guitar and banjo?"

In the summer of '97, the instruments were loaned out for exhibition and performance at The British and Irish Country Music Festival. I told Glen about this, and in June of that year he wrote a personally signed letter to the British and Irish County Music Festival about our meeting. The letter is a tribute to my dad, who sadly never did get to realize his dream of knowing Glen's opinion of his guitar and banjo. However, I know he would be very proud of what he had to say.

The story took on a new twist in August 1999 when I was contacted by Rudy Fischmann, a producer of *Ripley's Believe It or Not!* He invited me to participate in a segment for the new series that was due to premiere in January 2000, saying, "The story of all the matchstick instruments was truly remarkable and definitely fit into the *Believe It or Not!* mold." They decided the segment would be best structured around the playing of the instruments. The $64,000 question was; who would give a performance? I mentioned that Glen had played the guitar and banjo during his U.K. tour in '97, and he was due back again in September for another concert tour. I never expected anything to come of this. I was stunned when I received a call from Rudy, telling me he had contacted Glen, who said he would be delighted to get involved with the segment. I couldn't believe it. Was I dreaming? It really was unthinkable to me that one of the world's greatest performers had agreed to play my dad's guitar on American TV.

I realized my dream was about to become a reality when I received an invitation to interview Glen and hear him perform with the matchstick guitar. I arrived at his hotel in London, where a room was set up by the film crew. With the camera rolling, a very nervous Tony Hall greeted Glen. Glen made the interview very easy for me with his friendly, relaxed manner and charming personality. Nothing was too much trouble (even though he was performing his final concert of the tour at the London Palladium in a few hours time). He did everything the director wanted. I asked if Glen would perform "Amazing Grace" for the segment, and he readily agreed. During our interview, I told him the reason why I had especially requested this tune: my eighty-five-year-old mum had been in very poor health for a long time, and I said it would be a tremendous boost to see her favorite performer sing this song. I said, "My mum's name is 'Grace' and she is one 'amazing' lady." Glen turned to face the camera and said, "We'll dedicate this to you, Grace. If you see this. God love you." Words cannot express the tears of joy these sentiments brought to my mum and our family. At that time, my mum was struggling with the final stages of terminal cancer, but she managed to see Glen's tribute on tape before she passed away.

DAWN THOMPSON (FAN):

On the weekend of August 15/16, 1977, the same weekend Elvis died, some friends and I went to the Illinois State Fair to see the Bay City Rollers. I don't really know how, but we found out the names of the hotels the guys were registered at. We picked one, and set out to find us some Rollers!

One of my girlfriends was more "equipped" than any of the rest of us. She was prepared to break into their room. She thought that surely it was the best suite in the hotel, so off to work she went on the door lock. We stood guard at the ends of the hall. While we waited there, a young girl who worked at the hotel came by and informed us that they were on another floor. We tried to get to that floor, but security was naturally heavy.

Feeling very discouraged, we went down to the lobby/snack bar area and called a taxi. We sat there drinking chocolate milkshakes and waited. Lo and behold, who walked in a few moments later but Leslie and Eric! God, Les looked sooo sexy. All he had on was a snug pair of jeans and tennis shoes. They were surprised to see us, but not wanting to get roughly escorted out, we stayed pretty cool for four fifteen-year-olds face-to-face with their idols. They chatted with us briefly, and we took a few photos. Then off they went. I had been unable to do anything but stare. Once they were gone from sight, I cried like a baby. I hated that I was so starstruck that I couldn't speak.

GLEN SCRIVENER (FAN):

I saw Jethro Tull at Hammersmith Odeon on their "Stormwatch" tour. A handful of fans gathered after the show at the stage door, hopeful for sightings of the band. These fans had scant reward when the band zoomed past in a limo, out into the lonely Hammersmith night. Save one that is. John Evans, who was one of the keyboard players, greeted the fans on his own, and happily chatted to all. He debated with one, I recall, about whether he had actually played at the Sunderland Empire. Having signed all the autographs, he simply turned round and walked away down the street into the darkness. I wondered if the rest of the band had forgotten him?

ALLEN EDGE (FAN):

The odor hung around ominously. Foreboding? Perhaps. Fear? Maybe. Call it what you will. We shall never really know for sure. That night in that narrow alley, whatever it was stalked nostrils desperate for something fresher. Yet, in those moments that followed no change would come. No fresh pastures would materialize out of the thin air. The protagonists at either end of that alley were already set on their destinies. It was too late to stop now. Two worlds were about to collide. Two lives mapped out years before were now ready to discover what had lain in store for all those years. On either side of them, the ramshackle shanty pulsed with offers of refuge. Lights shone from caravan windows. The shadows formed offered them an escape. Beseeching them to accept a way out. Yet, in reality, the flickering lights merely emphasized the steely resolve etched deep across each of their faces. The easy option was spurned. The get-out clauses rejected out of hand. These were men who simply never turned back. This was their Tombstone. Their Dodge City. This was their alleyway of fate.

As they drew nearer, their eyes met. Bizarrely, it revealed disparate appetites for the momentous rendezvous about to unfurl. The one oozed relish. The other meanwhile, in stark and sobering contrast, reeked of dread. It was suddenly clear the stench of foreboding had emanated from one source alone, that those seemingly corresponding resolves had been fed by differing fuels. At once, an upper hand had been established. The rule of the jungle would apply here as anywhere. And this alleyway was no place for the fainthearted. The protagonist relishing his fate was now sprightly, hungry even, seemingly eager to pounce. The other was cagey, as if almost frozen in the glare of the spotlights from those caravan windows on either side. He glanced almost desperately either side at the lights that shone on him. Now he would have taken any one of them to make his exit. To transport him away in some mythical ray. Now he prayed for a door to open to invite him in. Any light. Any door. Anything. A hole in the ground, even, to swallow him.

It was too late to stop now. Perhaps it had always been too late. The sprightly one, the younger of the two, was too nimble. Moved far too fast. Even before his older adversary had time to realize what was happening, he had flashed out his arm from his side and grasped the hand of his adversary. It was as firm a handshake as he had ever conjured up. "Don't mind I hope, Van, lad. Respect mate!"

As they loosed go after what seemed like a shake that would last forever, the younger man walked off into the night. Smiling. Content. An overenthusiastic fan off, perhaps, to bother others of similar repute amidst that backstage shanty. Garth? Richard? Rick? Meanwhile, Van Morrison stared disbelievingly at his hand, molded as if putty. He wondered to himself whether he'd ever be able to play the piano again.

MATTHEW GREENWALD (JOURNALIST):

I was a musical oddball in my Southern California high school in the late '70s. While everyone was grooving and head-banging to Fleetwood Mac, the Eagles ,and Led Zeppelin, I was plowing through the used records stores picking up such psychedelic and folk/rock fodder as the Doors, Dylan, the Beatles/Rolling Stones/Buffalo Springfield lexicon. But perhaps my biggest early passion was Love, led by Arthur Lee. I hunted down their hard-to-find sides and devoured what I could locate, reveling in their strangeness and beauty. I learned to play guitar from their records.

I first got to see Arthur Lee live in 1978 at a small club called The Relic House, and he was amazing. Later, I caught shows at The Whiskey, The Alligator

Lounge, and many other venues. Some were better than others. One of the weirdest was a 1981 show at The Whiskey, where Bryan MacLean (fellow Love cofounder) was the opening act. Arthur was in the audience—seemingly orbiting somewhere in the vicinity of Saturn—when he suddenly threw a cup of coffee up at MacLean while he was playing. Bryan, ever the trooper, wiped it off, complained that he "didn't like it with that much sugar," and kept on playing. Arthur's set saw him withering around on the floor of the stage, speaking about John Belushi's recent death, handing microphones out to the audience, and other nonmusical antics. He culminated his aborted "set" by jumping off the lip of the stage, running out through the crowd and out the front door. Between Clark and Hilldale, literally.

Cut to 1993. I was working at a branch of Apple Computers as a telephone-customer service representative. The office was in Sherman Oaks, right next door to a miniature golf/arcade place called, oddly enough, The Castle (which was also the name of Love's 1966 communal home on Commonwealth Road near Griffith Park). Not being much of a fan of miniature golf or arcade games, I had yet to set foot on the property. But one beautiful spring day, I had an early shift, which meant a ten AM lunch. I had a quick bite to eat, grabbed a cuppa, and decided to take a stroll around the grounds till I felt at home. The place seemed deserted. As I walked around the course, I heard a couple of voices off in the distance. I looked, and there were two middle-aged guys, casually dressed, playing miniature golf, laughing and talking. One of them looked like Arthur. They got a little closer to where I was, and I looked at 'em and said to myself, "No, Arthur Lee does *not* play miniature golf at ten AM." But he did, and he was.

I had met Arthur very, very briefly after a couple of shows I'd attended years earlier, along with a clutch of other fans. It never went beyond, "Hey, great show Arthur." "Oh, thanks, man." I walked towards them, and at about twenty feet caught his eye and politely and quietly said, "Arthur?" "Yeah, it's me. Who are you? Wait, I've seen you before man. You come to my *shows* sometimes." "All the time, Arthur."

We spoke for a few moments—Arthur's friend was as thrown as I was at this bizarre meeting—about upcoming records (Arthur informed me that he had a new single coming out soon, which would be "Girl On Fire," on his Distortion Records) and some of his shows I'd seen. I shook his hand, thanked him for all the music, excused myself, and went back to work with my head reeling.

About a year later, I went to another show somewhere, and afterwards I saw

Arthur about to get into his car, but first he looked at me at about fifty feet, pointed, and said, "Hey, miniature golf!" It became a running gag.

A couple of years after that, I began a career as a music journalist and somehow got a hold of Arthur for a brief telephone interview. Before the interview, I told him who I was, mentioned how we met, and he said, "So ya wanna go play some miniature golf or what?"

KATHIE MONTGOMERY (FAN):

My best friend, an L.A. record company executive, invited me to a Neil Young benefit concert in San Francisco at The Boarding House. In and of itself, this would have been a very special event, but to add to the thrill, Neil was filming for his movie *Human Highway*. The night promised adventure, and I was dressed to kill.

After the concert, invited guests were to join a movie banquet scene with the actors downstairs. Cameras roamed about. After visiting the elaborate ladies' room, I emerged to walk gracefully across the large lobby to my friend, aware of the cameras and being oh-so-cool. Imagine my puzzlement when the look on her face began alternating between horror and hysteria. My concentration was broken by a woman's voice behind me. "Miss, you've got toilet paper on your shoe." Now, I didn't just have toilet paper on my shoe, I had a ten-foot ribbon trailing me, firmly rooted to my perfect boots' heel. A small Spanish dance ensued and I extricated myself from the offending banner. When I reached my friend, all she could do was blurt out, "I can't take you anywhere," while trying not to let hysteria take her over.

Now, this event might have stayed in the family had it not been for those pesky cameramen. Neil was too fine a gentleman to embarrass a lady publicly but nevertheless knew a good shot when he saw one. Toward the end of *Human Highway*, there's an animated sequence of a "lovely young woman" in her finest dress walking gracefully through a field of flowers. Floating into frame, as though blown by a gentle breeze, comes a piece of toilet paper! More and more pieces of toilet paper join the breeze. As they begin to overtake the frame, a telephone booth appears and the "lovely young woman" moves inside it for shelter, allowing the toilet paper clouds to just blow by. Thank you, Neil.

Index

ABOUT THE AUTHOR

Marley Brant has been employed in the entertainment industry for the past twenty-eight years as an artist development executive, publicist, biographical writer, music and television producer, and author. Brant's entertainment affiliations are extensive, and she has worked with a wide variety of rock and country artists; actors; directors; on numerous television, radio and film productions; toured with major rock acts; and assisted in the successful development of new artists.

Brant's expertise working with artists was recognized when she was appointed assistant national director of artist development and publicity/artist relations and tour coordination with Chrysalis Records. Employed by Paramount Television, she worked closely with the casts and crews of many of Paramount's premier television series and mini-series. Brant was account executive for several films, as well as the music programs *Fame, Solid Gold,* and *The Tom Jones Show* while working at ICPR, and she coproduced the album *Gram Parsons and the Fallen Angels: Live, 1973,* which resulted in a Grammy nomination for Gram Parsons and Emmyou Harris in the category of "Best Country Performance by a Duo or Group with Vocal". Brant served as co-creator, associate producer, and historical consultant on "Outlaws, Rebels and Rogues," the first installment of TBS's three-night television series The Untold West.

Brant is the author of six books including *Southern Rockers: The Roots and Legacy of Southern Rock* (Billboard Books, 1999) and *Freebirds: the Lynyrd Skynyrd Story* (Billboard Books, 2002).